UNDERSTANDING ORGANIZATIONS
Theories & Images

SAGE has been part of the global academic community since 1965, supporting high quality research and learning that transforms society and our understanding of individuals, groups and cultures. SAGE is the independent, innovative, natural home for authors, editors and societies who share our commitment and passion for the social sciences.

Find out more at: **www.sagepublications.com**

UNDERSTANDING ORGANIZATIONS
Theories & Images

Udo Staber

Los Angeles | London | New Delhi
Singapore | Washington DC

Los Angeles | London | New Delhi
Singapore | Washington DC

SAGE Publications Ltd
1 Oliver's Yard
55 City Road
London EC1Y 1SP

SAGE Publications Inc.
2455 Teller Road
Thousand Oaks, California 91320

SAGE Publications India Pvt Ltd
B 1/I 1 Mohan Cooperative Industrial Area
Mathura Road
New Delhi 110 044

SAGE Publications Asia-Pacific Pte Ltd
3 Church Street
#10-04 Samsung Hub
Singapore 049483

Editor: Kirsty Smy
Development editor: Robin Lupton
Editorial assistant: Nina Smith
Production editor: Sarah Cooke
Marketing manager: Alison Borg
Cover design: Francis Kenney
Typeset by: C&M Digitals (P) Ltd, Chennai, India
Printed by MPG Printgroup, UK

MIX
Paper from
responsible sources
FSC® C018575
www.fsc.org

First published 2013

Library of Congress Control Number: 2012947231

British Library Cataloguing in Publication data

A catalogue record for this book is available from the British Library

ISBN 978-1-84920-740-9
ISBN 978-1-84920-741-6 (pbk)

Contents

Preface

This book has both an intellectual and a personal history. Its intellectual history comes from my experience with sharing my academic insights about organizations with a wide variety of students from different age groups and social and national backgrounds. The students constantly reminded me that there is no single understanding of a given organizational phenomenon and that context matters a great deal in understanding. This book's personal history stems from my practical involvement, as a worker, consumer, and consultant, in many different types of organizations and in many different countries. I have observed how organizations struggle with various types of problems. In many cases, these problems were structural in nature, but were experienced as personal failures. Ineffective solutions were often not the result of deficient skill training on the part of organizational participants, but were caused by deep-seated misunderstandings, stemming from differences in personal disposition or social background. I have written this book with a view to the value of pursuing alternative interpretations of organizational phenomena, hoping that the analysis helps readers better connect abstract theoretical concepts to "facts" as they may apply to their own life experiences. A practical test of this book's value is whether it helps readers view organizational matters more clearly, or at least differently.

When writing this book, I also had Bernard Mandeville's *Fable of the Bees* in mind. The structure of an aggregate like an organization is the result of the actions of individuals who may or may not have some larger collective goal in mind, but, in the end, these individuals are what they are: self-interested, but also sociable; competitive, but also cooperative; dependent, but also controlling; and vulnerable, but also resilient. Moral sentiments aside, and metaphorically speaking, organizational participants behave like bees, busily constructing a place for themselves, in an uncertain environment filled with natural enemies and potential cooperators. There is an important difference, however. Like bees, they "dance to each other," but, unlike bees, they also reflect about their dancing, in search for better understanding.

This book is aimed at advanced undergraduate and graduate students in the fields of organization theory and organizational behavior, with applications in areas like human resource management, strategic management, and small business and entrepreneurship. It should also be of interest to students in sociology, psychology, economics, political science, public administration, social anthropology, and history. It is intended to provide readers with an up-to-date and accessible resource for study, debate, and inspiration regarding a broad range of phenomena in organizations, large and small, in business, government, and the non-profit sector. To make the most of this book, readers should have a basic understanding of the principles of social science analysis and the kinds of questions addressed by social scientists.

I want to thank the many friends, colleagues, and anonymous reviewers who have taken the time to comment on drafts of various parts of this book. I am also grateful to the editors at Sage who have helped me through the long process of writing and revising. My eternal thanks go to my wife, Rosemarie, who selflessly organized much of my non-professional life and buffered my workspace from the pressures of an often unpredictable environment.

1

Introduction: Organizations Matter

Learning Objectives

This chapter will:

- Identify the defining features of organizations

- Distinguish between organization and organizing

- Introduce three theories as conceptual frameworks for analyzing organizational phenomena

1. Introduction

Organizations are essential building blocks of social life, so much so that we refer to society as "organizational society" (Perrow, 1991) and to action as "organized action" (Knoke, 1990a). When chaotic situations follow structured paths, revealing **rules** and procedures, we speak metaphorically of "organized chaos" (Thiétart and Forgues, 1997). When the basic rules of social order are violated, we speak of "organized crime" (Raab and Milward, 2003). Organizations are tools for solving a variety of problems in economy and society, but they can also be a source of new problems, inviting organizational intervention for handling them. It is difficult to imagine a world in which organizations are not significantly involved in the way people make a living, get entertainment, receive education, manage their leisure, represent their **interests**, or have their health restored. The idea of **organizing** is a central element in the cultural toolkit of modern society, describing how people arrange competencies and activities when they classify ideas, prioritize tasks, assemble resources, or look for patterns in ambiguous situations. For most people, organizations and organizing serve an instrumental purpose; they turn to organizations because they "provide meaning and order in the face of **environments** that impose ill-defined, contradictory demands" (Weick, 1993: 635). For social scientists and other academically motivated people, organizations are interesting in their own right, because they affect the human condition in fundamental ways, independent of the particular products and services they produce in a particular instance.

The general objectives of this book are twofold. First, one needs to understand the role that organizations, as entities ostensibly designed for order and stability, play in market societies in which short-term orientations and flexibility imperatives have come to dominate productive activities in many fields. The integrating function of organizations is sometimes forgotten in areas where people are asked to take on more responsibility for their own fate – to become more self-reliant, self-disciplined, and self-managed. Even so, organizations remain basic building blocks of society, aggregating individual interests and administering social order. By creating new resources, they generate wealth and shape the distribution of power and social status. They also affect people's life chances by destroying wealth and by allocating resources in ways that restrict access to material and social opportunities. Organizations not only *affect* society; they are *part of* society. By arranging opportunities differentially through distributing positions and rewards, they produce, reproduce, and transform the **structure** of the society in which they are embedded. This book discusses some of the fundamental ways in which organizations relate to economy and society, with a view to their differentiating and unifying, and constraining and enabling features "across indefinite time-space distances" (Giddens, 1991: 16).

The second aim of this book is to push for a multi-theoretical analysis of organizations, to suggest that differences in perspectives and understandings are not something to be deplored, but to be embraced. The study of organizations has grown over the last few decades into a lively subject of theorizing and empirical research, with applications in a variety of areas, including human resource management, strategic management, entrepreneurship, and public policy. **Organization science** is an exciting field of inquiry in which social scientists debate the nature of organizations, how they should be studied, and what the key problems are that should be attended to. Problems range from micro-level concerns, such as how to accelerate decision processes, to macro-level concerns, such as how to coordinate the activities of an organization's subcontractors. Organizational scholars have developed a wide range of theories and theoretical perspectives for analyzing specific phenomena. The study of organizations is itself organized in that organizational matters are grouped, using criteria such as levels of analysis, assumptions about human nature, and

logics of action. Most scholars in this field are specialized in their use of theories and methodological techniques. This specialization has contributed to the rapid growth of organization studies by cultivating the simultaneous development of specialized topic areas. In the following chapters, three theoretical frameworks – highlighting the economic, institutional, and evolutionary elements of organizations – will be reviewed and applied to a broad range of areas in which organizations are active.

The next section of this chapter will look at the defining characteristics of organizations, with special reference to the dynamic interplay between organization as a structural form and organizing as a process, mediated by human **agency** and social relations, and given meaning by **actors** in the specific context in which an organizational unit, organization, or organizational population operates. The numerous ambiguities and **paradoxes** in organizational life remind us of the importance of revisiting conventional understandings, and they encourage us to enlarge the scope of theoretical lenses with which we study or think about organizations. **Metaphors** are a popular method by which people make sense of organizations and organizational behavior, but they are analytically incomplete. More insightful than metaphors, for understanding complex and dynamic social entities like organizations, is an analytical approach that accommodates multiple theoretical perspectives. This chapter briefly introduces organizational economics, institutionalism, and evolutionary theory as three theoretical frameworks that have spawned major research agendas during the last few decades. While these frameworks differ in core concepts and assumptions about human nature, they address common problems and, when taken together, hold the promise of integrating different insights about a wide range of organizational phenomena.

2. What are organizations?

The everyday use of the term "organization" denotes a **rationally** designed, thoroughly structured social entity whose members work cooperatively towards an explicitly stated common goal. The reality of most organizations, however, differs from this "idealized" depiction. An empirically more realistic and scientifically more sensitive definition of organizations characterizes them as continually evolving activity systems, oriented towards precarious collective goals, and struggling to maintain a distinct identity in an uncertain environment on which they depend for vital resources. Given change and uncertainty, the order and stability that some researchers impute to organizations may not match the perceptions of organizational participants.

Organizations are socio-economic entities, in which calculative elements (e.g., costs, benefits) mix with cultural ideas (e.g., values, meanings), and categories (e.g., member/non-member, white-collar/blue-collar) are used whose boundaries are rarely clear-cut and stable. As social entities, organizations negotiate economic exchange with reference to **normative** criteria like fairness and equity. As such, they differ from markets in which exchanges are coordinated with reference to prices. Yet, organizations also contain market elements, for example in the form of **internal labor markets** as a mechanism for allocating workers to jobs and setting prices for skills. Organizations differ from other social groupings, like families and religious communities, in that they can more easily replace their members without risking survival. Yet, they also include social elements with community character, for example in the form of structures that sustain friendship cliques and **social networks**. In organizations, individuals acting as if they were autonomous are normally less effective than individuals acting somewhere in-between close-knit social groups (e.g., families) and arm's-length relationships (e.g., global investment markets). Communal features may be essential to the maintenance of the organization's social fabric and identity, but disruptions, stemming from interpersonal conflicts, misunderstandings, or improvisation, are an ever-present possibility in organizations that struggle to survive in volatile environments. The interaction of economic and social forces in an ever-evolving organizational context makes it difficult to study organizations in the way natural scientists approach their subject matter, seeking law-like, universal explanations in the form of unambiguous "if–then" (e.g., "the more of X, the more of Y") statements. Instead of organizational behaviors with law-like consistency, we find tendencies, probabilities, exceptions, and surprises. Organizations are best seen as entities for which "but–also" explanations (e.g., "X may lead to Y, but under certain conditions it may also lead to Z") are appropriate. Few organizational phenomena are so clear-cut that they permit no alternative explanations. Much of the "evidence" collected in research – no matter how carefully designed empirical studies may be – is compatible with different interpretations.

As those who are athletically inclined know, being a good athlete requires more than having a set of skills and the will to succeed. Skills need to be learned and improved, and motivations need to be nurtured and adapted to fit new circumstances. Similarly, an organization is more than a building with a structural foundation, a group of individuals with skills, and a set of plans for construction. An organization has a formal structure, supported by rules and regulations, but it is not a finished entity. Rather, it is a project under construction, involving actors who negotiate options, mobilize resources, coordinate inputs, and monitor performance. One can usefully distinguish between the *organization* as an entity with a structural form and pattern, and *organizing* as action and a process of adapting the organization to new conditions, while noting that structure and action are mutually constituted and that neither structures nor processes are ever final.

2.1 Organizing as process

Organizations are in continual flux, although some aspects of organizations can show remarkable persistence. Interpersonal rivalry, demographic changes in the workforce, protests against felt inequities, and so on, always threaten to undermine existing structures and to unsettle well-tried **routines**. Some changes are minor and they occur slowly; other changes amount to deep transformations in the organization's strategic purpose, technology, or authority system. Individuals matter because they keep things in motion through the actions they take when they join forces with like-minded others, collect new resources, or monitor their rivals. From a process view, individuals are interesting not primarily in terms of differences in attitudes and behavioral dispositions, but more with a view to their ongoing efforts to maintain or change their condition in the organization. Investigators taking a process approach study not so much *why* individuals engage in certain actions than *how* they act, looking for temporal patterns evident in sequences, paths, chains of events, disruptions, formations, and so on.

The idea of organizing leads to the understanding of organizations as **social constructions**. Organizations are socially constructed in the sense that there are individuals who, on the basis of preferences and capabilities, and in interaction with others, negotiate goals, evaluate requirements, make decisions, and enforce sanctions. People are not necessarily aware of all the details of what they are doing. They may not explore all possible options, may act out of habit, and may justify their behavior *post hoc* in light of the outcomes of their actions. Their behaviors, planned as well as haphazard, contribute to the reality in the organization to which they then adjust. Organizational realities can differ widely across space and time, contingent on the demands that participants face in specific contexts. For example, when convicts are sent to prison, they have to learn to survive in a different physical reality, and nurses adjust their occupational realities when a new technology is introduced. New realities are the *provisional* end points of variations in organizing activities.

Process has become the mantra of "postmodern" organizations, the antithesis of the stifling traditionalism of organizations in earlier periods. This is the organization of programs and procedures, in which everything of value is legitimized through a process language: process management, group process, learning process, optimization process, and process optimization. Some scholars go as far as to *define* organizations in processual terms, highlighting the actions that "create, maintain, and dissolve social collectivities" and suggesting that "the ways in which these processes are continuously executed *are* the organization" (Weick, 1969: 1, emphasis in the original). Organizing involves series of events and social interaction processes through which adaptation, learning, and innovation take place, without ever reaching a final end-state.

This is most apparent in hazardous work settings like firefighting and aircraft carriers (Weick, 2001), but it also describes what happens in more routine situations, where individuals change the features of an organization, however slightly, every time they reassemble at the workplace and go about their daily tasks (Birnholtz et al., 2007). In the process of getting a little more experienced, learning new things, and discovering new problems, they contribute in one way or another to the organization's development. The anecdote below reveals a dynamic situation, involving a sequence of interpretations and interactions between a car rental agent and an irate customer. Both sides in this heated exchange are trying to bring order to the situation by structuring their social interaction towards a particular end. The organization in this instance is emerging through a process of sense-making, as Martin is using his understanding of an irresponsible organization to give meaning to the employee's behavior, while the employee is using her understanding of rule-based organizations to accommodate Martin's behavior. The outcome is a fragile state of affairs, rather than the kind of order and stability one often associates with the **concept** of organization.

ANECDOTE 1.1

It was the first skiing vacation in the Austrian Alps that Maureen was about to take with her family. Because she could only take five days off from her job in Liverpool, she had carefully planned her trip to Austria. She did not want to leave anything to chance. She had reserved her favorite car model with an international rental agency in Liverpool, where she was promised that the car, equipped with snow chains and a ski rack, would be ready for her to pick up at Vienna airport.

When Maureen arrived at the counter of the rental agency in Vienna, the lady there told her that she didn't have the vehicle Maureen claimed to have booked and that it did not include the equipment she said she had ordered. Maureen explained to the agent that she had made the booking two months ago and that she had been promised the delivery of the car fully equipped for travel in deep snow. The agent seemed indifferent to Maureen's plight and, shrugging her shoulders, she remarked in nearly fluent English, "Well, I'm sorry, but that was in Liverpool. We are here in Vienna." "But this is the same agency," Maureen retorted as politely as possible. "Sorry, I can't help you," the agent insisted. "We don't have a car for you." Maureen quickly became impatient. It was already afternoon and she wanted to reach the resort town before nightfall. "Doesn't your office in Liverpool forward reservations to your unit here in Vienna?" she asked. "Isn't that the whole point of making reservations ahead of time?" "Yes," the agent snapped, "I know how this works." "So what's the problem?" Maureen asked. "The problem is that you must have given them the incorrect information," the agent replied sternly.

Meanwhile, Martin, Maureen's Austrian friend, who had come to the airport to meet her, had come over to the counter. He asked firmly: "I don't really care about who is to blame. I want to know what you do when a reservation goes wrong? Don't you have some sort of cooperative arrangement with any of the other rental agencies at the airport? Maybe they have the vehicle that my friend here wants." Looking at him in disbelief, the agent told him that there were no such arrangements. "I can't just dream one up," she said. "Well, maybe you could just ask the agency next door," Martin suggested. "No, I can't," she snapped back. "That's not our policy here." Maureen's German was good enough to understand that Martin had become furious about what he called "outrageous behavior" and an "abusive attitude" on the part of the rental agent. "I don't care about your company policy," he insisted. "When something goes wrong, it's your business to make it right. Can't you be a bit flexible?" "We have procedures, you know, and my job is to follow them," she said. When Martin told her that he wouldn't go away until the matter was resolved, she handed him a slip of paper on which she wrote the phone number of the agency's office in Liverpool. "Here is a number you can call." At this point he pounded with his fist on the counter, shouting something about "lousy service" and announcing that he would complain to the management of this company, both in Vienna and Liverpool, and that, if necessary, he would write a letter to the local association of tourist bureaus, the airport authority, and the Vienna city marketing office, and anyone else who he thought should be interested in the way customers are treated by this company. He was still shouting long after the agent had disappeared into a back room, never to be seen again.

This story suggests that organizations should not be taken for granted, not even organizations as large and mature as international car rental agencies. Organizations are continually constructed, both by members and customers who, in the process of interacting with one another, create outcomes that are not always the best ones possible, for reasons related to deficient information, differential bargaining power, human emotionality, and so forth. Organizations are not merely the formal system of hierarchies, rules, and standard operating procedures that we normally think make organizational life predictable. More often than not, organizations are in a constant process of becoming something other than what is set out in strategic plans, mission statements, goal-setting exercises, and the like. If organizational structures hold up over time it is often only because people improvise, compensate, self-correct, or acquiesce. From an organizing perspective, an organization is never a finished product but is the precarious result of a never-ending process of changing and adapting.

2.2 Organization as structure

While the concept of organizing conjures up the image of a river, denoting flow and fluidity, the concept of organization may be visualized as a river bed, anchored in a location and giving flows direction. The organization has a structure, giving it a specific form and pattern, and is measurable in terms of levels of hierarchy, degrees of task differentiation, or number of written rules

(Blau and Schoenherr, 1971). If individuals matter in the structural *form* that an organization takes, it is more in terms of their interdependence in the workflow than their psychological disposition or cognitive capacity. From a structural perspective, individuals' understanding of their membership in the organization is embedded in the other-directedness of their actions. The car rental agent in the above anecdote (1.1) defends her actions with reference to her position relative to others in the organization's system of policies, rules, and procedures, and relative to the customer who, presumably, does not understand the organization's rules.

The organization as structure refers to relationships between positions rather than positions *per se*. Organizational positions are locations occupied by people performing such roles as project leaders, departmental employees, or task force members. Positions have a natural structural interpretation because they are defined *vis-à-vis* each other rather than in terms of content, such as whether the position contains technical expertise or discretionary power regarding the spending of money. In structural language, a person occupying a position is connected to others in some way. The position of a top executive is "distant" from that of a sales clerk not because these individuals perform different tasks or use different knowledge, but because they sit in different locations in the organization's pattern of social relations. Although they may differ in the level of decision-making **authority**, they may be *structurally* similar in their relationships to some of the other individuals in the organization. For example, they may both personally know the head of the finance department or they may both obtain coaching from the same consultant. "Structural equivalence" means that the individuals occupy the same location in the relational system of the organization, even though they may never meet physically or may be unaware of each other's existence.

2.3 Human agency and social relations

An organization's relational system does not exist on its own but is "made to happen" by individuals who have some reason for whatever they are doing. Relational systems are constructed by agentic individuals who interpret events, make decisions, or distribute favors. The distance in power between the executive at the top of the organization and the sales clerk at the bottom of the hierarchy may be insurmountable formally, but this does not mean that the sales clerk is completely at the mercy of the executive. Subordinates can protest against felt injustice, recruit the help of others to negotiate a better deal for themselves, or withdraw into "inner exile." Superiors with formal authority can exercise power only to the extent that subordinates comply with their commands. Even discretely bounded categories like male/female, black/white, or native/foreign are not fixed properties, but require human agency to translate perceptions and labels into action to maintain the meaning of differences and similarities. Structures make a difference only once they are given meaning through human action, while action always takes place within and in response to existing structures (Giddens, 1984).

Agency means more than individuals acting out some purpose and *doing* something; it also includes the capacity to understand the conditions and reasons for their actions. Individuals behave as agents if they act self-reflexively, within a broader structure of rules, positions, and conventions, which guide behavior without determining it (Giddens, 1984). "True artists" (Bain, 2005), "real craftsmen" (Sennett, 2008), and "born teachers" (Ogbonna and Harris, 2004) are often mentioned as examples of human agents who attach a strong sense of self to their work and who forcefully negotiate their identity in an often hostile economic environment. The aggregate outcomes of their actions, such as government subsidies for a stagnant industry or a new accreditation system for a profession, may not be intended by anyone in particular, but without their actions nothing may have happened. Agency is the thread that weaves economic transactions, social structures, and institutional contexts together, relationally and dynamically.

The concern for agency in organization studies is part of the "relational turn" that has taken place across the social sciences in recent years (Emirbayer, 1997). From a relational perspective, aggregate phenomena, such as income inequality or bureaucratic rigidity, are not primarily a function of *personal* attributes (e.g., charisma, resilience), but are the result of contestation, negotiation, competition, and cooperation within a dynamic system of *social* relations between differentially endowed actors. In organization studies, the concept of **relation** refers not only to interpersonal relations in a work group and to relations between organizations and environments, but also to relations between humans and artifacts (e.g., architects and buildings, programmers and computers) and between non-human entities (e.g., tasks constituting jobs, texts constituting websites). **Narratives** (e.g., stories about successful entrepreneurs) consist of relations between ideas, with a structure that defines a beginning and an end, as well as turning points and new directions in-between (Mohr, 1998). Relational systems, such as statements in company reports, events in organizational initiation rites, or decisions in an employee recruitment process, can be examined with a view to the evolving connections between the constitutive elements (Pentland and Feldman, 2007). The goal of a relational representation of organizational phenomena is to provide insight into their social construction across time and space, enabling researchers to simultaneously consider issues of substance (e.g., knowledge), form (e.g., structure), and process (e.g., adaptations).

2.4 The dynamic interplay between action and structure

Variations in organizing actions extend to variations in **organizational form**, although there is no one-to-one relationship between the two. In one case, organizing efforts may lead to flexible structures supporting spontaneous communication between workers; in another instance, the same organizing behaviors may trigger new structural constraints through the clarification of formal procedures. The difference in outcomes may be due to resource availability, the technology in use, the personalities of individuals, or some other factor. Although there is no one-to-one relationship between action and structure, they are not independent of each other. Viewed dynamically and across the micro–macro-level divide, structure is the source and outcome of processes as well as the medium through which processes unfold (Giddens, 1984: 16–28). Decision-making processes, for example, have structural outcomes regarding the distribution of power and information. Conversely, the way in which decisions are made – how fast or how consistently – is shaped by structural features, such as the composition of the decision group in terms of people with similar and different skills. While differences in human psychology and cognitive capability are important, their impact is mediated by the relational configuration of the entity under investigation. If one ignores this aspect in the characterization of organizational behavior, one no longer has enough structure to interpret the interactions among the organization's participants.

Structure is inextricably and dynamically linked to action as both its medium and outcome. Individuals draw on the organization's structure, in the form of rules, resources, and incentives, and in doing so they reproduce or transform these same properties (Giddens, 1984). For example, people who have a secure position in the organization's employment structure are more likely to report a case of witnessed harassment than people who are in a more peripheral and temporal organizational position (Folgerø and Fjeldstad, 1995). Their intervention may stimulate the creation of formal rules of conduct to prevent harassment, but new rules may lead to the perception in the workforce that there exists widespread harassment in the organization, with the effect of intensifying the reporting of real or imagined cases of harassment, and then leading to a further tightening of rules. In this way, the organization becomes more structured over time, with new rules and resources spent on enforcing the rules, and with outcomes that may or may not be in line with the actors' original intentions.

There is nothing inherent in the interplay between structure and action that would lead only to *functional* outcomes, from the point of view of the organization or its individual members. High-rise apartment buildings, such as those shown in Exhibit 1.1, may be designed for clean, safe, and efficient living, but the same design may also give rise to social alienation, crime, and vandalism. Architecturally and culturally diverse urban spaces, like those

Exhibit 1.1

shown in Exhibit 1.2, may be planned for human enjoyment and entertainment, but they may also cause overcrowding and pollution. An organization is not merely a formal arrangement of purposively planned activities. It is also the result of forces arising spontaneously out of the social interactions among the participants. Some parts of an organization are expected, preferred, or prescribed; other parts are downplayed, not observed, or avoided. This means that it is not sufficient for the investigator to simply state the functional or dysfunctional results of particular organizational forms. The analyst also needs to identify the processes which account for the construction and transformation of organizational forms in a specific context.

Exhibit 1.2

2.5 Organization and context

Organizations and organizational units are not stand-alone entities. All social interaction in and between organizations occurs within a larger context, which can itself be the subject of investigation. Context is that which "surrounds" a particular phenomenon and is analytically distinct from the phenomenon itself. Interactions evolve across levels that are contextually "nested" within each other. "Nesting" means that higher levels in the system contain lower levels and that levels become increasingly inclusive as one moves up the "hierarchy" from component entities, such as decisions and rules, to organizational populations, such as industries and regional business clusters. Hierarchy of levels does not mean that higher levels are more important or more real in any way than lower levels. It does mean, however, that phenomena are generally more complex and often more disorderly at higher levels, given that at higher levels there are more contexts and a greater variety of interrelated **variables**. Organizing is generally more diverse at higher levels than at lower levels. Individuals can less easily influence outcomes at the organizational level than the immediate job level, and it takes more time for individuals to affect what happens in industries than it takes organizations to make a difference at the industry level. Still, individual actions are consequential for higher-level phenomena; they keep the organization in motion, while the organization's structure provides the context in which the actions unfold.

The fact that external environments vary in the terms on which different types of resources are available to organizations explains much of the wide variation in organizational forms (Hannan and Freeman, 1989). Consider the many differences between museums and churches, or the differences between consulting firms and machine shops. These organizations differ in mission, authority structure, knowledge base, and task complexity, and they differ in how the details of these elements, as well as the processes connecting them, play out in specific instances. The practical day-to-day challenges of, say, maintaining order, may be tied to situational specifics, such as the nature of a particular customer. The recalcitrant customer described in Anecdote 1.1 may very well be one that the employee of this organization has never encountered before, causing her to retreat behind existing organizational rules rather than experiment with new behaviors and accept the risks associated with improvisation. In a less rule-constrained organization, the employee might have been more willing to try out new approaches to dealing with "difficult" customers, but testing this expectation requires the incorporation of contextual contingencies. Without the presence of customers posing unique challenges, the employee might never learn the benefits and costs of alternative behaviors in a different context. That is, to understand particular actions, one also needs to know the context in which the actions occur.

Contextual variations draw attention to the limited applicability of particular organizational models. For example, **mechanistic** models of organizational structure, which emphasize strict rules and centralized decision-making, may be more appropriate for technical organizations specializing in aircraft maintenance than they are for religious organizations mobilizing people's ideas about spiritual issues. People studying organizations should always ask questions about the conditions under which a particular **practice** or structural feature will make what kind of difference and for whom. For this, they need a **theory** or, preferably, several theories with which they can develop non-obvious hypotheses and then put them to an empirical test. And those who work in organizations and are looking for predictability, efficiency, legitimacy, or some other outcome should be aware of the impact of situational specifics. For this, they also need a theory that helps them understand what they are doing and why they are doing it. Some organizational settings are so complex and volatile that people have difficulty distinguishing between what is a unique and non-recurring situation and what is a regular and generalizable pattern. Effective theorizing includes statements about *how* context affects the phenomenon under investigation, rather than merely acknowledging the existence of context or describing contextual differences. Regarding the rental agent's behavior in the anecdote above, an analytically insightful question would ask why and how a different context, such as a different type of customer or the absence of a customer's friend, would trigger different behaviors. Understanding the **mechanisms** by which different features of the context exert influence would make organizational models regarding the effectiveness of particular structures or behavioral routines more accurate and robust (Elster, 2007).

3. Thinking about organizations metaphorically

People who look for general patterns in an organization may find it difficult to appreciate the details of its inner workings. Rather than engage in a systematic analysis of some complex phenomenon, which would require them to examine how some event or process results from or leads to a larger set of interrelated variables, they often use metaphors as a short-cut to understanding. Metaphors are implied comparisons, used to represent an ambiguous concept in terms of another, more familiar concept. Metaphors are popular in general parlance, but also researchers employ metaphors to communicate the essentials of a difficult phenomenon (Oswick et al., 2002). For instance, the machine metaphor ("This team runs like a well-oiled machine") draws attention to the close interdependencies among the constitutive elements of an entity to highlight predictability and efficiency. Some people may use this metaphor to emphasize the organizational order of residences like the massive apartment complex shown in Exhibit 1.1. They may view the uniform architecture as an indicator of things that are characteristic of hierarchical controls ("knowing one's place") and formal standards ("following the rules of the house") in large-scale organizations, and they may interpret machine-like structures as comforting if they offer order and accountability. Others may draw the opposite inference from this metaphoric depiction; they may criticize the hierarchy and discipline in a machine-like order as dehumanizing and emasculating.

Organizations that are designed to work like machines may have efficient processes but they are not always effective in consequence. People may think of organizations with machine-like forms as "sinking ships," running aground because of their inability to initiate fundamental change or to effect change quickly. Or, they may believe that machine-like structures eventually turn into "treadmills," forcing individuals into routines as if they were climbing up a never-ending staircase. In contrast to the machine image, the metaphor of organizations as "garbage cans" conjures up the idea of chaos, but, in specific contexts, the consequences of chaos may be benign. People may perceive the diverse mass of people, buildings, and artifactual contraptions at San Marco Square in Venice (Exhibit 1.2) as disorderly, but it is also colorful and lively, attracting innovations. The buildings represent a variety of architectural styles, with cultural meanings imported from different historical epochs and regions in the world. The individuals who had them erected, over the course of several centuries, could not foresee the diverse functions they serve today (e.g., eating and drinking, art exhibitions, award ceremonies, film locations). If there is any order at all in this diverse assembly of buildings, purposes, and people, it is likely the result of **organic** adaptation, rather than deliberate mechanistic planning. The dynamic coherence of organizations with an organic form results from the interdependence of differentiated elements and from the ability of each element to adjust to the requirements of its own context, which may help organizations survive in changing environments.

Metaphors can be helpful as a sensitizing device, encouraging people to question old wisdoms and conventional assumptions, but they may also cement current thinking. Organizations that feel like "a golden cage" can turn into an "iron cage," but this may only tell part of the story. Metaphors focus on what is considered essential in a given phenomenon, but they may also obscure certain aspects by leaving out what people are not familiar with or what they are not looking for. Metaphors treat the organization *as if* it had the characteristics of the entity one is familiar with. By highlighting familiar features, they illuminate what one believes is central to an organization and what one thinks one knows about the organization already. For example, when people characterize the presumed "disorganization" of a parliamentary assembly as a "circus," they may not only reinforce their assumptions about complex decision processes in a political entity like a parliament, but they may also ignore the potential flexibility and innovativeness of circus-like structures. To the extent that such structures permit resource redundancy, encourage cognitive diversity, and support constructive rivalry, they may be ideal for situations requiring innovation, improvisation, and imagination.

Metaphors thus draw attention to the perspectival nature of organizations. What matters is how we see things, and that depends on the perspective we take. Organizational reality is never clear enough to permit a single true representation, so that the observer needs to make a choice between available perspectives. This is not necessarily a bad thing. To the extent that different theoretical perspectives overlap and complement each other, there is some common ground on which fruitful debates can take place. Perspectival diversity provides a richer environment for learning and innovation than adherence to a single perspective. Different perspectives make accessible different kinds of information and thus provide a foundation for alternative understandings. In the complex world of organizations, applying a single perspective carries the risk of becoming corrupted by a hegemonic view, ending in a blind alley, and forgetting that all theorizing is a project of construction, a process of sorting out key concepts and of distinguishing genuine phenomena from noise. Consider the limitations of trying to make sense of the image shown in Exhibit 1.1 from a single perspective. Economists may emphasize the resource efficiency of accommodating large numbers of people in tightly structured high-rise facilities. They may note the cost savings of clear rules for negotiating and enforcing contracts, but may ignore the disruptive power struggles in contract negotiations. Theorists taking a sociological perspective may attend to the relativity of claims about efficiency. They may argue that preferences are shaped by concerns about social status, but may ignore the economic costs of maintaining status differentials relative to the benefits. Cognitive theorists may focus on human perceptual errors to explain why some residents in this housing complex feel anonymous, but they may overlook the role of social biases in perceptions. While each perspective adds important insights, there is the danger that scholars who build a research program solely on the basis of a single perspective get caught within the narrow confines of the perspective they have chosen. It is often through the synthesis of different theoretical perspectives and the borrowing of concepts from related or competing perspectives that deep understanding is obtained (Whetten et al., 2009). Difficult situations, such as those depicted in Anecdote 1.1, are an invitation to move beyond common-sense reasoning and speculation, and to engage in detailed theoretical analysis (Merton, 1967).

4. Organizations as a field of theoretical inquiry and empirical research

Many scholars take an **empiricist** approach and pursue organization studies as if it were a natural science, seeking to discover objective realities and general laws for explaining them. Others reject the natural science approach in favor of a view of organizational realities that is constructed by **intendedly rational** people and is difficult to grasp with law-like generalities. These realities come with all the ambiguities and surprises that construction "from the ground up" implies. Many scholars value **theoretical pluralism**, noting the complexity of organizations as settings where economic, social, cultural, political, and psychological forces interact, with outcomes that are often impossible to predict. Others believe in the incommensurability of **paradigms** that are grounded in different assumptions about the subject matter and in different views about what counts as research. Some scholars deplore the lack of consensus in organizational theory, while others would be surprised if organization scientists should ever reach consensus about anything.

Researchers often work with abstract concepts like **bureaucracy** and routines in order to arrive at general principles of organization that hold across time and space. The problem with universal concepts is that while they may cover important general ground, they tend to leave the proverbial "black box" untouched. The black box of organizations contains many different processes and mechanisms. Bureaucratic organizational structures, for example, limit individual discretion, but they also empower people and enable action. Routines contain rules that provide stability, but these are also the subject of negotiation and the target for change. Abstract concepts may also cut across problem areas in which different mechanisms are at work. The mechanisms that causally link, say, organizational rules to innovation in professional organizations (e.g., law firms) may differ substantially from the mechanisms linking rules to innovation in non-professional organizations (e.g., video stores). Unpacking concepts, as well as the mechanisms that causally link concepts, is necessary if we want to understand organizational realities in different situations. In the end it is reality, or at least a particular interpretation of reality, that needs to show if the concepts that scholars work with provide useful insights.

As in social life in general (Tilly, 2006), the members of organizations do not always know exactly what they are doing and why they are doing it. When asked about the reason for their behavior, they often match their answer to what they think the person asking them wants to hear, and they rarely collect the data necessary to test their assumptions. Even highly educated managers are often not aware of the main research findings in their field of expertise, or they fail to implement the recommendations flowing from that research (Rynes et al., 2002). When dealing with difficult situations, people tend to engage in **heuristic** decision-making, relying on cognitive short-cuts such as common sense, intuition, single-case observation, or their own experience (Kahneman, 2011). They may behave habitually or they may conform to what they think the majority are doing in a particular situation. In some cases, making a decision on the basis of intuition or habit may indeed be preferable, for example, when there is not enough time to consider all possible variables and alternative options. In other situations, this produces highly sub-optimal outcomes; important problems are not solved, or new ones are created. Academic scholars would suggest that the employee in the anecdote above (1.1) reflects on the likely consequences of adopting a different behavioral approach towards this customer, based on a theoretical understanding of human behavior in different contexts. In this particular instance, understanding might come, for example, from theories about human cognition, decision processes, or organizational routines.

A central aim of this book is to help readers appreciate the value of a multi-perspective analytical approach to the study of organizations. Openness to diversity of perspective is useful for both scientific progress and for applications in organizational practice, although it is not easy to weave through the multitude of theories and theoretical perspectives current in the field of organization studies (Baum, 2002; Clegg et al., 1996; Scott, 2004; Tsoukas and Knudsen, 2003). Arguably, some of the perspectives in use do not constitute a logically coherent set of concepts and statements. They are better thought of as "orientations" to specific aspects of the organizational world, but this does not necessarily limit their usefulness. Also, perspectives may blend into another in ways that can make it difficult to apply them separately in particular instances. It is, however, possible to distill several general *frameworks* that differ in main premises and arguments and which have attracted sustained attention in organizational scholarship in areas such as organizational design, strategic management, change management, human resource management, innovation management, and entrepreneurship. In this book, three such theoretical frameworks – emphasizing the economic, institutional, and evolutionary dimensions of organizations – will be applied to problem areas ranging from the interactions between individuals to the relationships between organizations and environments.

Organizational economics, institutionalism, and evolutionary theory can be considered theoretical frameworks – or theory groups – in the sense that they assemble interrelated concepts under the same umbrella and provide a reference point for interpreting empirical observations. When applied together, they are useful for organizational analysis in at least two ways. First, they draw attention to the recursive relationship between action and structure, providing insights into the fundamental question of how organizational reality is constructed, and with what effects. In doing so, they attend to the close links between organizations and the people in them, highlighting the **emergent** aspects of organizations. Actions always emerge out of pre-existing structures, in an evolving context that shapes but does not determine outcomes (Sawyer, 2001). The results of emergent systems cannot normally be predicted even under the best conditions and even if one has full knowledge of the pre-emergent properties of the organization. The interplay between economic, institutional, and evolutionary forces guards against excessively **deterministic** accounts of organizations as mere dopes of environments to which they respond automatically.

Second, economic, institutional, and evolutionary frameworks address the problem of relations between actors, rather than only the attributes of actors. Studying relations affords a look into the black box of organizational life, taking into account the interests of individuals and organizations as **causal agents**, without treating them in isolation from the context in which they are embedded. Organizational phenomena cannot be reduced to individuals alone, as individual behavior in and between organizations is always mediated by social relations. It is not only the existence of a connection that matters, but also the nature and quality of the connection. Friendship ties may work differently than gossip ties, and it makes a difference if social ties in project teams, interest associations, or strategic alliances are underpinned by pecuniary motives, institutional regulations, cultural meanings, or some other consideration.

Social relations, and the dynamic interplay between action and structure, figure prominently in organizational economics, institutionalism, and evolutionary theory, although researchers may approach them differently in specific instances, focusing on different details and sorting them in different ways. In a study of career development in and between organizations, for example, investigators might highlight different structures of opportunity and mechanisms of "getting ahead." Career is an example of general concepts that appear in a variety of research programs and are studied from different theoretical perspectives. Individuals have careers (e.g., employment and skill development), as do work teams (e.g., formation and stagnation), professions (e.g., legitimation and institutionalization), and ideas (e.g., generation and diffusion). Economic, institutional, and evolutionary processes play a role in each of these areas, but the explanations of origins and outcomes, and the mechanisms connecting them, differ between perspectives. From an economic perspective, careers evolve through employment episodes, reflecting the worker's economic worth to the organization (Masters and Miles, 2002). From an institutional perspective, career advancement is affected by social institutions such as family, education, and health care (Kalleberg, 2009). And evolutionary theorists view career development in terms of the distribution of job opportunities in the organization's job ladder (Miner, 1990). Theorists who work within these theoretical frameworks focus on different mechanisms through which career development affects a person's life chances, and they may arrive at different conclusions. It is not only *what* scholars see but *how* they see it that gives each framework its distinctive flavor, while being open to accommodation between different perspectives. The following section provides a brief summary of the key concepts and arguments in each of these frameworks, as they will be used throughout the subsequent chapters in this book.

4.1 Organizational economics

Standard economic theory has little to say about organizations, even though it is mostly through organizations that things of economic value are produced and distributed. In classical economic theory, the producers of goods and services are assumed to operate in perfectly competitive markets for products, labor, and capital, where organizations are merely an epiphenomenon in a system driven by the price mechanism. In neo-classical economic theory, the organization is treated as if it were a single person, a self-interested, rational, and internally coherent actor competing with others in markets on the basis of invariant rules. Resource competition is expected to lead to an optimal distribution of specialized and efficient actors.

Organizational economics departs from this depiction by problematizing the organization as a more or less heterogeneous entity that does not normally act as a simple price-taker in perfectly competitive markets. It views the organization as consisting of individuals who pursue interests that do not automatically add up to a consistent organizational goal. People are seen as constrained in their capacity to act as economically rational decision-makers because of limited information-processing capabilities (March and Simon, 1958). Organizations require an efficient hierarchical control and incentive system to align the interests of all participants and to improve the quality of decision-making. Incentives are specified in formal contracts (e.g., employment contracts, profit-sharing arrangements) and informal agreements (e.g., goal-setting agreements, special awards), detailing the rights of each individual, the performance criteria for the evaluation of their contributions, and the payoffs they can expect from the wealth the organization produces. The economic problem is that the negotiation and enforcement of contracts and agreements involves costs, which increase when the partners to the exchange have conflicting interests or interpretations. Small, family-owned and -controlled firms tend to face lower costs in this regard than large organizations, where specialized knowledge is widely diffused among individuals with different skills and orientations, but the division of interest between the owners of property (principals) and the employees (agents) introduces extra costs in all organizations. The principal's problem is how to devise a system of incentives that leads the agent to behave in ways consistent with the principal's interests. Uncertainties and trade-offs arise because principals cannot normally achieve complete control over the work process, because of limited expertise, time constraints, and institutional regulations imposed from the outside. They may, therefore, delegate control to managers and supervisors, but delegation may itself create agency problems, raising coordination and control costs.

Achieving organizational efficiency means more than maximizing utilities in the allocation of scarce resources (Barney and Ouchi, 1986). Organizational economists ask the more basic question: Why do organizations exist in the first place? Given the costs of hiring employees, supervising them, evaluating their performance, settling disputes, and so on, it may be more efficient for organizations to purchase needed inputs on the open market than to produce them inside the organization. The economic answer to the question of externalizing (via the market) or internalizing production (via organizational hierarchy) turns on the problem of minimizing the transaction costs associated with coordinating economic exchange relations.

The various strands of organizational economics, dealing with property rights, principal–agency problems, and transaction costs, have proven useful for organizational analysis because they address a wide range of problem areas related to cooperation and control within and between organizations. Still, to many scholars, organizational economics does not go far enough to the extent that it takes an exclusively efficiency-based approach to organizations and treats the individual as driven solely by economic self-interest, while neglecting non-economic considerations, such as social status, justice, and reputation. These issues are taken up in institutional theory.

4.2 Organizational institutionalism

While there is no single, agreed-upon definition of **institution**, most scholars think of institutions as commonly shared and taken-for-granted cultural meaning systems (Jepperson, 1991), such as the idea that organizations have the right to hire those individuals they think will add value to the organization. Institutions play a central role in organizational life, by providing an evaluative and regulatory framework, through which organizations acquire reputation, credibility, and **social legitimacy**. Institutional conformity, stemming from the desire to "look good" in the eyes of constituents, helps organizations survive in uncertain economic environments (Scott, 2008).

Organizational forms are often not uniquely "optimal" in any meaningful sense because they are constructed in response to a variety of sometimes inconsistent institutional pressures. The expectation that, say, older job applicants be given the same opportunity as young applicants may collide with the expectation that older workers be given less physically demanding jobs. Some institutional expectations are of a general nature, exposing different kinds of organizations to the same demands, regardless of economic need and benefit. The expectation that employees be offered maternity leave may be as strong for car dealerships as it is for hospitals, even if the former organizations employ far fewer women than hospitals do. A central prediction in institutional theory is that organizations existing in the same institutional environment tend to adopt similar forms to signal compliance with institutional demands, even if this means some sacrifice in efficiency.

The various strands in institutional theory differ with respect to whether emphasis is placed on institutions seen as relatively stable relational structures constraining action ("This is how things are done"), or as a terrain for contesting rules and regulations ("This is how things should be done"). In the former case, institutions are studied as fundamental elements of social structure, with powerful effects on organizations. Ideologies and traditions limit the range of options from which organizations choose solutions that fit their particular circumstances. In the latter case, institutions are studied more as "social constructions" and sites of political struggle between actors who differ in interests and power. In both cases, however, institutions are considered means of social control (Berger and Luckmann, 1966).

Institutional theorists also differ in their view on organizational adaptation. To some theorists, adaptation is the *result* of organizational conformity to existing institutional pressures. These theorists take a more static approach to institutional effects, similar to organizational economists who characterize organizational forms as arrangements matching existing situational requirements. Other institutional theorists are interested more in the way adaptation works, studying adaptation as a *process* of interpreting, learning, and adjusting. They view adaptation as a process of organizations acting purposively, within a local context of cultural beliefs and social structures, carving out a niche that fits their unique circumstances. On the whole, the broad scope of institutional theory provides insights for the analysis of organizations as social constructions in which the normative and cultural aspects of social relations often prevail over narrow economic criteria. Similar to organizational economists, institutional theorists argue that organizations should not be taken for granted – although for reasons having to do more with cultural and social than with efficiency concerns.

4.3 Organizational evolution

Evolutionary theory addresses not only purposeful behavior, regardless of whether actions are motivated by economic efficiency or by institutional considerations. It also pays attention to the unexpected and improbable in organizational development, in order to cover all possible actions – both planned and *ad hoc* – and outcomes of actions – both intended and unintended (Aldrich and Ruef, 2006). The goal is to study the entire range of variation in organizational forms, resulting from the interplay of organizational actions and environmental conditions.

A distinct contribution of evolutionary theory to organizational analysis is that it takes into account both successes and failures in organizational behavior. Evolutionary theorists take an open-ended, non-teleological, and value-neutral approach to organizational development, suggesting that no organizational form is, or can ever be, historically privileged over other forms. If certain structures and actions do improve things for the organization, there is nothing immutable about the criteria by which improvement may be defined, and there is nothing inevitable about the course of organizational development, given the state of the external environment. By furnishing vital resources for organizations, environments affect the probability that particular organizational forms are created, replicated, and diffused. This does not mean that all organizations are completely at the mercy of their environments. Organizations explore emerging opportunities, exploit available resources, and extract rents from their investments, and some organizations shape the terms on which resources are available for other organizations. Organizations are engaged in a competitive struggle over scarce resources, but they also cooperate with each other to minimize competitive pressure. Organizations can also learn from past mistakes and transmit what they learn to subsequent generations of organizations.

The evolutionary approach seeks to explain changes in organizational forms as the result of processes involving variation (producing differences), selection (choosing a variant), and retention (storing the selected variant for future use). These processes occur at hierarchically nested levels, from the intra-organizational level of ideas, beliefs, and actions, to the inter-organizational level of organizational populations. Some of the new variations in organizational forms are unplanned, resulting from chance and trial-and-error behavior. Other variations are deliberate, resulting from actions that are part of an overall strategy, although purposeful actions can also lead to dead ends, depending on the state of the environment. Evolutionary theory categorically rejects the teleological notion of movement towards a predetermined end-state. The generality of this theory, based on the universal principles of variation, selection, and retention, makes it useful for studying the development of organizations across time and space.

In summary, while organizational economics, institutionalism, and evolution offer distinct approaches to the study of organizations, they also overlap in certain aspects, suggesting possibilities of integration. For example, the concern in evolutionary theory for competitive processes provides a link to the economics of competitive organizational strategy with respect to such issues as new product development and technology transfer. Organizational economics also includes a stream of research on evolutionary adaptation as a continuing process that may never reach a state of equilibrium (Nelson and Winter, 1982). The link between evolutionary and institutional theory is provided by a common concern for cooperative interaction within and between organizations (Zucker, 1989). Much research has shown that the economy is not separate from the institutional sphere, and that the same kinds of evolutionary processes drive developments in both economic and institutional domains (Scott, 2008). The vast literature on organizations is replete with studies of phenomena that are examined with concepts from organizational economics, institutionalism, and evolutionary theory, sometimes in the same study. The research brief below provides an example of such a phenomenon, indicating the advantages of taking a multi-perspective approach. This study shows that many firms do not employ certain kinds of human resource management techniques even if they are well-grounded in scientific research. Firms that do use them may do so because they expect them to enhance their social reputation, rather than to improve their market performance. The conditions under which human resource management techniques are adopted can be interpreted with reference to arguments from organizational economics, institutionalism, and evolutionary theory.

RESEARCH BRIEF 1.1

Human resource management (HRM) techniques, such as job enrichment, empowerment, and total quality management, are normally praised for their economic benefits. The common view is that such techniques improve the performance of organizations by reducing coordination costs and stimulating innovation. Organizations that adopt them are assumed to benefit in the form of higher profitability and improved survival chances.

Contradicting the generality of these assumptions, the study by Staw and Epstein (2000) suggests that few organizations employ popular human resource management techniques. They are not even used by all of the largest corporations, and those firms that do use them are not always high performers in their respective markets. Drawing on data from company citations in newspapers and magazines, this study found that executives of the 100 largest industrial corporations in the United States are often rewarded for adopting popular management practices simply because they are considered socially desirable, improving a firm's institutional reputation. The concern for reputation imposes strong evolutionary selection pressures on the decision to adopt the newest management techniques. Firms that introduce popular HRM techniques can expect to increase their reputation in society, but they do not necessarily lead to higher financial returns.

These findings can be interpreted from several theoretical perspectives. From an institutional perspective, organizations do not necessarily adopt the technologically best or economically most efficient techniques but, instead, adopt those techniques that enhance social legitimacy. In principle, reputation can be an important source of competitive advantage, consistent with

(Continued)

economic reasoning about the allocation of resources to activities that improve the firm's market performance. However, the pursuit of social reputation may divert scarce resources away from other important activities. The question is: How long can firms afford to maintain comparatively inefficient programs until they are required to prove that these programs are economically beneficial? This question relates to the adaptive value of organizational structures and practices. From an evolutionary perspective, firms may be able to deviate from accepted economic performance standards without punishment in the short term. In the long run, however, environmental pressures will likely sanction firms that do not meet the extant criteria for survival. As this study shows, these criteria are not only economic ones. While in the institutional domain, literal market mechanisms do not exist; there are institutional elements, like traditions and conventions, which get winnowed in the evolutionary selection process as well.

From a methodological point of view, this study has several limitations, as noted by the authors. One limitation is the use of data at the corporate level. Human resource management innovations typically occur at the plant level and unit level. Aggregate data at the corporate level, and data based on newspaper accounts, may not provide a true picture of the reasons and outcomes of such innovations. Another limitation is the focus on distant outcomes such as returns on equity, rather than more proximate outcomes, such as employee satisfaction or product defects. The adoption of management techniques may well have economic benefits, if measured in terms of behavioral outcomes at the level of employees, such as work productivity and absenteeism.

5. A look ahead

Organizations are studied for many reasons and from many different points of view, reflecting personal interest, situational demands, and theoretical debate. The following chapters in this book show how arguments from organizational economics, institutional theory, and evolutionary theory can be applied to a broad range of organizational phenomena and at various levels of analysis. The theoretical frameworks will be discussed with a view to the synthetic possibilities of taking an integrative approach. Readers are encouraged to apply these frameworks as orienting devices that help order and give meaning to research findings. In line with Lewin's (1951: 169) classic statement that "there is nothing more practical than a good theory," they should feel encouraged to think in theoretical terms. The idea is to engage in theoretical reasoning to better conceptualize problematic situations in everyday organizational life and to discover potentially useful new avenues of dealing with them. The objective of a "theory sensitizing" approach is to give readers an opportunity to gain some insight into the exciting debates going on in organization studies, while also getting a glimpse of the vast empirical work being done in this field today. Empirical evidence comes from the burgeoning literature on organizations in fields such as strategic management, entrepreneurship, human resource management, and organizational design, and in disciplines like sociology, psychology, economics, political science, and economic geography.

Each chapter includes a "research brief" to provide an example of the kinds of questions organizational scholars ask and the kinds of data they collect to test theoretical arguments. In many cases, research findings contradict or qualify common assumptions about organizations and organizational behavior, regarding rationality, decision-making, social interaction, and so on. In the spirit of science, scholars work hard to construct arguments that are open to refutation and replication through an appeal to logic and evidence, but they are normally limited by the availability of valid and reliable data. The "research briefs" indicate some of the methodological difficulties that scholars normally encounter in their investigations, suggesting that the available evidence should be understood as tentative rather than conclusive. Like other social sciences, organization studies struggles with methodological problems and inferential challenges that may lead researchers to reject good ideas and accept false ones. The methodological standards in the natural sciences are appealing to many organizational scholars, but they are not attainable in most of the organizational settings they study. Arriving at valid and reliable scientific conclusions through controlled experiments is unrealistic in most areas of organizational life, for reasons related to the sampling of units from ill-defined populations, the various social biases that contaminate data collection, and the measurement of variables whose meanings often differ across the sampled subjects. Most organizational research is non-experimental, given the near impossibility in organizations to achieve controlled conditions. Still, researchers may do their best to approximate experimental methods as closely as possible. They may construct random samples, verify the measurement of variables, distinguish between causation and association, and rigorously apply advanced statistical techniques, but they still often turn up findings that are difficult to explain.

Complex research findings are often difficult to convey to readers who prefer simple conclusions over elegant statistics or long texts with many conditional statements and "but-also" qualifications. Visual images, such as those shown in this book, can be very useful in this regard. They can spur one's "sociological imagination" (Mills, 1959), for the sake of better understanding, by encouraging the observer to shift perspectives and to consider alternative interpretations. The diversity of symbols and artifacts shown in Exhibit 1.2 may appear as psychologically "rich" or anthropologically "mythical" at first glance, but, upon further analytical reflection, it may turn into perceptions of economic inefficiency or political chaos. The photograph shows many people from different walks of life, but it says nothing about the consequences of such diversity. It may even show patterns of movement, but it does not reveal whether these patterns facilitate or constrain social interaction, as the individuals pursue their various personal goals. Although first glances have intuitive appeal, alternative understandings cannot be ruled out. Visual images are sometimes "worth more than a thousand words," but they cannot provide more than initial insights into the complexity and dynamics of organizational worlds.

It is also worth noting that much of what organizational researchers do is to some extent philosophy rather than science. Aristotle considered philosophy the discipline which tells us how to distinguish a good argument from a bad one. In the literature on organizations, there are plenty of both, and they are often difficult to distinguish. To develop good arguments, organizational researchers may closely follow the canons of good science, but the reader may sometimes wonder why *these* hypotheses, *these* data, and *these* statistical techniques. Researchers often do not explain why they pursue a particular topic, other than suggesting that exploring the relationships between a particular set of concepts contributes to good organizational design, innovative business strategy, or better economic development policy. Readers may suspect that the choice of topics and research questions is often a matter of personal preference and that a researcher's choice of theory often stems from an interest in "winning" some academic debate. There is also the distinction between the value-neutrality and value-relevance in social science (Weber, 1949). A factual statement regarding, say, the positive relationship between work performance and payment may easily be understood as suggesting that compensation systems *should* be designed such that employees work harder and the organization's survival chances are increased. A given research finding is value-neutral in the sense that its scientific validity stands regardless of the value judgments that may be applied to it. However, the same finding may also have value-relevance in that it reflects the personal interests of the investigator and the practical implications that the users of the finding derive from it. Facts do not speak for themselves; they are interpreted and applied, in ways that may deviate far from what researchers may have intended with their particular study. Undoubtedly, personal and value-based choices feed into many of the phenomena that organizational scholars study and the diverse implications that organizational practitioners derive from research. Some observers may consider this unfortunate, arguing that it detracts from the rigors of the scientific enterprise; for others, personal choice and perspectival diversity is what makes this field so exciting and innovative, and worthy of debate.

The remainder of this book is organized into seven chapters. Chapter 2 sets the stage for discussions in the subsequent chapters by reviewing the central concepts and arguments of each of the three theoretical frameworks. Organizational economists focus on questions related to the efficiency of different governance structures; institutional theorists highlight the cultural meanings of organizational forms and evolutionary theorists study the adaptive complexity of organizations in variable and changing environments. Together, these frameworks contribute to a more rounded understanding of organizational phenomena than what a single perspective can achieve, although they do not add up to an overarching "grand theory" of organizations (Merton, 1967).

Chapter 3 examines organizations with reference to the external environment from which they draw vital resources for survival. Organizational forms emerge in large part as a response to requirements from environments, which include other organizations whose actions create uncertainty for the **focal organization**. Much of what organizations do in their exchange with other organizations is intended to reduce the uncertainty associated with resource dependence. The central problem that organizations face in this regard is how to interpret environmental demands correctly and how to translate the interpretations into organizational forms that are responsive to these demands, without foreclosing opportunities for difference and innovation.

In Chapter 4, organizations are examined with a view to their location in different kinds of spaces. Space is not just a passive and static backdrop to organizational action, as if organizations merely existed in one location or another, or pursued strategies that have only one meaning. Rather, organizations exist at different geographic scales and in different social and **symbolic** spaces, with meanings related to a range of criteria, such as legitimacy, morality, and rationality. Spaces link local and immediate exchange to the wider institutional aspects of economic and social life, with implications for the identity of organizations.

In Chapter 5, organizations are conceptualized as temporal entities. Organizations are not fixed in the here and now; rather, they evolve, in a context that evolves together with them. There are no durable essentials in organizations; things are not what they are because that is their nature. Rather, there are variations and differences, and the aim of theorizing is to explain the emergence and evolution of these differences over time. Whatever form an organization has at a particular moment is a form *for the time being*. It is neither the best possible form nor the final form. There are always interruptions, irritations, and new discoveries which can move the organization onto a different path, with uncertain outcomes. The idea of temporality is to change the analytical perspective away from static interdependence to dynamic agency, from allocation to innovation, and from the existence of options to the process of adapting.

Chapter 6 discusses the formal and informal structural properties of organizational forms, emerging out of adaptation processes. The structural form of an organization reflects a solution to the question of how to balance the need for task specialization with the need for coordination. Rules, procedures, and hierarchies lay out the structural foundation for actions, without determining what actually happens on a day-to-day basis. Formal structures are brought to life by informal relations, infused with personal prejudices, emotions, and motivations. Structures do not exist by themselves; they are created, negotiated, and transformed into something else, contingent on such factors as human nature, task complexity, and environmental conditions.

Chapter 7 discusses knowledge as an organizational asset, but this asset has to be created and applied to obtain force. Knowledge cannot be taken for granted, given the limited cognitive capacities of people and the costs of collecting and diffusing information. The problem for organizations is how to align their structural form with the distribution of different forms of knowledge in people's heads. The challenge is to create adaptable organizational forms to ensure that knowledge *becomes* available wherever and whenever it is needed.

Chapter 8 summarizes the above issues with a view to the embeddedness of organizations in social structures, both as a source and outcome of change. Organizations are social actors, exerting significant influence in cultural, social, and political matters through structuring employment opportunities, shaping the **social capital** of local communities, and creating an environment in which individuals construct their personal identity. The chapter concludes with thoughts about the shift from the "organized individual," who is strongly connected to an employing organization, to the "unorganized individual," who builds his or her own work biography outside a specific organization, in the context of the emerging "new economy," characterized by organizational restructuring towards greater flexibility.

Recommended further reading

Adler, P. (ed.) (2009) *The Oxford Handbook of Sociology and Organization Studies: Classical Foundations*. Oxford: Oxford University Press.
This collection of articles argues for the relevance of classical thinkers in sociology for contemporary organizational analysis. Classical ideas on such concepts as liberalism, solidarity, and rationality are applied to organizational issues such as domination, cooperation, and change.

Edwards, R. (1979) *Contested Terrain: The Transformation of the Workplace in the Twentieth Century*. New York: Basic Books.
The author chronicles the development of workplaces in modern organizations, involving shifting combinations of simple, technical, and bureaucratic forms of control. The analysis links organizational forms to stages in the development of market-based economies.

Morgan, G. (1997) *Images of Organization*. Thousand Oaks, CA: Sage.
The author argues that all theories of organization are based on implicit metaphors, and that exploring alternative metaphors can open up new ways of thinking about organizations.

Perrow, C. (1992) Organizational theorists in a society of organizations, *International Sociology*, 7: 371–380.
A sociological-critical analysis of the role of theorists in the study of organizations.

 ■ **Practice questions for Anecdote 1.1**

1 If you were the rental agent, how would you deal with this customer's demands?

2 As the rental agent, how would you handle the potential conflict between having to maintain organizational order and seeking a flexible solution to this customer's problems?

3 If you were Martin, the customer's friend, how would you communicate with the rental agent to improve the situation?

2
Theorizing Organizations

1. Introduction

The broad reach of theorizing organizations is not surprising, given the complexity of the subject matter, which encompasses structures and processes, actions and contexts, and relationships cutting across levels of analysis, from cognition at the individual level to inter-organizational relations at the level of communities. Scholars study identities, hierarchies, decisions, rules, and so on as **ontological** matters, on the assumption that such entities have a consistent existence and can be unambiguously specified. They are also interested in **epistemological** questions regarding, for example, the degree of certainty in conclusions drawn from the analysis of the same ontological matters in different settings.

Some researchers use a single perspective to investigate a narrow question, such as whether employees on long-term contracts are more or less likely than temporary employees to share information with colleagues. Others draw on several perspectives in the same study to explore the interconnections between different problem areas, such as the processes by which managers' perceptions of external **stakeholder** demands translate into organizational change programs. Investigators often take analytical concepts from adjacent disciplines, where they are already well tested, to be methodologically efficient, or they use them as "bridging concepts" to avoid seeing phenomena in isolation. Resource dependence theorists, for example, who study the uncertainties that organizations face when they require resources controlled by other organizations, draw on reasoning from political science to explore the contestability of organizational design (Pfeffer and Salancik, 1978). Researchers working from the knowledge-based perspective draw on identity theory in social psychology to explain the conditions under which individuals share knowledge (Kogut and Zander, 1996). Organizational demographers use arguments from cognitive science and social exchange theory to investigate the impact of management team diversity on the competitive strategy of organizations (Hambrick et al., 1996). And learning theory is used by social network theorists to investigate the diffusion of information across organizational boundaries (Kraatz, 1998). Such cross-disciplinary work requires much diligence in the use of concepts developed for different contexts, but it increases the likelihood of new theoretical insights for understanding complex situations.

Organizational scholars sometimes borrow ideas from different areas of inquiry to create a more encompassing explanatory scheme which sorts the empirical observations and guides the collection of data. Their goal is to identify competing and complementary arguments in the search for logically adequate and empirically grounded explanations for organizational phenomena. In doing so, they may draw on perspectives that employ similar streams of argumentation and build upon each other. Social identity theorists, for example, use ideas from the interpretive approach to explain the construction of organizational identity, and motivation theorists use interpretivist arguments to study how individuals select cues from their social situation to make sense of task requirements. Resource dependence theorists draw on interpretivism as well to explain how actors perceive demands from the organization's environment. And institutional theorists employ interpretive arguments to explain how actors create the organizational rules to which they then respond. Interpretation is central to human agency and to the relational aspects of organizational structure and action, explaining how choices are developed, evaluated, and renegotiated by individuals in an ongoing dialog with unfolding situations (Emirbayer and Mische, 1998; Meyer and Jepperson, 2000; Powell and Colyvas, 2008).

Although it is unlikely that there will ever be a "grand theory" (Merton, 1967) in organization science, synthesizing everything to be known about organizations, there are certain strands which can be usefully drawn together. Perspectives with the same epistemological roots, for example, may be subsumed under schools of thought, theory groups, or frames of reference. As theoretical frameworks, they provide orientation by sorting ideas and concepts into consistent categories, integrating related streams of research, and permitting comparison across different research contexts. In areas of inquiry as diverse as organization studies it is often useful to search for possibilities of integration across different perspectives. Without at least some concern for integration, scholars risk propagating a highly fractionated view of organizational phenomena. A lack of appreciation of links between perspectives can also lead to a certain degree of research inefficiency, if scholars fail to consider ideas produced in areas other than their own and then simply "rediscover" what is known already.

The aim of this chapter is to review three theoretical frameworks that, over the last few decades, have become central points of reference in organizational analysis: organizational economics (regarding costs and benefits), institutionalism (regarding norms and values), and organizational evolution (regarding adaptation and change). Taken together, these frameworks are sufficiently broad to capture the central elements of organizations as continually evolving activity systems, oriented towards collective goals, and struggling to maintain a distinct identity in an uncertain environment from which they draw vital resources. They also share common links to the relational view on organizations. The central ideas in these frameworks are summarized in Table 2.1.

Table 2.1 Key ideas in organizational economics, institutionalism, and evolution

	Economics	**Institutions**	**Evolution**
Key concepts	Governance	Meaning	Change
Assumptions about humans	Self-interested, opportunistic, intendedly rational	Sociable, socially biased, conforming	Mindful, future- and past-oriented
Units of action and interpretation	Exchange, transaction	Ideas, norms, symbols, values	Rules, routines, competencies
Goals of organizational design	Administrative efficiency	Accountability, predictability, social legitimacy	Adaptability, external and internal fitness
Key causal mechanism	Instrumental rationality	Meaning construction, negotiation	Contribution to fitness

2. Organizational economics

Organizational economics has its origins in debates that economists have had since the 1970s – with precursors in Barnard's (1938) **inducements–contributions** calculus and March and Simon's (1958) writings about the rationality of self-interested individuals – about whether firms are homogeneous organizational entities and whether they operate in markets that are sufficiently competitive to weed out inefficient firms (Barney and Ouchi, 1986). Organizational economists differ from the standard neo-classical view in that they do not take the firm – or more broadly, the organization – as given and do not treat it as a "black box," with structures and practices that are irrelevant to the firm's position in markets. In contrast to the standard neo-classical economic approach, which presumes that individual actors are perfectly rational and firms are driven solely by profit maximization goals, organizational economists propose a rather weak model of optimality. Individuals, so their argument goes, are constrained in their **instrumental rationality** because they do not have access to complete information and are not fully capable of processing the information available to them. Akin to **rational choice theory**, individuals are considered intendedly rational; given the constraints of information and time, they simplify the decision problem rather than seek the best possible solution (March and Simon, 1958).

The perspectives falling within the framework of organizational economics are oriented to the guiding question: "Why are there *any* organizations?" The answer to this question employs the concepts of exchange, cost, efficiency, and governance. Any production system involves the exchange of entities such as labor, commodities, services, and information. Exchange implies costs (e.g., searching for information, negotiating deals, evaluating outcomes), motivating the actors to select an efficient form of governance for coordination and control. Organizational economists have developed several approaches to the question of what kinds of governance forms help to reduce the uncertainty associated with exchange, each addressing a specific aspect of this question: property rights, principal–agent relations, and transaction costs (Barney and Hesterly, 1996).

2.1 Property rights

The standard economic approach views markets as the most efficient solution to the problem of coordinating economic exchange. The "invisible hand" of the price mechanism in markets that are competitively structured and populated by calculatively rational economic actors is thought to ensure that exchange is swift and equitable in the sense that the least efficient actors are weeded out – at least in the long run. Organizational economics emerged out of a critique of this view, asking why there are any firms at all. If markets are the most efficient way to manage exchange, why would there be complex organizational systems, like corporations? These are costly to maintain because one cannot assume that individuals always cooperate voluntarily and contribute equitably to collective efforts (Coase, 1937), not even in organizations pursuing non-economic goals, like schools and social clubs.

According to Alchian and Demsetz (1972), the concept of **property right** offers an explanation for the existence of organizations by providing an institutional framework for defining the conditions of ownership and control of productive assets and for evaluating the costs of control in an organization relative to the costs of governance in the open market. Producers will establish an organization only if they expect the benefits of "internalization" to exceed the costs. Creating an organizational system for allocating scarce resources and monitoring their uses involves various costs. For example, individuals may pretend to possess valuable skills or they may claim to be committed to a work team, thus creating a "**moral hazard**" for the principal. If they have an incentive to exaggerate claims about their performance, they cannot be trusted and need to be monitored closely. In this case, the rational principal will assign monitoring functions to select individuals, acting as supervisors or managers, to observe, evaluate, and sanction the efforts of each producer. Creating such roles is efficient up to a point beyond which the marginal costs of monitoring exceed the marginal benefits from reduced shirking. However, this solution to governance introduces the problem of creating efficient incentives for the monitor to expend effort on monitoring. The person assigned a monitoring role may want to shirk as well, by distorting information about the details of his or her monitoring activities. A solution is to reward monitors by giving them "property rights," that is, the right to exclusive usage of resources (e.g., money, labor, equipment, information), including the right to negotiate contracts, determine payment for their contributions, and extract the residual income from the value created by those they monitor (Alchian and Demsetz, 1972). The assignment of such rights leads to the creation of an organizational hierarchy, stretching from lower-level supervisors and project leaders, to department heads and top managers.

Based on the assumption that individuals are motivated to maximize the returns from the rights given to them, the question is, how are these rights distributed in an organization and how do the actors put them to use? What is the structure of property rights that maximize the efficient use of resources? The distribution of property rights among the members of an organization determines the structure of behavioral opportunities. One might hypothesize, for example, that publicly owned organizations are less efficient than privately owned organizations if the former lack transfer rights and incur higher control costs. Changes in the economic environment, such as the intensity of market competition, or in the institutional environment, such as foreign trade regulation or antitrust legislation, can lead to efficiency gains or losses for organizations, depending on their effects on the incentive structure for owners and controllers (Bishop and Thompson, 1992).

2.2 Principal–agent relations

In large-scale organizations, it is unlikely that those who own property are in full control of the use to which their property is put. To the extent that principals lack time or expertise to exercise control, they may delegate managerial control to others, the agents. This leads to a principal–agent relationship in which the agents may be able to exploit or circumvent the principals' control attempts. To protect themselves from exploitation by agents, who may be opportunistically inclined, principals may want to specify contractually all expectations they have of agents managing their assets (Aoki et al., 1990). In practice, however, it is rarely possible to write complete contracts, covering all contingencies that might arise. There may be uncertainty about the future, and it may be too costly to enforce contract specifications that are open to interpretation in changing environments and when there are many agents involved. Contracts cannot effectively compensate for the stochastic elements one finds in many organizational settings (Holmstrom, 1982).

The agency problem is the possibility of an opportunistic agent acting against the interests of principals who are then motivated to act *as if* the agent will indeed behave opportunistically. Principals will want to create organizational structures to protect themselves from exploitation, while minimizing the agency costs (i.e., monitoring and sanctioning agent behavior) associated with such structures. If they cannot exercise "process control" by verifying agent behavior directly, they may attempt to monitor the *results* of behavior, by exercising "output control." However, this does not solve the agency problem if performance outcomes are difficult to measure, or there are disputable definitions of "good" performance. In this case, the labor market in which managerial competencies are traded may be the only mechanism to discipline managers, but the efficiency of this mechanism depends on the availability of appropriate metrics and reliable information about managerial skills. In cases where such information is absent, principals may rely on social indicators, such as the reputation of agents. For example, company shareholders may appoint to the governing board directors considered experts in a particular field (Singh and Harianto, 1989), and the stakeholders of universities may resort to university ranking schemes as indicators of quality management (Gioia and Corley, 2002). Reputational indicators, however, are subject to their own limitations, as argued by institutional theorists.

2.3 Transaction cost economics

The transaction cost economic perspective complements property rights and agency theory with a concern for the costs of exchange taking place in organizations relative to the costs of exchange in markets (Williamson, 1994). The basic unit of analysis is the individual transaction implicated in the exchange of goods, services, or information. Transaction costs arise from the preparation of an exchange relationship, leading to an informal agreement or a formal contract. They include the costs of identifying appropriate partners, assessing their trust-worthiness and likely contributions, and negotiating the terms of the exchange. Other costs arise after an agreement has been forged, such as the costs of monitoring the partner's compliance with the terms of the agreement, enforcing compliance, and adjusting the terms of the exchange, if necessary.

While property rights and agency theories are more concerned with the dis-tribution and use of authority, the transaction cost approach focuses specifically on the organizational boundary question, asking about the conditions under which transaction costs in the open market are so high that it is more efficient to bring exchanges into the organization, where they become subject to hierar-chical control (Eisenhardt, 1989). From the transaction cost perspective, markets are only efficient to the extent that the actors have full information about each other's competencies and commitments, and are able to assess the value of the exchange. Transaction costs are higher in situations of uncertainty if, for example, the actors cannot rely on prices as a source of information about the value of the exchange or if they cannot assess the trustworthiness of the exchange partner. Uncertainty forces them to expend more resources on coordinating exchanges than they otherwise would. Hence, they have an incentive to design governance forms that minimize transaction costs. One option is to internalize those exchange relations that entail the greatest degree of uncertainty and to external-ize the more routine activities, thus either expanding or constricting the organi-zation's boundary for different activities.

Given the assumption of bounded rationality and opportunism, actors will always be under pressure to devise governance structures that economize on transaction costs. The general answer to the question "Why do organizations exist?" is that organizational authority systems emerge to resolve the problems of market-based governance under conditions of uncertainty. Two conditions are particularly relevant as sources of uncertainty: transaction frequency and transaction-specific investments (Williamson, 1985). Regarding *transaction frequency*, the more often an exchange takes place between two partners, the greater is the incentive to find an economical way to manage the relationship. One-time exchange is not worth worrying about; it can be handled through "spot" contracts specifying inducements and contributions, as when a tourist purchases a snack at a hot dog stand. However, if there is a high probability that the exchange will occur again, there is an incentive for the actors to enter into a long-term relational agreement. For example, two lawyers specializing in different fields, who expect to be working together on the same type of projects again in the future and who know that their collaboration will require much time investment, may decide to create a formal partnership because this saves on transaction costs from not having to renegotiate the terms of the relationship for every project.

Transaction-specific investments refer to the resources the partners invest to maintain the relationship. For example, the actors may contribute special skills that are of value only in that relationship, for example because the skills are tied to the specific needs of a joint customer. Asset-specific skills, which cannot be transferred readily to other people or organizations, increase the degree of informational and behavioral interdependence between the actors, which in turn increases uncertainty if the actors behave opportunistically. Organizations provide a solution to this problem to the extent that they can impose formal rules and hierarchical controls or can rely on informal controls, as will be discussed in Chapter 6. When transactions involve high asset-specificity and recur frequently, the partners have an incentive to create long-term organizational arrangements providing reliability and information transparency, rather than relying on short-term contracts mediated through the price mechanism of markets. Robust organizational forms would be expected, for example, in the surgical department of a hospital, where it is critically important that staff coordinate their specialized skills flexibly and equitably in line with evolving patient needs, task requirements, and technological possibilities. Organizational structures that provide clear rules and support collegial behavior and consensual decision-making among the medical staff tend to be more efficient in this case than short-term, arm's-length market relations (Witman et al., 2010). Once the actors work under common ownership and the same organizational roof, they have less incentive to seek personal advantages over each other.

2.4 Summary

Organizational economists have made significant contributions to our understanding of organizations. Compared to the standard economic approach, which treats organizations mostly as a "black box" or assumes that organizations are singular and coherent entities, the perspectives dealing with property rights, principal–agent relations, and transaction costs come much closer to organizational reality, taking into account the bounded rationality of actors and the problem of uncertainty. They discuss organizations not as monolithic entities but as aggregates of individuals with different capabilities and utility functions. Their specific contribution to organizational analysis is the concern for costs and benefits, the separation of ownership and control, and the conditions under which exchange relations are better coordinated hierarchically in organizations than through the market price mechanism. The organizational economics framework, however, is often criticized for its axiomatic approach to economic criteria (e.g., efficiency, utility maximization), at the expense of viewing organizations and markets as "social constructions" replete with cultural meanings, social biases, and flawed interpretations. Organizational economics is most useful for studying organizational settings with actors who are motivated mostly by material concerns. These are primarily economic enterprises, but may also include organizations offering their members social or cultural returns, to the extent that the members evaluate these returns in terms of "more" or "less" and are willing to pay a "price" for goal achievement. Still, any economic approach to organizations is limited if the individual and organizational actors are abstracted out of their social and institutional context (Granovetter, 1985). In organizational economics, questions concerning, for instance, the political enforcement of contracts or the social definition of property are either not problematized at all or are addressed only indirectly, with recourse to other theories, such as institutional theory. Institutionalist thinking has gained some currency in economics but has largely remained within the economic tradition of viewing actors as basically self-interested and competitive (Hodgson, 2004). Institutional theory has much stronger grounding in sociology, political science, and history, where it is used to contemplate how "things came to be what they are" and how actors quarrel over how "things should be."

3. Organizational institutionalism

Broadly defined, institutions are relatively persistent rule systems, allowing people to act collectively on the basis of common understandings. Distinct rule systems can be found in areas like government, business, family, education, health, and religion. Each of these areas consists of a web of meanings and values which specify how its participants should act and relate to one another. Social and economic processes are considered institutional if they have a rule-like quality providing coherence and stability. Institutions penetrate organizations in the form of cultural ideas, social conventions, and cognitive frames with which problems are evaluated and solutions are devised, based on understandings of what is socially acceptable in a given instance (Scott, 2008). Hospitals, for example, admit patients on the basis of socially defined rules classifying different categories of patients for specialized treatment; universities handle student grievances using rules distinguishing a legitimate from an illegitimate grievance; and sports clubs use rules specifying acceptable forms of fundraising. Institutional rules are often infused with values and ideologies, which individuals or groups may use to **rationalize** their vested interests, as when funeral undertakers argue that selecting a "bottom-price" funeral arrangement would indicate a lack of respect for the departed.

Institutional theory has a long and rich history in the social sciences, with broad applications in organizational analysis at both the micro-level of cognition and interpretation (Powell and Colyvas, 2008) and the macro-level of society (Zucker, 1987). Institutional theory extends into every corner of society, drawing on broad-sweeping ideas of such thinkers as Marx, Weber, Durkheim, Mead, Simmel, Tönnies, and Veblen regarding the functioning of markets, the role of laws, and the nature of social organization. Institutional theorists study the non-economic aspects of organizations as well as those things that are hidden from view if one thinks of organizations as merely instrumental entities. While there is no single unitary perspective in institutional theory, there is general agreement on the view of organizations as entities existing in social, political, and symbolic realms, subject to demands that are not always consistent with the material and technical requirements of production. It makes a difference for understanding organizations if one views them as tools for powerful elites to promote their interests or as entities following a logic of their own. Organizational economists take the former view, when they argue that the principals devise governance systems to protect their investments. Many institutional theorists take the latter view, suggesting that organizations often develop on their own terms, to the point where they may be able to escape economic requirements because they are taken for granted by their main constituents. When this happens, organizations have the quality of a "**social fact**" (Durkheim, 1982) in the sense that they are accepted independently of people's specific preferences.

3.1 Organizations as rationalized systems

The distinct insight of institutional theory is the view of organizational environments as a web of cultural elements providing meaning and legitimacy. Organizations are considered legitimate if there are undisputed explanations for their existence, roles, and jurisdictions. They gain the status of "rationalized systems" by absorbing, interpreting, and enforcing cultural values so that they can act as coherent entities (Meyer and Rowan, 1977). Institutional theory thus offers an antidote to the calculative rationality that economists normally impute to organizational actors. It suggests that models of rationality are themselves cultural notions, emerging out of the values and norms prevailing in a given social setting. In the educational sector, for instance, the key values revolve around the meaning of education in its various manifestations of training, schooling, and special needs instruction (Meyer, Boli and Thomas, 1994a). The specific meanings of education may be subject to contestation regarding the social value of particular ideas, or the pedagogical value of certain kinds of examinations, but there is general consensus on the social significance of education *per se*. In other fields, the key values may be more precarious, as in the mental health sector in many countries, where institutional rules are too weak to confer undisputed legitimacy on a given organizational form of detecting mental disorders and restoring mental health (Shorter, 1997). The result of ambiguity regarding the definition of mental health and the value of different therapeutic techniques is an organizationally fragmented sector that includes different professions with distinct interests and ideologies, competing therapeutic technologies, and different funding arrangements, as well as diverse populations of organizations (e.g., specialized clinics, counseling centers, self-help groups) with structures and goals that often have little to do with what goes on in everyday patient care (Meyer, 1994).

Some organizations may survive on the basis of "rationalized myths" (Meyer and Rowan, 1977). For example, when medical specialists promulgate the belief that standards of health in society will decline if tighter government regulations on fee structures are introduced, they may be creating a myth that rationalizes their vested interest in professional self-control. "Rationalized myths" are most likely to arise in settings where it is difficult to measure performance and cause–effect relations. In such settings, organizations often use rituals (e.g., award ceremonies, retirement parties) or engage in actions with symbolic value (e.g., architectural building designs suggesting progressiveness, product names indicating innovativeness) to save face or to promote confidence in what they are doing. Mental health clinics employ "admission suites," and youth summer camps use initiation rites, to create an illusion of consensus around the legitimacy of the organizational form they employ. Myth-like statements such as "Quality first" or "We care about people" obtain their force not from their truth value but from the fact that people think that everyone else believes in them. "Rationalized myths" are examples of institutions that have an impact not necessarily because they provide the "correct answer" regarding how best to solve certain problems, but because they carry values that people accept (Stinchcombe, 1997). Organizations reproducing themselves through myths may have forms that are far removed from efficiency-based evaluation. Mental health organizations, for example, may claim that they are effective because they follow government-mandated admission procedures or because they protect the idea of sovereignty of the individual, without having to prove that patient health is indeed improved through the therapeutic methods applied (Scheid and Greenley, 1997).

Organizations can enhance their survival chances by demonstrating that they act as legitimate participants in society. If they enjoy the status of institutionalized organizations, they can expect continued support from customers, government regulators, and investors even if there is no agreement on how to measure their economic contributions. If, on the basis of "rationalized myths," they can convince their institutional constituents that they take social expectations seriously, they may be able to conduct their operational affairs without having to document that they do in fact meet these expectations. This is not to say that compliance with institutions is incompatible with economic performance. Organizations may adopt product quality standards, customer complaint procedures, policies to curb sexual harassment, and so forth not only because this promotes the *image* of caring about quality or equity but also because it may in fact confer economic advantages (Beck and Walgenbach, 2005). Even organizations for which values (e.g., justice, political correctness) are at the center of their *raison d'être* (e.g., planned parenthood clinics, labor unions) can derive economic utility from value conformity. Social movement organizations and business interest associations may offer their members meaningful participation rights, while also providing material incentives to remain in the organization (Aldrich et al., 1994). And corporations may adopt human resource management techniques not only to present the image of a "modern organization" but also to improve their social standing in the hope that this helps to attract qualified managers and employees (Staw and Epstein, 2000).

3.2 Institutionalization processes

In contrast to the static approach of organizational economists who study the appropriateness of particular governance structures under existing conditions, institutional theorists take a more dynamic view, examining the processes by which organizations adopt particular structures. They ask about the origins and diffusion of institutional rules, and the strategies by which organizations adapt to them or alter them to suit their specific purposes (Scott, 2008). Institutionalization describes a process of constructing reality based on rules and standards that both enable and constrain human action. At the point where a particular reality is no longer questioned, it becomes objectified and internalized as being "true" (See Berger and Luckmann, 1966). Institutionalization may occur in a variety of ways. Organizational members may internalize standards through the acceptance of rewards or through peer pressure, or they may imitate the strategies and structures of other organizations. The outcomes of institutionalization are organizational forms that are independent of the preferences of particular actors and that no longer need to be maintained through explicit acts of social control (Zucker, 1977).

Institutional theory predicts that organizations that are subject to the same institutional forces will over time adopt similar forms. For example, the central role that family and village play in East Asia is taken as an explanation for the particular way businesses are structured and organizational authority is distributed in that part of the world (Wilkinson, 1996). In the typical Korean or Japanese enterprise, authority is based on moral superiority, in addition to technical competence. Employees in East Asian organizations are expected to participate in collective events, such as company-endorsed recreation or award ceremonies, to a far greater extent than is the norm in Western organizations. Institutional pressures rooted in tradition and custom are evident in the way East Asian corporations discourage employees from forging strong social ties with employees from other companies (Chai and Rhee, 2010). In Western companies, by contrast, it is far more acceptable that employees develop social ties with people outside the employer's domain. In industries that place a premium on innovation, such as the higher-education or the multimedia sector, employees may even be *encouraged* to maintain ties with outsiders in order to gain access to valuable knowledge (Benner, 2003).

Guided by the fundamental question, "Why are organizations so similar?," institutional theorists have identified three mechanisms by which organizations adopt forms in line with institutional expectations: coercive, normative, and mimetic (DiMaggio and Powell, 1983). *Coercive* forces typically emanate from the state via regulation, public ownership, or legislation. In the educational sector, for example, coercive pressures are evident in government regulations on standards for curriculum development, student evaluation, and teacher promotion. In the airline industry, safety standards are attached to landing rights granted by governments and airports. *Normative* forces operate through shared interpretations of values, attitudes, and identities. In contrast to coerced compliance, normative forces require no externally imposed motivation for conformity. Rather, the actors are internally motivated to do what is expected, or they rely on intermediary organizations, such as professional associations and labor unions, to aggregate and promote normative standards. In the educational sector, it is often through informal contacts between teachers and local employers that curriculum needs are interpreted. Lastly, *mimetic* processes are driven by organizations emulating other organizations. Many universities, for example, have introduced professional programs that mimic those of private educational institutes, and fashion shows are organized worldwide along presentation standards that are copied across events. Imitation of other organizations, particularly those that are perceived to be successful, is a common low-cost strategy for organizations in situations of uncertainty.

Coercive, normative, and mimetic processes may occur in the absence of evidence that they help organizations improve their economic performance. Organizations may be rewarded more for their similarity to other organizations than for their operational efficiency. Similarity may help them attract employees with particular competencies or may enhance their reputation as reliable social systems. Organizations may staff teams on the rotation principle to minimize bribery, but this practice can have severe efficiency costs. Managers may seek the advice of professional consultants and external coaches not because they can furnish indisputable evidence that their advice will bring economic success to the organization, but because the act of seeking advice allows them to say to the organization's stakeholders that they are doing *something* to improve their situation (Kieser, 1997). Organizations may develop expensive procedures (e.g., for performance evaluation) to signal to the public that they are serious about meeting social expectations through mechanisms such as "optimization" and "lifelong learning." Similarity in organizational form does not imply that organizations never diverge in the way they handle problems specific to their local environment. Schools, for example, will often deviate somewhat from institutional standards in order to maximize the flexibility required by the uncertainties of daily life in the classroom (Meyer, Scott, and Strang, 1994b). Medical clinics may maneuver between competing institutional logics, where health restoration is practiced with reference to technical, social, and economic criteria (Reay and Hinings, 2009). Institutionalization is best viewed as a fluid process that helps reduce uncertainty, without eliminating it, not least because organizations compete with others as they struggle to shape the very institutions that impact on their condition.

3.3 Constructing institutions

There is no singular and uniform approach within the institutionalist framework. Theorists differ foremost in their view of institutions as a set of relatively stable constraints or as a contested terrain. A common distinction is that between an older and a newer version of institutional theory (DiMaggio and Powell, 1991; Stinchcombe, 1997), although in research practice these two versions are often difficult to separate. Theorists working with the older version of institutionalism tend to take a view of institutionalization as essentially a political struggle between actors with competing interests. Organizational adaptation to environmental change is seen as a process driven by conflicts of interest between individuals and coalitions who use the organization as a strategic device to further their goals. Political struggles often have unintended consequences, which may say more about institution-building than the purposive actions themselves. Professional architects, for example, may engage in activities – in the name of "artistic freedom" or "professional rigor" – that are intended to produce innovations, but they may end up creating "silent hierarchies" and "invisible walls" (Brown et al., 2010). In the newer version of institutional theory (neo-institutionalism), the emphasis is less on conflict and change, and more on the persistence of institutional structures and their enduring impact on organizations. Institutions are seen as involving powerful forces at the macro-level of society, embedded in ideologies and state structures, and heavily constraining organizational options. In some cases, institutional forces are so strong that individuals are not even aware of any alternative actions they *could* take. Mental asylums (Goffman, 1961), spiritualist consulting (Zaidman et al., 2009), and religious sects (Bennett, 2006) are examples of organizations trying to create a "totalizing" experience for their participants.

In recent years, institutional theorists have paid more attention to the micro-level and cognitive elements of institutions, emphasizing human agency and choice within institutional constraints (Ingram and Clay, 2000). The immense growth of the global economy, it is argued, has softened institutional controls over the flow of goods, money, and labor, leading to more fragmentation and less predictability in the organizational world (Sennett, 2006). In line with these changes, many scholars are turning away from the assumption that institutions are mostly self-reproducing. They are paying more attention to the mechanisms by which institutions are maintained and extended into the future, or are adjusted to fit changing circumstances. Their argument is that institutions must be actively maintained, or they risk disintegration. To this end, many organizations employ expensive rituals to reinforce rules and expectations. Organizations may also attempt to create new institutions to reduce uncertainty in a hostile environment, as in the cultural sector where there is intense competition for limited resources and where organizations juggle economic goals with symbolic and aesthetic considerations (Amin and Thrift, 2007). Institutions play a central role in the cultural economy, by providing orientation through regulations, technological infrastructures, and social conventions. In a music cluster in northern Italy, for example, music academies, music events, and collective interest associations are constructed to achieve some degree of order for freelance musicians in an otherwise intensely competitive market (Sedita, 2008). The anecdote below (2.1) describes the problems an artist experiences who works in an industry that lacks the kind of institutional support that professionals in fields like law and medicine normally enjoy.

Sam had just moved from Toronto back to his small hometown in the Canadian Prairies to be closer to his family and friends from school. His friends back home had told him that as an artist with his kind of talent he could be innovative anywhere, but in his hometown he would also have emotional support of the kind he would not get in the "big city." Soon Sam realized that his move to this small rural town was a big mistake. He had many close friends there, but he missed the formal recognition as an *artist*. Not only was "this place just too straight to be different," as he called it, but it also lacked the kind of organizations that would give his work the legitimacy that people in other professions normally enjoy.

Sam thought that his identity as a professional artist was on shaky ground in a place that had none of the diverse arts organizations he was used to in Toronto. Being close to such organizations was important to him. Unlike lawyers, doctors, and engineers, who obtain formal training, licenses, reputation, and income in a well-established sector of organizations, he had only recourse to arts organizations that led an extremely precarious life in the economy. He felt that art was not given the social respect that professionals in other fields received. There were no socially accepted criteria for distinguishing the professional artist from the art hobbyist. He had been told by many people that artistic talent was a gift, not a skill that could be taught. He hated it when he met people who remarked that he was "just an artist."

All that Sam could do to gain respectability was to create his own reputation as a professional. To make his identity as a professional credible he had to confidently assert himself by making himself as visible as possible. His small, rural hometown was not the place to achieve this goal. This town did not offer him the opportunities he had in Toronto where he interacted with many other artists, people from the media, and organizers of workshops and special events. Being around old friends was nice and comforting, but he missed Toronto where he had access to art dealers, art critics, art collectors, art historians, and art schools.

A micro-level perspective on the construction of institutions forces attention to the motivations and capabilities of individual actors who work within existing institutional constraints but are not blind prisoners of institutions. Sam, in the above anecdote, prefers to be in Toronto where he can choose between a multitude of organizations relevant to his particular interests. Institutional environments are a dynamic complex of individuals, roles, rules, and meanings, producing variations in structures and enactments (Meyer and Jepperson, 2000). Many recent studies, designed from an institutionalist perspective, have taken an interpretive and **constructivist** stance to examine how exactly people create rituals, negotiate rules, or save face when confronted with failure (Powell and Colyvas, 2008). Such studies contribute to a more balanced approach to the tension between stability and change, and between structure and action in institutions. Research on institutions conceived at the micro-level of individual cognition and action, such as the study reported in the research brief below (2.1), views organizations as social constructions that acquire some stability only through the active engagement of organizational participants. This study shows how individuals contribute to the reproduction of a society's social class system by participating in a traditional organizational ritual in a leading university (Dacin et al., 2010). The findings suggest that institutional outcomes like legitimacy and reputation are not automatic but the result of people actively communicating ideas and negotiating over resources. Research on the micro-foundations of institutions and on the agentic aspects of institution building returns attention to power and politics as the issues that are at the center of the older version of institutional theory (Zald and Lounsbury, 2010).

RESEARCH BRIEF 2.1

Many studies of organizational phenomena conducted from an institutional perspective have either ignored the question of maintaining institutions or have assumed that the reproduction of institutional rules and routines is largely automatic, given the definition of institutions as taken-for-granted elements and entities. To show how institutions are linked to the actions of concrete individuals, Dacin et al. (2010) examined how micro-level interactions between people in organizational rituals contribute to the maintenance of larger societal institutions.

The authors studied how the ritual of college dining (the "Formal Hall") at the University of Cambridge contributes to the maintenance of the British social class system. Rituals are highly structured and dramatic episodes of repeated interaction and communication in which the participants develop shared understandings of some reality. This study shows how the dining ritual socializes the participants into particular values and teaches them the roles they are expected to play. By hiding disagreement and conflict, this ritual also motivates participants to maintain order and build a common identity, and to refrain from resistance to established social class values and the entitlements that go with social class. The dining ritual carries symbolic and cultural material that individuals draw on in their daily interactions also outside the university setting. This organizational ritual thus has wider societal implications, supporting the maintenance of social class distinctions across time and space.

While insightful in the specific instance of one particular organizational mechanism of institutional reproduction, it is not self-evident that the findings of this study can be generalized beyond the context under investigation. As the authors themselves note, this context is unique in many ways. The University of Cambridge is one of two universities in the United Kingdom that are most closely associated with social class. It is one of the two oldest universities in the English-speaking world and has, until quite recently, been overwhelmingly dominated by white, male students from privileged social backgrounds. The basic function of this university – to prepare students for life in the upper echelons of British society – has essentially remained unchanged. Uniqueness of context speaks to the limitations of a single case study, especially since, as in this empirical instance, longitudinal data are not available to explore the long-term dynamics of institution building. It is, therefore, not possible to test alternative explanations for the institutional outcomes investigated here. Nevertheless, this study highlights the details of an important institutional mechanism – organizational rituals – that occurs in many other organizational contexts as well (e.g., company birthday parties and initiation ceremonies) and that contributes to the reproduction of macro-level institutions, such as ideologies and social class beliefs.

3.4 Summary

The central insights of all variants of institutional theory lie in the departure from the standard economic view of organizations as activity systems driven by the economic calculus of self-interested individuals. For institutional theorists, organizations do not exist only for instrumental reasons. Although their professed goal may be to maximize profits, they normally do not create forms oriented solely to the needs of efficient production. Rather, they are social systems held together by shared interpretations of acceptable norms of collective conduct. On the other hand, institutional theorizing is problematic to the extent that organizational actions are treated as *purely* social and it is assumed that social interaction has benevolent outcomes simply because the actors are familiar with each other or share the same experience. Although institutions impose powerful constraints, through the "rule of law" or through ideologies, organizational responses are often sub-optimal, haphazard, and contested. Recent studies have contributed additional insights into our understanding of the role of institutions in organizational life by exploring the micro-level actions by which institutions are constructed, reproduced, or transformed. By attending to the agentic aspects of institution building, one can move beyond the more reactive elements of institutional imitation and conformity. The idea that organizations may succeed or fail in their relationship with institutions is taken up explicitly by the evolutionary approach to organizational analysis.

4. Organizational evolution

Organizations always operate with some degree of uncertainty, no matter how well designed their structures are or how clearly their goals are specified (Aldrich and Ruef, 2006). In environments that are constantly shifting, organizations work with incomplete information, new problems arise, and old solutions are no longer effective. Much of organizational decision-making occurs by way of trial and error and improvisation, with results that are normally not the best ones possible. On the other hand, there may be outcomes of flawed actions that actually *improve* an organization's fate, depending on the state of the environment. From the evolutionary perspective, the relationship between organizational actions and outcomes is largely indeterminate. The more skilled or motivated individuals do not necessarily outperform the less "fit" individuals, and the more efficient organizations do not necessarily outcompete the less efficient organizations, an insight shared with institutional theory. Organizational evolution is a probabilistic process, not a deterministic one. What sometimes appears to be a sequence of decisions leading to a particular outcome may simply be something that individuals discover in retrospect. Evolutionary theory explains organizational developments without the assumption that individuals are economically rational or that they assign socially "correct" meanings to their actions.

Evolutionary theorizing in organization studies has its origins in nineteenth-century explanations of social change as a process driven by the gradual replacement of old entities with new ones that are better adapted to the new conditions (Tylor, 1871). The evolutionary idea is that the replacement of outdated entities with new ones can be explained by features of the relevant environment, without having to take recourse to notions like special creation, purposive design, or moral imposition (Dennett, 1995). Applied to organizations, this means that the success of entities like rules, routines, technologies, and work groups does not depend on the intelligence of organizational designers, strategy leaders, or governing board members, but on properties of the relevant environment which favor particular combinations of the elements constituting an organization. Scholars working in sociology (Runciman, 2009), anthropology (Richerson and Boyd, 2005), psychology (Campbell, 1969), and economics (Nelson, 2006) have extended Darwin's theory of biological evolution (as a natural selection process of descent with modification) to the study of change in the cultural realm of ideas and beliefs, and the social realm of action and interaction. Evolutionary processes are considered sufficiently general to apply to all systems (biological, cultural, and social), although the details of these processes vary across particular instances (Hodgson and Knudsen, 2006). Human behavior is subject to genetic *and* cultural influences. Inventions like the preferential hiring of women for certain kinds of jobs are of a social and cultural nature, and are not the result of changes in the human genetic code. It is well known that men and women can perform equally well in a variety of work roles, but it is also known that the different strategies that men and women may adopt for accommodating their work behavior to their unique psychologies is partly the result of evolved psychology (Nicholson, 2010).

Organizational evolution is not the same reproductive process as it occurs in biology, given the human capacity for learning and transmitting new knowledge to members of the same and subsequent generations. Still, there are certain principles of variation and inheritance that allow the conceptualization of organizational change by the same evolutionary algorithm that has unified our understanding of biology. We know that organizational evolution has taken place when changes in the frequency distribution of units (e.g., beliefs, skills, practices) in a population of such units – bounded in such entities as routines, groups, organizations, or industries – have occurred such that the population as a whole is better adapted to current conditions in the relevant environment. When evolutionary theorists speak of evolutionary change, they merely mean that an adaptive change has taken place; they do not mean that this change is an improvement, in a value-laden sense, in some behavior, attitude, or structure. The aim is to explain the evolution of organizational forms with a view to their adaptive complexity, innovativeness, coherence, or some other feature, rather than to evaluate this feature as "good" or "progressive," which would require criteria that themselves have meaning only within a specific environment. Characterizing the emergence of a particular organizational form as "inevitable" or "bound to happen" requires knowledge of the form's previous history and the ongoing constraints, with reference to the relevant comparisons and possibilities, but such complete knowledge is rarely available.

4.1 Generic processes of evolution

Darwinian evolution is essentially about replicating populations of slightly different combinations of units in changing resource environments, rather than changes of singular self-organizing systems. Evolutionary processes, thus conceived, are generic and applicable to any unit and environment. The units may be decisions or competencies, and the environments may be labor or capital markets, or the capacity and willingness of individuals to attend to the information contained in units, such as rules and skills. The Darwinian paradigm characterizes evolution as a movement away from a previous state of a system towards a new and different state, driven by four generic processes: variation, selection, retention, and the competitive struggle for resources. Evolution in a social system, like an organization, work group, or business cluster, is possible if there is sufficient variation in the population of units constituting the system, if selection can operate because there is competitive pressure, and if the selected units can be passed on to subsequent generations (Aldrich and Ruef, 2006).

4.1.1 Variation

The processes generating differences between the units in a population are central to any evolutionary explanation. Without variation, there can be no selection and, therefore, no possibility of improving the adaptive fit between the population and its environment. If all units in a population were exactly identical, simple random selection would determine which units were replicated and which were not. If there is variation and some of the units are better able to acquire resources than others, then those variations with the adaptive advantages will be more likely to be replicated. For example, a skill that is easy to learn is more likely to be passed on to newcomers in an organization, if learning new skills produces a selective advantage in the relevant environment. If variation is to enable evolution, it has to create new opportunities for the organization to adapt to changing environments. Variations must also be able to fail. In an evolutionarily "fit" organization, outdated ideas are given up, inappropriate rules are discarded, and old skills are forgotten if they are no longer useful in a new environment.

Variations exist within organizations and between organizations. At the organizational population level, such as an industry or business cluster, there may be significant differences in control structures, strategies, and practices. The Catholic Church, for example, has more strictly hierarchical decision-making structures than worker cooperatives, and Islamic mosques translate "salvation" into different organizational practices than the routines used by Protestant churches or Buddhist temples (Dyck and Wiebe, 2012). Within organizations, variations may exist between individuals in their personalities, interests, and competencies, and between departments in **task technologies**, work cultures, and evaluation systems. Variations are created through deliberate actions, as when organizations develop new quality control techniques to outcompete rival organizations. Variations also result from chance events and faulty decisions. The organizational equivalents of mutation in the biological domain are improvisations and trial-and-error experiments stemming from opportunistic behavior, interpersonal conflicts, or simple curiosity. Much of the variation generated in organizations is "blind" in the evolutionary sense of individuals not anticipating correctly the outcomes of their actions (Campbell, 1969). Organizational strategists and planners may act intentionally, contemplating constraints and options, but they cannot know the consequences of their own or other people's discoveries and subsequent decisions until they have made them. The selection of variations follows from the consequences of actions rather than from intentions.

4.1.2 Selection

Variations that improve a unit's survival chances are positively selected so that, over time, the advantageous variations become more prevalent in the population. Selection criteria vary depending on the type of environment in which a population exists. For example, schools are subject to institutional expectations with respect to social needs and cultural values, whereas video stores are exposed to competitive pressures driven by consumer tastes regarding the meaning and cost of entertainment. If selection criteria favor, say, production flexibility, as in the hypercompetitive fashion industry, then adaptive organizations will develop structures and processes that deliver flexibility, and organizations with rigid structures will eventually be weeded out by market competition, holding everything else (e.g., government wage subsidies, trade protection) constant. At the organizational population level, the results of market selection are evident in the different failure rates of organizations. At the level of individual organizations, political selection criteria may lead to different dismissal rates for different categories of employees, while selection criteria based on technology may generate different disbanding rates of jobs with different skill requirements.

In contrast to predictions from organizational economics, but in line with institutional theory, selection criteria do not always reward the most efficient organizational forms. In some cases, for example in environments with clientelist political traditions, powerful individuals may use coercive measures to maximize their own returns or to extend "personal favors." In other environments, social norms may prevail over economic efficiency criteria, as in the area of international relations (e.g., ASEAN, European Union) where justice and diplomacy are important considerations. Evolutionary theorists distinguish between selection criteria that are internal and those that are external to the organization, but they may be empirically related in a given instance. Internal and external criteria may co-evolve in the sense that the entities in which they apply have a causal impact on each other's ability to survive. The development of the German dye industry up to World War I is an example of such co-evolution, as firms' selection decisions on research affected, and were reinforced, by curricular developments in the German university system (Murmann, 2003). Internal and external criteria are not always consistently or functionally related. For example, internal selection may be driven by organizational leaders' desire to hire people similar to themselves. This practice may create **organizational inertia** by producing a homogeneous and closed **organizational culture**, preventing the organization from adapting quickly to deep changes in the environment. From an evolutionary perspective, selection processes may not create the best of all possible worlds. Evolution always produces winners and losers, and stories of success normally provoke anti-stories of alternative explanations, all of which keep the system in motion.

4.1.3 Retention

Selected variants can only be used on future occasions if there are mechanisms to preserve and reproduce them. Without the ability to retain what has been discovered, any gains would dissipate quickly. Retention mechanisms in organizations include files, job descriptions, and records of meetings. Learning theorists suggest that retention mechanisms help the organization economize on information processing in situations that require significant cognitive investments (Miner and Mezias, 1996). At the level of organizational population, retention mechanisms are embedded in linkages between organizations through which knowledge is diffused and resources are shared, such as formal production cooperations (e.g., joint ventures) and informal social ties (e.g., social networks between former work colleagues). Resource dependence theorists postulate that organizations which are mutually dependent, because they draw on the same environmental resource pool, tend to enter into alliances to soften the impact of competitive selection (Pfeffer and Salancik, 1978).

4.1.4 Competition

Resource scarcity leads to a competitive struggle between the units in a population. Different types of resources are relevant at different levels of action. At the cognitive level, ideas may compete for human attention in brainstorming meetings; at the organizational level, work groups may compete for financial support; and at the level of organizational populations, industries may compete for government subsidies. Competition ensures that there is a continuous push for change and innovation, producing winners and losers, thus contributing to new variations. The survival of a single unit in a population may not be consequential to the survival of the population as a whole, depending on how tightly coupled the units in the population are – the closer the linkages, the stronger the population-level implications of changes in any one unit. Variations across units contribute to the pool of competencies in the population, but they do not determine the population's collective fate. The survival of a chain organization in fast-food, banking, or maid services is not normally jeopardized by the closure of a single outlet (Winter and Szulanski, 2001).

In sum, the processes of variation, selection, and retention do not occur in sequence but function simultaneously and via feedback effects. Retention processes enable the replication of selected variations, for instance by improving imitability. They can also constrain the emergence of new variations, for example by reinforcing routines that make it difficult to absorb inconsistent information. In a changing environment, selection criteria are themselves subject to evolution, altering the conditions for variation and retention. Organizational evolution proceeds through the diffusion of units available for selection. Institutional mechanisms of diffusion include imitation, instruction, and strength of habit, subject to actors' opportunism and bounded rationality. Similar to organizational economists, evolutionary theorists focus on the competitive constraints in diffusion, noting mechanisms such as bankrupty and takeovers, but they also emphasize that competition is not the only selection force. Organizations often collaborate either out of a sense of social obligation, as in communities of cooperatives (Staber, 1992), or for economic reasons, as when firms collude to increase market power (Pfeffer and Salancik, 1978). Impediments to efficient evolution arise when the actors disagree on goals, protect their vested interests, or misinterpret new opportunities. Organizational evolution is not a mechanistic sequence of actions and responses, but is affected by the perceptions and interpretations of individuals acting alone or in unison with others. Evolutionary mechanisms always contain a significant element of uncertainty, leading to indeterminacy of outcomes.

4.2 Evolutionary indeterminacy

From an evolutionary perspective, any "improvement" in organizational form is relative and differs from optimization by some absolute standard. Evolution denotes changes that may or may not be *intended* by the actors, and the direction, magnitude, or speed of changes cannot be specified in advance. Organizational evolution is best understood as the result of the actions and interactions of "intendedly rational people making what sense they can of their various situations, pursuing their various aims, and often acting in ways that they have difficulty explaining, even to themselves" (Weeks and Galunic, 2003: 1320). Evolution is driven by the interplay of actors, who are differentially endowed with resources and motivations, and variable conditions in the economic and institutional environment. Evolution is not an efficient optimization process, but a context-dependent and, in many ways, deeply flawed process of adaptation, with uncertain outcomes (Carroll and Harrison, 1994).

The evolutionary process rules out the kind of determinism familiar in standard economic theory, which presumes a moving equilibrium in the variables of interest. It is also inconsistent with the determinism inherent in standard **contingency analysis**, which views situational factors as an imperative force in organizational development and argues that the suitability of a given organizational form is determined by the goodness of fit between itself and the current environment (Lawrence and Lorsch, 1967). And it opposes those neo-institutional theorists who argue that institutions are powerful and persistent to the point where they leave no meaningful choices to organizations. Evolutionary change occurs neither fully randomly nor fully predictably. On the one hand, much of what happens in organizational evolution involves errors, surprises, and chance events, although organizational planners and strategic managers often adopt a rhetoric of deliberate intervention (e.g., in press releases, on websites, on television talk shows), presenting themselves as individuals making decisions with foresight and strength of will. Organizations contain significant elements of randomness stemming from interest conflicts between individuals and units, flawed decision-making structures, and fragmented organizational cultures. On the other hand, organizations also contain elements of order, in the form of authority hierarchies, formal rules, and standard operating procedures, that help keep the organization on a directed path. The normally espoused *raison d'être* of organizing is to create selection and retention structures that enhance predictability and accountability, but the appropriateness of particular structures can be known only retrospectively. Evolution is an emergent process, in the sense that units at higher levels of action depend on units at a lower level without being reducible to, or predictable from, lower-level units (Blitz, 1992). For example, personal dispositions like ambition and creative talent may contribute to an organization's innovativeness but they do not determine whether the organization is indeed innovative and whether innovativeness enhances organizational survival. The outcomes of organizing are not independent of the interests and capabilities of individual actors, but neither are they fully determined by them.

4.3 Summary

According to evolutionary theory, as used in organization science, organizations are not like organic systems, but they share the variation–selection retention algorithm common to all evolutionary systems (Campbell, 1969). To be useful for an understanding of organizational life, evolutionary theory must achieve at least three objectives. First, it must explain the dynamics of how organizational forms change over time. In doing so, it must recognize the underlying variability of the components making up organizations and populations of organizations. In particular, it must appreciate the impact of human agency, leaving room for cognitive diversity, discretionary possibilities, and changes in actors' capabilities and preferences. Second, it must address the mechanisms that generate persistence as well as change, rather than merely describing statistical regularities of the "if–then" sort. And third, it must consider the ever-present possibility that organizations evolve in ways that do not improve their performance and do not serve the interests of all their members equally well. Most organizations fail eventually, and many others produce outcomes that are not in the best interest of everyone. An organization exists not necessarily because it serves the interests of its designers, although the designers may *think* that it should. And an organization does not exist because it constitutes an effective solution for some kind of social problem, although planners may *propose* that it does.

The inclusion in the analysis of dysfunctional elements in organizations helps to avoid the **functionalist** reasoning evident in studies that attempt to explain the occurrence of an entity in terms of its beneficial outcomes. An organizational rule may not achieve what it is supposed to achieve; an individual may not contribute to the work group as specified in the employment contract; and a hierarchical system of control may not be efficient even if it is endorsed by everyone in the organization. If one defines the structure of an organization by its purported functions, there is the need to explain the non-occurrence of functions as well. One would also need to suggest functional alternatives, as well as the mechanisms by which evolutionary processes produce different outcomes, both adaptive and non-adaptive. A distinct contribution of evolutionary theorizing is that it takes into account the entire range of possibilities, leaving open what the actors in organizations make of these possibilities in a given instance.

5. Common relational elements in organizational economics, institutions, and evolution

Scholars working within an economic, institutionalist, and evolutionary framework address specific questions about organizations and employ a distinct set of analytical concepts, but they also share commonalities that offer a possibility of integration. One of these commonalities is the concern – albeit not always stated explicitly – for relations between units, as opposed to the attributes of units. The growing interest in organization studies in relations has gone hand in hand with the "cultural turn" in the social sciences (Emirbayer, 1997), with scholars attending to the meanings of social action and to the ways in which individuals construct meaning (Pachucki and Breiger, 2010). The conventional – and, in managerial practice, also the most popular – approach to organizations and organizational design and governance emphasizes the structural architecture of relationships between actors differing in relevant attributes (e.g., age, education), and proposes that this configuration (e.g., who in a group occupies what position, who has what kinds of decision-making rights) shapes individual and collective action in predictable ways. The relational approach, by contrast, attends to the mutual constitution of structural relations and the meanings of relations, with a view to what people do when they discover contradictions or obstacles, renegotiate the content of ties, or change partners (White, 1992). From a relational perspective, the structure of relations affects their meaning, while at the same time being shaped by the meanings that the actors ascribe to relations. Structure and meaning are co-constitutive of one another.

Consider, for example, the assembly of individuals shown in Exhibit 2.1. This assembly is a social collectivity in the sense that the members have a common goal, in this case gaining admission to a tourist site. While waiting, some of them converse with others, including people they have never met before. They exchange ideas, tell stories, and some of them might make plans to meet again in the future. A conventional **structuralist** study of, say, group diversity would focus on the group's configuration in terms of individual differences, such as nationality or occupational background, and would *infer* from these differences something about collective behavior, such as whether the individuals will likely stage an organized protest if this tourist site remains closed for the rest of the day. By contrast, a study conceived in relational terms would also investigate the meanings the individuals assign to their membership in this group, with a view to how they construct these meanings out of their social relations. Some of the individuals who share the same ethnic background might assign a new meaning to the concept of ethnicity, depending on what they hear in their discussions with others. For some of them, interaction with different people might open new opportunities for viewing

Exhibit 2.1

themselves as something other than tourists. Others might move closer to people they perceive as similar to themselves, to survive in a setting where they feel like "strangers in a strange land." The mutual constitution of meanings and relations will likely differ depending on the situation (Godart and White, 2010). In a different context, the same individuals might exhibit very different behaviors. If they were to meet in, say, an organizational project team, they may define their interaction primarily with a view to technical requirements (Kilduff et al., 2000).

The point is that individuals are always embedded in a context-dependent web of structures and meanings from which they derive their identity in relation to the identity of others in the web (White, 1992). Simply knowing that individuals in a group differ in some attribute says nothing about the group's collective orientation. From a relational perspective, one also needs to study how they make sense of that attribute in light of how it relates to the distribution of other attributes in the group, such as whether the discourse among the participants reveals any overlaps in the meanings of the same and different attributes. A relational perspective suggests that social entities evolve through the dynamic interplay between meanings and structures. Relational structures emerge out of the meanings the individuals assign to them, while in turn shaping the meanings connected to the structures in which the individuals are embedded. As individuals switch between the various social, cultural, and economic domains in which they are active, opportunities arise for constructing new meanings and relational structures (Mische and Pattison, 2000). For example, when students move between places of study, home, and work, they adjust the meanings of the situations in which they are located as well as the identities that are invoked by the movements (Burke and Franzoi, 1988). Research on work groups has shown that racial similarity increases cooperative behavior to the extent that group members interpret such similarity as confirming their work-related identity (Milton and Westphal, 2005). In a different context, racial similarity may lead to different outcomes, although the actors are the same. In complex organizations, one should not be surprised that people's interpretations of their condition change in line with co-evolving relational structures.

The concern for relations is reflected in many of the ways in which organizational scholars draw on arguments from evolutionary theory, institutionalism, and organizational economics. For example, evolutionary theory draws attention to the temporality of organizational relations by asking about the origins of variations and the dynamics of selection processes. Selection criteria are not immutable but are the result of struggles between individuals over the "correct" meaning of the criteria. The competitive struggle for meanings is embedded in, and made possible by, existing relational structures, while the structures evolve through the replication and transformation of people's mutual orientations and actions. If a consistent pattern of collective behavior emerges, it might be the result of convergent evolution under common selective pressures in a tightly bounded environment. Alternatively, it might be the outcome of different retention patterns, such as lateral transmission (e.g., through the importation of new ideas from outside a group) or vertical transmission (e.g., mentors passing ideas on to the next generation of organizational members).

Institutional theory adds to this understanding by exploring the rules and conventions that channel human attention, and the mechanisms for enforcing expectations. Institutional thinking provides a framework for explaining the conditions under which change is evoked, imposed, or acquired. When change is evoked, individuals respond automatically to a change in environmental circumstances. When change is imposed, individuals comply with the expectations set by powerful institutions. And when change is acquired, individuals observe, imitate, or learn from salient others. In each case, individuals assign meaning to relations, based on the existing structure of relations. Thus, the acquisition and use of meaning systems always involve social structures plus institutional rules for defining what kinds of relations are appropriate in a given context. Individual choices are impossible without such relational rules. For example, some of the people shown in Exhibit 2.1 may prefer the "first-come-first-serve" queuing rule, while others may refer to the "I paid for it" domination rule, expecting the organizational leadership of the tourist site to impose a system of orderly admission. A problem arises in settings where the actors differ in their understanding of institutional rules ("What is order?") or where they refuse to submit to institutional forms of domination ("I was here first!").

Similarly, but with a view more to the material utility value of orientations, organizational economists note that individuals' preference functions are not exogenously given. Instead, they emerge out of the transactions through which individuals procure scarce resources, evaluate contractual obligations, and define property relations. For example, when the partners to an exchange relationship perceive a risk that the other actor will behave opportunistically, they have an incentive to restructure the relationship by adding institutional safeguards, such as contractual clauses or third-party dispute resolution arrangements. Situations that are so complex that they cannot be interpreted unambiguously may motivate the actors to invest in long-term relationships to develop common understandings, whereas unfulfilled **reciprocity** claims may cause them to look for new partners outside the industry. Regarding the group of people waiting for admission to the tourist site (Exhibit 2.1), organizational economists would predict the pure market to fail as a coordination mechanism, if the individuals have distinct identities, there is no shared history of cooperation, and some of the individuals are inclined to behave opportunistically by cutting in line or pretending physical disability. When information ambiguity is extreme, it may overwhelm all rational control attempts, leading to collective behavior dominated by chance events. From an evolutionary perspective, these are situations that provide fertile ground for mutation through the reinterpretation of norms and the renegotiation of roles. Organizations in the creative sector (e.g., advertising, architecture) illustrate settings where the possibility of such mutations is actively pursued. In other industries, organizations try to prevent such mutations by imposing tight formal structures, although such structures may provoke unplanned behavioral deviations with potential adaptive value.

6. Conclusion

Each of the three theory camps discussed in this chapter constitutes an overarching framework, combining related streams of research and providing a platform for integrating arguments from diverse perspectives. The arguments qualify as theory in that they propose causal schemes linking concepts, specify boundary conditions, and permit falsifiable hypotheses (Bacharach, 1989). While these frameworks all view organizations as social entities adapting to changing requirements in relevant environments, they differ in their approach to the details of how organizations respond to these requirements. Whereas organizational economists focus on the demands for more efficient structures and practices, institutional and evolutionary theorists argue that many of the most fateful forces in the organizational world are the result of socio-cultural pressures in the form of traditions, norms, and ideologies.

All three frameworks emphasize external forces, but they are also mindful of the fundamental fact that organizations are composed of individuals who construct – through cognitions, actions, and interactions – organizational forms as locally shared systems of meaning from the ground up. Meaning systems involve various types of perceptual choices: people discount the future, rationalize the past, and reframe current situations. The concern for human agency also turns on the question of evidence in the development of explanations for observed organizational phenomena. All social science researchers struggle with problems related to the interpretation of empirical observations. If one accepts the psychologist's characterization of people as individuals who are often mistaken about the causes of their own behavior (Wilson and Brekke, 1994), then one should not be surprised that even the methodologically most diligent organizational researchers refrain from claiming that they know what their study subjects are *really* thinking and are *therefore* doing. Any theoretical statement can only be an approximation of the "truth," and all evidence in favor of one or the other explanation must be considered tentative (Popper, 1959). Given available data, one may not be able to conclude, for example, that someone behaves cooperatively in a work group because the existing incentive system guards against shirking (the property rights explanation of economists), because the person imitates high-status individuals in the group (the institutional explanation), or because such behavior brings adaptive advantages to both the person and the collectivity (the evolutionary explanation). Motive-based explanations of behavior are problematic because they are fairly immune to direct empirical verification (Reskin, 2003), as individuals are often not aware of the reasons for their behavior (Tilly, 2006).

Although organizational researchers risk making interpretive mistakes of a kind that may not arise in the study of material matters in fields like physics or chemistry, it should not prevent them from developing alternative explanatory hypotheses and to subject these to the best empirical tests they can muster. The goal should be to construct theoretical arguments that are open to refutation through an appeal to logic and evidence. This is what has been happening in organization studies for the last few decades and what has made this field such a lively area of research and debate. The discussions in the following chapters will show how theorizing from an economic, institutional, and evolutionary perspective advances our understanding of a range of substantive organizational problem areas. They indicate the usefulness of these perspectives for understanding phenomena in all types of organizations, including economic enterprises, cultural organizations, interest associations, ideological organizations, and organizations where it is difficult to disentangle the material and social motives of their members.

Recommended further reading

Burrell, G. and Morgan, G. (1979) *Sociological Paradigms and Organisational Analysis*. London: Heinemann.
Similar to social analysis in general, organizational analysis can be organized along two dimensions: philosophical assumptions about the nature of society and the nature of social science. This classification system has proven useful for organizing many of the theoretical perspectives in use in organization studies.

Hofstede, G. (1996) An American in Paris: The influence of nationality on organization theories, *Organization Studies*, 17: 525–537.
The author proposes that organizational researchers from different countries and cultural regions of the world work with different theories. It is, therefore, difficult to achieve consensus on any theory of organizations.

Pfeffer, J. (1993) Barriers to the advance of organizational science: Paradigm development as a dependent variable, *Academy of Management Review*, 18: 599–620.
Compared to the natural sciences, the study of organizations is paradigmatically not well developed, lacking consensus about concepts and methodologies. The author views this as a barrier to the development of a successful organizational science.

Stern, R. and Barley, S. (1996) Organizations and social systems: Organization theory's neglected mandate, *Administrative Science Quarterly*, 41: 146–162.
The authors link the study of organizations to the social context in which it has developed, arguing that the location of organizational scholarship in a business school environment has led to reduced attention to organizations' role in the broader society.

 ■ **Practice questions for Anecdote 2.1** ■■■■■■■■■

1 What could Sam do to build for himself an institutional setting that would give him the recognition he seeks as a professional artist?

2 How would you build a social network in a small rural town to increase your economic opportunities as an artist?

3 Identify some of the transaction costs Sam faces when setting up an arts show in his home town.

3

Contexts and Environments

Learning Objectives

This chapter will:

- Discuss the external environment as a contextual feature of organizations
- Discuss the structure of environments in terms of interdependence and interconnectedness between organizations
- Discuss environments as a source of uncertainty for organizations

1. Introduction

When couples experience serious marital problems, they may seek advice from specialists outside their family, and when neighborhood residents demand improvements in the local transportation infrastructure, they often expect external organizations to provide the necessary resources. Similarly, organizations cannot normally on their own generate all resources they need for survival. Many material, social, and informational inputs are located outside their boundaries, in an environment populated by other organizations with which they compete and cooperate. Volatility in the terms on which external organizations make resources available creates uncertainty for the focal organization. To reduce uncertainty, it enters into exchange relationships with those organizations on which it is resource dependent (e.g., in the form of supplier contracts) or with which it shares resource dependencies (e.g., in the form of interest associations).

Variations in the way organizations manage environmental uncertainty have become a distinct subject of inquiry since the 1980s, when organizational scholars began to pay more attention to entire production systems rather than individual organizations. The early writings on organizational management – associated with the **scientific management** and **administrative schools of thought** in the early 1900s – focused on matters internal to organizations. This was in contrast to the "classical" sociological work on organizations by theorists such as Durkheim, Marx, Michels, and Weber, who linked formal organizations to the social structure of society and argued that they were central to the cultural transformations taking place in modernizing societies (Giddens, 1971). Curiously, the "classical management" theorists (e.g., Taylor, Fayol, Urwick, Barnard) did not attend more closely to the ways in which forces in the wider society impacted on organizations, even though they wrote about organizations at a time when Western society was in great upheaval. Many of the innovations in organizational forms at that time were responses to the turbulence created by dramatic environmental events (e.g., World War I, the Great Depression) and the social upheavals associated with industrialization (e.g., mass migration to cities, emergence of the factory system).

Even today, many scholars study organizations as if they were closed systems, holding the external context constant or ignoring it altogether. In doing this they miss factors that, although they may have no direct impact on internal organizational matters, are consequential because they interact with the phenomenon under investigation. For example, managerial efforts to reduce worker absenteeism rates may fail despite a well-designed organizational incentive system (e.g., flexible working time arrangements for employees with young children) because they ignore contextual factors, such as the culture of the local community in which the organization exists. The local culture may be such that frequent absenteeism from the workplace is considered socially acceptable. In this case, the effect of local culture is to moderate the influence of the organization's incentive system. Organizational members may be tightly embedded in the local community's social structure through their social ties to actors in families, churches, neighborhood clubs, and so on, which function as a channel for the enforcement of cultural norms regarding "appropriate" employee conduct. For researchers, this means that empirical studies should not merely *control* for variations in contextual factors, by holding them constant. Rather, they should *explain* their influence, by exploring the mechanisms by which context exerts influence (Johns, 2006).

This chapter begins with a discussion of environments as the context in which organizations evolve. Organizational action is inseparable from the environment and cannot be understood if it is analyzed separately. Two themes are especially noteworthy here: one pertaining to *what* organizational researchers study when they attend to environmental context, and the other theme relating to *how* they conduct these studies. Regarding the *what* question, researchers have developed several classification schemes to identify dimensions of environments. Of central interest here is the interdependence and interconnectedness between a set of organizations, as the structural sources and outcomes of uncertainty. Regarding the *how* question, scholars working within the organizational economics, institutionalist, and evolutionary frameworks have examined different aspects of the organization–environment interface. Much of this research has been dedicated to understanding how organizations translate environmental uncertainty into organizational forms for reducing uncertainty.

2. Context matters

In one of the most widely cited books in organization studies in the late 1970s, the authors suggest that "much of the literature on organizations still does not recognize the importance of context" (Pfeffer and Salancik, 1978: 1). Their key argument was that if one wants to understand the actions of organizations, one must understand the context in which they occur. Until the 1970s, many scholars had merely acknowledged the various manifestations of environments in such forms as industry structure, government regulation, and market demand. Some researchers argued in favor of viewing organizations as "open systems," but they directed their attention mainly to internal matters, such as leadership style and communication structure (Katz and Kahn, 1966). And those who incorporated "environmental variables" in their research designs treated them mostly as contextual givens rather than a subject in their own right. In one of the earliest explicit statements about the organization–environment interface, Aldrich (1971: 281–282) noted that organizational forms were usually "investigated without regard to their contributions to fitness in varying or diverse organizational environments." The typical approach, practiced for example in the early organizational strategy literature, was to emphasize the importance of being in the right industry and then to decide whether to compete on the basis of cost advantage, product differentiation, or some other criterion. Eventually, scholars began to pay more systematic attention to forces in the environment, investigating their influence on organizational dynamics and exploring adaptive strategies (Aldrich, 1979; Meyer and Scott, 1983; Miles and Snow, 1978; Pfeffer and Salancik, 1978). This research has produced numerous insights into the organization–environment interface, branching into diverse areas of inquiry, from organizational strategy and entrepreneurship to marketing and regional studies. Today, few scholars would argue that the environmental context is no more than an extra-organizational explanatory adjunct.

The most common definition of context identifies "factors associated with units of analysis above those expressly under investigation" (Cappelli and Sherer, 1991: 56). Contextualizing organizational phenomena means linking observations to a set of relevant facts or points of view at a higher level of analysis. For example, to understand job search behavior at the level of individuals one may want to know whether job seekers are currently employed, or whether they are looking for their first job, because accumulated work experience affects perceptions of employability (Boswell et al., 2012). Or, to understand the likelihood of a business interest association disbanding, it is important to know whether it was founded in times of economic growth or in times of decline, because strategic decisions on how to respond to macro-economic conditions at the time of founding can lead to organizational structures that are difficult to change in the future (Aldrich et al., 1994). Context can impact directly on organizational phenomena or it can mediate the influence of variables. It can have a *main* (i.e., direct) effect on the phenomenon in question, as when multinational corporations design work systems tailored to the requirements of industrial relations systems in different countries (Geppert and Matten, 2006). Context can also have an *interaction* (i.e., mediating) effect, as when the influence of particular organizational practices depends on some contextual factor. For example, the presence of whistle-blowing legislation may harm an organization's public reputation only if it encourages employees to make complaints public (Perry, 1998). In this case, the influence of legislation on organizational reputation interacts with the impact of employee complaints, by increasing the effect of launching complaints.

The hypothesized impact of context can be taken up in the design of research studies through the selection of organizations for investigation and the measurement of variables. To understand, say, variations in the performance outcomes of different organizational forms, one needs to explore differences in a contextually varied population of organizations and explain how contextual differences are related to performance. The more contextually diverse the population of organizations, the more robust are statements about differences in performance. Explaining contextual effects requires the specification of mechanisms by which context produces effects at a lower level. For example, multinational companies operating in local markets with distinct local customer needs and institutions need to be flexible in their resource engagements, but flexibility can be achieved in different ways. In the television industry, for example, some internationally active content producers adapt to local conditions by imitating the existing organizational forms of local competitors. Others build complex network relations with a range of local organizations to create new forms of production (Sydow et al., 2010). Some of these differences in strategy can be explained with reference to different utility functions of the organizations involved. Institutional differences in the local context may play a significant role as well. How exactly organizations respond to the demands of their local environments also depends on how they conceptualize these demands.

2.1 Conceptualizing the environment

As a first step in conceptualizing the environment one needs to describe the phenomenon. Characterizing the environment has proven to be difficult in past research, not least because the environment is a social construct which is difficult to capture using standardized survey methodologies. Studying the environment as a social construct means treating it as an entity in terms of the way the actors under investigation *experience* environmental conditions, cognitively and in interaction with others who are similarly exposed to environmental demands. On the one hand, environmental forces, like market competition or social pressure from public interest groups, have an objective quality in the sense that they have an impact independent of how they are perceived. In that regard, they may operate as "social facts." On the other hand, environmental forces have *significance* for the organization only to the extent that they are interpreted as a cause for action. Local forces (e.g., protest activities of neighborhood watch groups) are more likely to be perceived as being relevant than forces in the more distant environment (e.g., government monetary policy).

2.1.1 Task and institutional environment

The early literature on organizational environment was concerned with the construction of **typologies**, by identifying dimensions of environments. A fundamental distinction that has proven useful for descriptive purposes is that between task environments and institutional environments (Meyer and Rowan, 1977). In task environments, organizational decisions are made with respect to the availability of inputs and the disposition of outputs; in institutional environments, decisions are informed by social and cultural considerations. Organizations experience task and institutional requirements in different combinations and intensities. For example, a hospital is subject to strong task demands stemming from the wide range of complex technologies used to restore a patient's health in areas like consultation, surgery, and rehabilitation. Hospitals are also subject to strong institutional requirements related to cultural notions of fairness and justice, enforced by government regulations and public media evaluations. Because hospitals cannot afford to ignore task and institutional demands, they construct complex organizational structures that give specialized attention to the interests of diverse stakeholder groups, including insurance companies, licensing boards, pharmaceutical firms, medical equipment manufacturers, and patient associations. To the extent that the identity of different groups of hospital employees (e.g., doctors, nurses, medical lab technicians, insurance specialists) is inextricably tied to the technical and institutional aspects of their work, they may interact directly with actors in the environment. Surgeons, for example, who are experts in the use of specialized equipment, may participate in procurement negotiations with equipment producers, and the licensing of medical technicians may be based on standards that are determined in interaction with insurance companies and medical schools. Powerful institutions may have a direct impact on professional identities, as in the case of health care reform in New Zealand, leading to a blurring of the identity boundary between hospital managers and clinicians, by forcing clinical staff to make medical decisions with a view to economically rational criteria rather than merely the health interests of patients (Doolin, 2002).

In comparison to hospitals, employees in a typical hair studio work in a simple task environment with a narrow range of technologies, leading to simple organizational structures and routines (Chugh and Hancock, 2009). Hairdressing salons are also subject to few institutional expectations regarding what is considered socially appropriate conduct towards customers. Hairdressers may construct an occupational identity more with a view to the specific needs of client groups (e.g., related to social class or age category) than to the institutional idea of hair care fulfilling a generalized social function. Given the comparatively minimal constraints of task technology and institutions, one would expect hair studios to be more flexible than hospitals in their interactions with customers. This does not mean, however, that they are less likely to fail, even if simple organizational structures enable greater adaptability in a changing market environment. If, on average, hospitals survive longer than hairdressing salons, it is because they have more market power and because the general public considers medical services socially indispensable and is, therefore, willing to tolerate a certain degree of resource inefficiency.

2.1.2 Environmental complexity and volatility

Another common approach to classifying organizational environments identifies complexity and volatility as sources of uncertainty (Duncan, 1972). Environmental *complexity* refers to the number and diversity of actors (e.g., competitors, suppliers, customers, interest groups) in the focal organization's environment, and the range of distinct demands they make on the organization. Fitness studios, for example, exist in a comparatively simple environment, normally serving a single type of customer with a limited range of expectations regarding fitness equipment, hygiene, and exercise instruction (Annesi, 1999). By contrast, universities serve a large variety of stakeholders with often competing interests, including funding institutions, accrediting agencies, and professional associations (Kerr, 2001). In cases where different stakeholder groups hold divergent expectations of organizational performance, organizations will tend to create specialized job positions or departmental units to handle their specific demands (Pratt and Foreman, 2000). Organizations operating in complex environments are also more likely to collaborate with similarly exposed organizations, forming industry alliances, creating interest associations, or sharing individuals on their governing boards (Pfeffer and Salancik, 1978). Colleges in the United States, for instance, routinely participate in consortia for purposes of joint marketing and government lobbying. The more closely affiliated colleges are with a consortium, the more likely it is that they respond similarly to environmental changes, such as developing new programs of study or introducing financial aid programs (Kraatz, 1998). Inter-organizational relations are seen as a mechanism for organizations to mitigate environmental uncertainty by learning from the experiences of similar organizations or by jointly controlling the flow of resources.

Environmental *volatility* refers to the turbulence in external conditions, such as rapid changes in consumer tastes, fluctuations in money supply, or turnover in the population of suppliers. A volatile environment means that the provision of vital resources is not assured and cannot be planned for. In some industries, environments change so slowly that organizations can easily adapt. The funeral industry in the United States is an example of an environment in which firms have not changed in their core features because consumers continue to prefer funeral ceremonies that follow traditional conventions (Torres, 1988). By contrast, the fashion industry operates in a highly volatile environment, where market demand is very difficult to predict but production must take place well in advance of sales (Schulz, 2008). To survive, fashion houses and textile producers need to experiment continuously with new designs, styles, fabrics, marketing techniques, and waste disposal methods. Many of the larger firms in the textile and clothing sector have adopted a "flexible network strategy," outsourcing production to specialized subcontractors and retail functions to department stores, and coordinating the network of subcontractors in the ever-changing mix of inputs and outputs. While the network strategy has become a general feature in this sector, the specific organizational form of networks can vary widely across countries, owing to differences in the institutional context related to labor training, industrial relations, licensing, and so on (Djelic and Ainamo, 1999).

Environmental complexity and volatility are analytically distinct dimensions, although they may be related empirically in specific instances, leading to different levels of uncertainty for organizations. Stable and simple environments, for example, imply little uncertainty. A crowded beach on a hot summer day represents a simple and stable environment for the sellers of ice-cream and cold drinks. There is little need for them to gather much new information and to make new decisions on how to bring products to the market. By contrast, organizations in cultural-product industries operate in highly volatile and complex environments. Firms in industries like film production and performing arts cater to a variety of customer groups with tastes that can change abruptly. To survive the tyranny of the entertainment market, organizations must be prepared to switch offerings and to assemble new project teams on short notice, given changing technological innovations, volatile labor markets, and resource-scarce funding environments (Perretti and Negro, 2007). The environment of Hollywood film producers, for example, has become increasingly uncertain since the 1930s. In response, the large studios switched from a control-oriented and property-based growth strategy, based on deeds of ownership or patents guaranteeing exclusive rights, to a flexibility-oriented knowledge-based strategy, based on the deployment of creative and collaborative skills (Miller and Shamsie, 1996). Organizing film production in networks of small, specialized organizations may enhance operational flexibility, but it also creates new challenges for coordination because of the transaction costs associated with managing the contributions of functionally interdependent but legally autonomous network partners.

2.2 Interdependence between organizations

Describing the elements of the phenomenon under investigation is an important part of understanding, but it is not sufficient if one wants to *explain* the phenomenon. To this end, organization theorists have gone beyond typologies of environments and have examined the conditions under which different organizational forms are effective in different environments. Specifically, they have studied the organization–environment interface in terms of the structure of interdependencies and interconnections among a set of organizations, arguing that the structural features of environments are both a source and outcome of inter-organizational relations.

Organizations are resource interdependent to the extent that their actions affect each other in some way. For instance, in many cities in northern Italy museums, galleries, and theaters are embedded in a network of specialized cultural organizations (e.g., auction houses, arts dealerships) and institutions (e.g., banks, professional associations, research centers) through which resources like money, labor skills, and ideas about culture are distributed, creating a high degree of functional interdependence (Lazzeretti, 2004). Art restorators depend on museums to provide them with work opportunities, while museums depend on restorators to enhance their reputation as places of well-preserved art and culture.

Functional interdependence arises from processes of differentiation and integration, as organizations carve out niches for themselves and coordinate their actions with others. Organization founders, for example, contribute to differentiation by exploiting new technologies, selling new products, or developing new labor skills. Differentiation reduces competition between organizations because they draw on different pools of resources. Competitive intensity increases when new organizations move into the same environment with a fixed level of resources. For example, when firms in different industries recruit labor from the same pool of skills (e.g., web designers working for advertising firms as well as film companies), there is a higher degree of competition between them than when they draw on different labor markets (e.g., a children's museum hiring clowns, and an art museum hiring multimedia specialists), with implications for organizational performance. A study of business foundings and failures in Denmark found that firms compete more in labor markets than one would expect from their degree of similarity in product markets (Sorensen, 2004). The rate of foundings was lower and the rate of failures was higher in industries with large overlaps in labor markets.

In addition to producing environmental differentiation, organizations also contribute to integration. Organizations often coordinate their activities through interest associations to lobby governments or to set industry-wide standards in production (Aldrich et al., 1994). In highly volatile environments, such as the life science industry, it is critical that firms have access to the latest information on markets and technologies. To mitigate the disruptive effects of competitive crowding, they collaborate in those areas where they don't compete head-on, such as basic research and finance. To enable close social interaction between scientists, collaborative ventures in biotechnology are often concentrated geographically in clusters, such as those in the Boston region and the San Francisco Bay area (Whittington et al., 2009). Firms occupying a central network position in such clusters tend to be more innovative than firms located at the periphery of networks because they can collect information more rapidly. However, even a peripheral position may produce certain advantages, depending on the type of organizations to which the firm is connected. For example, firms at the periphery of a production network may have special access to funding through venture capitalists or they may be linked to foreign government bodies. Understanding the effects of interdependence thus requires attention to the structure and content of network ties between organizations.

Competitive and cooperative relations between organizations involve different forms of interdependence – commensalism and symbiosis (Hawley, 1986). *Commensalism* refers to the interdependence of organizations with similar forms and functions. Organizations are similar if they seek similar resources from the environment, in the same metaphoric sense that people who "sit in the same boat" share the same fate. The question is: what happens when organizations experience commensalist interdependence? One possibility is that commensalism leads to direct competition for available resources, if the interdependent organizations cannot move to a different, more resource-munificent environment. Churches, for example, are in competition to the extent that they recruit members from the same population of people sharing an interest in religion (Koçak and Carroll, 2008). If religious demand is declining, individual churches may try to survive by offering new services. To avoid head-on competition, they may redefine their goals with a view to the specific preferences of different kinds of believers, thus contributing to differentiation in the population of churches. Greater diversity in the religious marketplace provides opportunities for churches to closely tailor their services to potential and current members (Perl and Olson, 2000). On the other hand, diversity in the environment also means that worshippers are exposed to competing understandings of faith and religion. Research shows that in the United States at the turn of the twentieth century, when the church sector became firmly established and when immigration rates were highest, religious diversity *reduced* people's church participation more strongly in the more urbanized communities, suggesting that the environment of churches had changed to a more pluralistic and secularized marketplace in which worshippers could come in contact with representatives of alternative faiths and non-religious groupings (Koçak and Carroll, 2008).

While commensalism refers to the interdependence of organizations with similar forms, *symbiosis* denotes the interdependence of dissimilar organizations. Symbiotically related organizations exist in different environments but benefit from each other's presence. An example of symbiotic interdependence are firms in the cultural products sector of urban conglomerations like Los Angeles and Paris where knowledge flows across functionally related industries in multimedia, design, advertising, fashion, and the arts (Scott, 2000). New ideas that emerge in, say, the fashion industry are applied and further developed in other industries, such as film production and advertising. The cultural products sector represents an **ecology** of interdependent specialized organizations and organizational populations, stretching into areas with overlapping artistic (e.g., theater, music), symbolic (e.g., photography, jewelry), political (e.g., interest representation, heritage preservation), economic (e.g., sports, entertainment), and media (e.g., talent casting shows, advertising) content. This ecology is rich in opportunities for new developments, fueled by interpersonal and **inter-organizational networks** through which ideas and material resources can flow, and guided by institutions (e.g., cultural consulting, city image marketing) providing legitimacy and reputation (Staber, 2012). The ecology is also rife with tensions (e.g., creativity versus efficiency) and competing logics (e.g., creative freedom versus economic viability), which keep the system in motion.

Organizations experiencing symbiotic interdependence often engage in collective action to promote common interests. The high-tech cluster in Silicon Valley, California, is often cited as an example of symbiotically related firms seeking to innovate through various forms of collaboration. In the early development of this cluster, local institutions such as economic development agencies, university laboratories, market research firms, law firms, and venture capitalists played an important coordinating role, by organizing information exchange between the firms (Saxenian, 1994). By contrast, in the technologically similar high-tech cluster in Boston, Massachusetts, coordinating institutions could not develop because firms were keen to maintain their decision-making autonomy, based on a local business culture of independence and competition. Silicon Valley's regional advantage also lies in the numerous social networks (e.g., professional, friendship, consulting), through which ideas flow between the specialized firms. These networks continue to flourish today, creating an open environment for developing new linkages, including ties with business people and engineers as far as eastern Asia (Saxenian and Quan, 2002). Such connections were lacking in Boston, where corporate hierarchies ensured that authority was more centralized, social networks remained largely within the firms, and local institutions were kept outside the firms. Interconnectedness between organizations is thus not a natural consequence of interdependence. The European Union is an example of a system of functionally interdependent national economies where coordination has been constrained by the absence of an institutional superstructure with sufficient authority to intervene in internal national affairs (Naurin and Lindahl, 2010).

2.3 Organizational interconnectedness

The structure of interconnectedness in an organizational population reflects a mix of competitive and cooperative actions intended to reduce environmental uncertainty. In uncertain environments, the pattern of adaptation is highly unstable, as in the evolution of the church sector in the United States (Koçak and Carroll, 2008). In some church populations, head-on competition was mitigated by secular changes in the demography of human populations (e.g., immigration, urbanization) and the rise of non-religious voluntary membership organizations (e.g., sports clubs, self-help organizations). Some churches collaborated with each other, promoting "faith" as the common goal; others distanced themselves from competitors by specializing in unique services, to avoid competitive crowding, leading to differentiation between church sub-populations (Kaufman, 2002). In some cases, whether churches competed or collaborated had more to do with the individual personalities of church leaders than with strategic organizational calculations. The choice between competition and cooperation may also be a function of the position of organizations in the value chain. When protecting the religious market from the intrusion of fraternal organizations, social clubs, and voluntary service associations, churches may collaborate, whereas in the delivery of services to worshippers they may compete.

Whether organizations behave more competitively or cooperatively in a particular instance is a question often decided idiosyncratically at the level of individuals. The individuals who sit at the boundary between the organization and its environment play a critical role in this regard. It is **boundary spanners** like human resource managers, strategy planners, and public relations specialists who identify the organization's stakeholders and interpret their goals. By connecting with organizations in the environment, they absorb uncertainty and feed their interpretations of environmental conditions into their own organization's decision-making process regarding strategy and structure (Aldrich and Herker, 1977). By selectively seeking information from the environment, interpreting it, and making decisions based on their sense-making, they "enact" the environment (Weick, 1969). From an evolutionary perspective, differences in boundary spanners' cognitive capacity and in their ability to implement their interpretations are an important source of variation in organization–environment relations. Two organizations may be similarly exposed to external pressures, but they may respond very differently because of differently capable boundary spanners. In one sense, then, inter-organizational cooperation and competition are psychological and political phenomena, influenced by boundary spanners' sense of rivalry, trust, and reciprocity (Kilduff et al., 2010) and by their positional power in the organization to translate external demands into a particular organizational strategy and structure (Pfeffer and Salancik, 1978). Given competing interests within and between organizations, this means that relations between organizations are always provisional and never final.

Interconnectedness is a structural feature of environments that obtains force through the ability of organizations to coordinate their actions with others. On the one hand, a high degree of concentration of organizations with similar goals, cost structures, and production functions can *reduce* the problem of interdependence because a smaller number of them must be coordinated. When concentration is high, there are weaker demands on efficient communication, and informal coordination may be possible, without reliance on formal contracts. By contrast, when concentration is low, formal controls may be necessary to achieve coordination, given the strong demands on communication in systems that include a large number of dispersed actors. In illegal inter-organizational networks (e.g., drug cartels, terrorist networks), for example, communication problems are especially serious because of the wide geographic area over which the activities of a large number of people are distributed (Raab and Milward, 2003). Formal coordination mechanisms are not possible in such networks because the actors attempt to keep their activities invisible. On the other hand, high concentration can also *increase* the problem of interdependence. In an environment that includes a small number of resource-munificent organizations it is more likely that the opportunistic actions of any one of them would upset the integrity of the system, creating power imbalances and interest conflicts. Whether such conflicts lead to system disintegration depends partly on the pattern of connectedness between the actors. If different stakeholder groups share common interests and are closely connected, it will be more difficult for the focal organization to resist their demands because it cannot easily play them off against each other (Rowley, 1997). Network studies of organizational populations have shown that the structure of interconnectedness can be consequential in many different ways and at various levels. It can stimulate or retard organizational innovation (Powell et al., 1996), enhance or slow down the development of regional economies (Asheim and Coenen, 2005), and shape the reproduction of a country's power elite (Maclean et al., 2010).

3. Theorizing environment and organizational adaptation

To explain variations in the structure and outcomes of organization–environment relations, researchers have drawn on several perspectives related to individual cognition and social exchange. One may broadly distinguish between perspectives that treat the environment as a determinant of organizational fortunes – the environment seen as an imperative – and perspectives that focus on the interactions between an organization and actors in its immediate task and institutional environment – the environment seen as contestable space. Within the latter perspective, scholars have increasingly emphasized human agency (Meyer and Jepperson, 2000), leading to a view of organizations with external boundaries that are highly unstable. Similarly, the relational turn in parts of organizational scholarship has shifted attention from entities (e.g., job, reward, skill) to connections between entities (e.g., transactions, negotiations, information flows) (Mutch et al., 2006). Together, the concern for agency and relations has opened up new opportunities for cross-fertilization between economic, institutional, and evolutionary perspectives, motivating scholars to study the role of environmental selection relative to internal organizational forces supporting or blocking organizational adaptation.

3.1 Organizational economics

Transaction cost economists have contributed to our understanding of the organization–environment interface by exploring the conditions under which transactions are internalized in an organization or externalized to the open market (Williamson, 1994). Environmental uncertainty complicates the decision situation for organizations. It increases the pressure on organizations to find a cost-effective way to reduce uncertainty, while requiring them to expend more resources than they would prefer, given their potential gains from exchange relations with actors in the environment. Strong linkages with government bodies and other institutional organizations can enhance the survival chances of organizations and organizational populations (Baum and Oliver, 1991), but building such connections requires patience and extensive resource investments, especially if the institutional domain is itself a source of uncertainty. The public policy arena in democratic countries is an example of an environment where decision-making is often described using the garbage-can metaphor, emphasizing fluid processes that involve many different organizations with divergent political interests (Knoke, 1990b). The actors often disagree even on the definition of the problem (e.g., "energy crisis," "Euro crisis") to be solved. Policy options cannot be winnowed quickly because resources and decision participation rights (e.g., in public projects like airport expansion or road construction) are broadly diffused among the relevant actors (e.g., coalition of residents, political parties). Under such conditions, any governance system that economizes on transaction costs will have a selective advantage. Any cost advantages, however, need to be seen within the constraints of institutional uncertainty, as, for example, in cultural products industries where policy initiatives to stimulate local economic development have to reconcile the economic logic of profitability and sustainability with the institutional logic of property rights and social legitimacy (Mommaas, 2004).

Environmental uncertainty creates an incentive for large organizations to disaggregate into autonomous units through outsourcing production or services (e.g., legal, accounting, employment testing) to respond more flexibly to market volatility. However, disaggregation also produces costs, leading organizations to consider transaction-relevant factors such as asset specificity and transaction frequency. For example, the decision of employers to hire workers on a temporary basis is influenced by the likelihood that they require them over the long term (Masters and Miles, 2002). If there is high uncertainty about future demand, employers will prefer to negotiate a series of short-term employment contracts as needed. However, there are costs associated with negotiating and enforcing short-term contracts, which limits the use of temporary workers in volatile markets. If employers cannot ensure a sufficient level of organizational commitment on the part of short-duration hires, but such commitment is required (given non-standard work tasks), they are more likely to employ people on a permanent basis, holding everything else constant. Also, if employers require workers with skills that are unique to the technology used in the organization (a case of high asset specificity), they have an incentive to create a long-term employment relationship, even if the market environment is uncertain. The extent to which organizations outsource activities is thus a function not only of the state of the environment, but also of the ability to coordinate the exchange relationships.

Research suggests that small businesses which use the services of external human resource management specialists tend to maintain multiple types of links with them to have access to a wider range of perspectives and expertise, as long as they can negotiate sufficiently detailed contracts with the human services providers (Klaas et al., 2005). In the film industry, production is organized through networks of small and highly specialized producers (e.g., audio-visual firms, film editors, costume designers, location scouts) who use short-term contracts to adjust to changes in the market (Cattani et al., 2008) and to meet the requirements of different film content and locations (Sydow et al., 2010). The specialized establishments can reduce their overheads and adjust their costs to fluctuating demand by hiring most of the required labor on a short-term basis. In this way, the entire film production system, involving product, labor, and distribution markets, becomes "flexibly specialized" (Storper and Christopherson, 1987). The coordination of the various specialized inputs is a key problem in such systems because there is no overarching control structure, in contrast to an organization with an administrative hierarchy (e.g., an integrated film studio). Film production, therefore, tends to be geographically clustered, to the extent that spatial concentration supports the timely exchange of information and other resources.

Much research has been conducted on the transaction cost implications of network-based coordination systems, such as the study (Lazerson, 1995) reported in the research brief below (3.1). The findings from this research suggest that networks by themselves do not always economize on transaction costs, given the investments necessary to maintain effective relationships between the network participants. Economic studies may mention the contribution of cultural factors (e.g., shared belief systems, traditions) to the transaction efficiency of networks, but the cultural setting is normally taken as a given or an add-on to economic exchange, rather than studied in its own right. This task is left to institutional theorists who examine how culture is implicated in relational structures and how exchange relations feed back into the construction of institutional environments.

The historical growth of large-scale industrial organizations, which centralize production in-house, has not led to the disappearance of small-scale, decentralized production systems. In many countries, there has even been a resurgence of local business clusters drawing on local resources and institutional support systems. The cluster of independent and mostly small artisanal producers of garments in a region in northern Italy studied by Lazerson (1995) is an example of a production system with organizational properties that are superior to those of an integrated organization. The system of highly specialized firms is held together by close-knit social networks of friends and relatives, which offers advantages in terms of quick response times, in an industry where products (e.g., fabrics, accessories) are diverse, tasks (e.g., fabric dying, button making, embroidery, sewing collars) are highly differentiated, and consumer tastes (e.g., regarding fabric style and durability) change often.

Transaction costs in this cluster relate to transportation of materials, communication between buyers and sellers, bargaining over prices, and monitoring quality of output. These costs are attenuated by a local cultural system that enforces trust and reciprocity among the producers. Mutual expectations of honesty are embedded in long-term relations between artisans and manufacturers who trust the artisans to protect their designs from misappropriation by competitors. Manufacturers are free to drop by their artisan suppliers to inspect work in progress, and workers can move to other employers where they are needed. Although subcontractors are responsible for any production errors, manufacturers normally refrain from charging them for minor mistakes in order to demonstrate their reciprocal good faith. The use of written contracts is rare. The base prices of commodities, technologies, equipment, and labor are public knowledge. They are discussed openly in cafés and piazzas. On the whole, this cultural system of norms and conventions helps to reduce environmental uncertainty for individual producers, while enhancing the competitive advantage of the production system as a whole.

However, caution is needed in generalizing from a single case study to clusters in other regions of the world, or to clusters in general. The way the sample of small business owners was constructed – by drawing respondents from membership lists of interest associations and by asking selected respondents for referrals – may have inadvertently led the researcher to study only business owners who knew one another well and collaborated closely. This is problematic if studying only respondents who are in a cooperative relationship, leading to conclusions about cooperative business behavior without evidence on the performance of businesses that do not cooperate with others in the system. Selecting on the dependent variable, in this case, cooperation and performance, diminishes what one can learn about organizations, many of which compete rather than cooperate.

3.2 Organizational institutionalism

Cultural, social, and political factors in organizational environments figure prominently in institutional theory, but theorists differ with respect to whether they view these factors as an external reality to which organizations respond or a reality that organizations construct through their actions and adaptations. Those taking the former approach attend more to the resilient aspects of organizational environments, focusing on the taken-for-granted rules and norms that constrain and stabilize behavior. For example, researchers studying how television program designers cope with the difficulties in predicting reactions in audience markets (e.g., viewers, advertisers, critics) might explore the use of traditional genre categories (e.g., sit-com, drama, documentary) or of actors' public reputations as criteria in program strategies (Bielby and Bielby, 1994). Institutional structures and routines may show persistence even in environments that have undergone significant changes. For example, the trust-based orientation to informal contracting in the business cluster reported in the research brief above (3.1) is interpreted in this study as the result of historically embedded cultural traditions (Lazerson, 1995). Social homogeneity in this cluster is reproduced through tightly structured kinship-based social networks which have been a traditional form of economic governance in this region for many centuries. In recent years, globalization pressures have intensified the search for more market-based solutions, motivating some of the larger firms to leave the region and to move the more labor-intensive production activities to regions with lower labor costs (Rinaldi, 2005). In other regions, global market forces have strengthened, rather than diminished, the role of local institutions in supporting organizational forms that preserve rather than change local traditions (Burroni and Trigilia, 2001).

The emphasis on order and stability leads to a view of environments as a reality to which organizations must adapt if they are to survive (Zucker, 1987), but adaptation may proceed in several ways (Scott, 1987). For example, organizations may simply adopt the policies that are mandated by external authorities, building faithfully those structures which meet institutional requirements. Firms in the United States that have formally institutionalized sick leave policies tend to be disproportionately located in states with legislation on gender-neutral workplace policies and in states where employment discrimination is defined to include pregnancy and marital status (Guthrie and Roth, 1999). Alternatively, organizations may imitate the strategies and structures of the most successful organizations, especially when they perceive uncertainty about the content of demands (Staber, 2010a). Some organizations engage in ritualistic behavior to connect with their environment, as a signal to the public that their structures are in line with social expectations. For example, universities that enjoy elite status in society often use rituals to reproduce recognized symbols of power and to affirm a shared identity among their members. The formal dining rituals at the University of Cambridge, for instance, are invested with rich symbolism (e.g., dining hall décor, ceremonial language, displays of high-status alumni) reflecting social class distinctions (Dacin et al., 2010). The rituals link the organization to its wider social context through a particular definition of exclusivity and demarcation from other social groupings.

In contrast to the view of environment as an external reality to which organizations respond and which they reproduce through compliance, imitation, or ritualistic behavior, the constructivist approach in institutional theory pays more attention to the origins of institutions than to their consequences. It views institutional environments as a site of contestation in which organizational actors mobilize resources and exert power to create and change rules to which they then respond (Hirsch and Lounsbury, 1997). Institution building can be observed in many social and economic domains. Areas like the advancement of women's rights, child labor regulation, carbon emission control, or consumer protection include a wide range of competing organizational actors and distinct logics (Djelic and Quack, 2003). Some of the institutional issues are decided on a national or even transnational level; others are dealt with at the level of organizational populations through interest associations. In all cases, however, a key question concerns the causal mechanisms by which institutions are created, transformed, or sometimes given up. In resource-scarce environments, economic mechanisms (e.g., competition, taxation) may predominate and efficiency considerations may prevail. In politically charged environments, political mechanisms (e.g., voting, lobbying) may be the main drivers of institutional change. And in cultural environments, symbolic mechanisms (e.g., narratives, mythologies) may make the difference.

Volatile environments are driven by a dynamic mix of different mechanisms operating at individual, organizational, and societal levels. Institutional analyses of changes in the organization of the Olympic Games, for example, include consideration of mechanisms at the level of individual actors, such as the personal visions of architects and municipal politicians regarding the images they want to project. At the collective level of organizations, institutional theorists may focus on the economically motivated actions of development agencies and corporate sponsors. And at the societal level, they may investigate the political actions of public media and temporary coalitions of taxpayers and neighborhood interest groups. Such analyses are based on the argument that actors are the key causal agents and that the resources (e.g., money, ideas, political connections) they work with are the ultimate causes of institutional outcomes because they provide the actors with varying degrees of power (Glynn, 2008). The organization of the Olympic Games has changed significantly over the years, varying with the national contexts in which they evolved. The key actors have used symbols (e.g., Olympic flame, logos, city image), visions (e.g., the Olympic spirit), money (e.g., corporate sponsorship, government subsidies), and local histories (e.g., tradition, heritage) as the resources to advance their specific economic and political interests. Political struggles between individuals, organizations, and institutions have transformed the Olympic Games from an originally religious ritual into a social institution, in the sense that they provide an enduring scheme for people to give meaning to such notions as excellence and identity. Variations in economic success are partly the result of local specificities related, for example, to clientelist politics and organizational incompetencies in planning, as in the case of the Athens Olympic Games, which have not generated the expected spinoffs for new industrial development (Gospodini, 2009).

3.3 Organizational evolution

To the extent that institutional theorists study not only outcomes but also the processes that brought them about, they share commonalities with an evolutionary explanation of organizational adaptation. The institutional view on environment as a system of beliefs, rules, and relations has kept alive an issue that stands at the core of evolutionary theory: the question of how organizations construct and maintain their identity as bounded entities that are distinct from, but not independent of, the environment from which they draw vital resources. Institutional theorists tend to view this question as an issue of institutionalization, in terms of the processes by which institutional rules and meanings create organizations as "enduring social groups" (Tolbert and Zucker, 1996: 180). To evolutionary theorists, institutionalization processes are important because they produce entities that are available for environmental selection. Only when an organization exists as an entity with a distinct identity and recognizable external boundary can it participate meaningfully in competitive and cooperative exchanges with other organizations. Without the protection afforded by boundaries, collections of people, competencies, and behavioral routines could not easily coalesce into *organized* action (Aldrich and Ruef, 2006). If individuals could join and exit an organization at will, it would not possess the internal stability necessary to deal with the demands of a changing environment. Commercial airlines could not survive if pilots who were trained for light, propeller-driven sightseeing planes were permitted to fly large intercontinental jet aircraft without passing through a long process of training and selection; and psychiatric clinics could not survive if they did not distinguish their formally licensed professional staff from self-appointed shamans.

Organizations may face a dilemma in boundary maintenance. On the one hand, they need to be sufficiently restrictive in boundary control to attract the kinds of resources they require, conjuring up the image of a nightclub employing specialized personnel to keep out unwanted customers and using strict hierarchical controls to tightly manage the organization's **labor process** (Sosteric, 1996). Given investments in identifying, recruiting, and developing new employees, acquiring new technologies, and designing task and role systems, organizations cannot afford to lose valuable employees every time new opportunities arise for them elsewhere. Rapid turnover in the workforce can harm organizational performance by depleting the organization's pool of competencies and by weakening its social fabric (Shaw et al., 2005). On the other hand, organizations also need to be sufficiently open to recognize new demands and opportunities in their environment. This requires boundary maintenance practices that encourage members to keep in touch with changes in the external world, without losing control over their actions (Brown and Eisenhardt, 1997). In the international advertising industry, for example, it is important for firms to be embedded in global networks through which information about markets and best practices can circulate. Advertising companies may participate in such networks, for example, by sending their employees to industry social events (e.g., award ceremonies) or by rotating employees between international work teams (Faulconbridge, 2006).

ANECDOTE 3.1

When Kathleen arrived in her office in Manchester the morning after she had returned from a long weekend trip to Montreal, she was greeted by her boss, Tony, with a snippish comment about her global mobility. "I guess you had a great weekend again!" Kathleen knew what he was referring to. From the beginning of her employment in this web design firm he had told her that he didn't like her to spend so much time away from the office. "I think you are much too friendly with your former colleagues," he said, referring to her previous job in agencies in Los Angeles and Montreal. "I'm afraid our rivals there want to steal our business there."

Kathleen saw this issue differently. She had a lot of experience in web design and knew how important it was to tap into the knowledge existing elsewhere, especially when clients keep moving their accounts. She considered herself lucky to have good connections to people working in the multimedia centers of the world. She also knew that she had to nurture her social relations, and this required much face-to-face contact. She considered herself an innovative worker who is always on the lookout for new ideas and new connections.

Tony had a different opinion about this. "Isn't it enough for you to have creative colleagues in our own firm? We hire very carefully to find people who really fit in. What kind of firm would we be if our people had to run off to outsiders every time they needed new ideas?" When Tony said this, he was not so much thinking about employees' emotional identification with the firm. He thought of himself as a pragmatic man, weighing the costs and benefits of employing people permanently and nurturing their development, rather than hiring them on a short-term basis to cope with market fluctuations. With employment flexibility he could better manage cash-flow problems, but he was afraid that the coming and going of short-duration hires would be too disruptive for his firm.

Tony was also concerned about employees behaving opportunistically when they were away from the office. When Kathleen was traveling, he had no control over what she talked about with her contacts. He had no idea whether she committed her energy solely to activities that would benefit his firm. What she told him did not exactly calm his fears. "What I do is not an exact science," she said. "I talk to lots of different people, and we share our ideas. Okay, I realize that we spend a lot of social time together. We go to the movies and sometimes we party. But who cares? I do whatever I can to keep my relationships alive."

The anecdote (3.1) above describes the dilemma of the manager of an advertising agency who expects employees to gather valuable knowledge through their interactions with people outside the organization, while also retaining their commitment to the organization. For this organization to survive in this highly competitive and volatile industry, it needs employees who are well connected to relevant actors outside the firm (Girard and Stark, 2003). However, the manager is afraid of losing valuable proprietary information to potential competitors if he permits employees to meet with outsiders as they see fit. Kathleen, the employee, believes that the time she spends socializing with her associates outside the organization helps her make more informed decisions in her project work. The problem is that outsiders are not only a source of valuable information; they are also a source of influence over the organization (Pfeffer and Salancik, 1978). Outsiders may co-opt the organization to push their own agenda. Research on corporate governance suggests that individuals from other organizations may use their membership in the focal organization's governing board to represent the interests of their home organization or to improve their own career prospects (Zajac, 1988). The risk of co-optation is especially great in emerging economies, like Indonesia, where businesses maintain close political ties to government bodies to obtain favorable regulation, import protection, and information about investment opportunities (Dieleman and Boddewyn, 2012), and in peripheral economies, like Greece, where political clientelism is a long-standing tradition (Spanou, 2008). Close political ties may be reliable, but they also carry the risk of misappropriation (e.g., corruption, extraction of excessive rents) or instability (e.g., political regime change). The challenge for organizations connecting with resource holders outside their boundaries is to find a balance of arrangements that are neither so tightly structured that adaptation to changing environments cannot occur, nor so loose and unstructured that organizational disintegration ensues. The organizational design solution to this stability–change and control–flexibility paradox is partly a question of contingency, such as whether the work tasks to be accomplished are simple and routine or complex and non-recurrent (Haas, 2010), as will be discussed in Chapter 6.

The problem of boundary maintenance speaks to the conceptualization of organizations as a meaningful social unit with a distinct identity (Hsu and Hannan, 2005). External audiences and stakeholders are critical in this respect. Consumers, regulators, investors, industry analysts, consultants, and so on constitute vital resources for organizations by defining the salient features that render an organization distinct from others. For museums, the central features of identity might include understandings of culture and education; for dental clinics, they might be based more on technology; for nightclubs, they might involve mystery; and for cruise ship operators, they might relate to understandings of fun and leisure. Worker skills and attributes can also be an important feature of identity, used by audiences to judge the organization's performance.

In film production, for example, companies screen actors and actresses according to recognized categories such as personality and physical appearance. Actors who succeed in associating themselves with a particular category (e.g., hero, victim, comedian) enjoy greater success in attracting producers' attention (Zuckerman et al., 2003). Serious violations of identity expectations, as when a film actor known for his action roles plays a "family man," can trigger devaluation for the actor, the film, and the film producer, leading to resource withdrawal by audiences and other stakeholders. Film producers that ignore well-established categories risk market failure and can incur heavy penalties at the box office (Hsu, 2006).

Organizations operating in a simple environment with a single audience holding a narrow set of expectations tend to define themselves around a single identity, such as music clubs or whole-food restaurants. Funeral establishments in the United States have been able to maintain a robust culture based on traditional routines of embalming and restoration, visitation and display, and cremation and burial (Torres, 1988). By contrast, when an organization's identity includes a variety of competing attributes, its boundary may become blurred over time, to the point where its **core competencies** are no longer perceived as distinctive, and organizational survival is at stake. Organizations that signal competing identities risk being misunderstood by their audiences and, ultimately, may be ignored. A private health clinic, for example, may define itself as both a "health services provider" and a "private business," mixing two potentially incompatible value orientations: a normative orientation emphasizing personal well-being and a utilitarian orientation emphasizing economic rationality (Doolin, 2002). To different audiences, the organization may appear as having one or the other identity, forcing the organization to deal with conflicting demands (Brickson, 2005) and thus raising transaction costs (Pratt and Foreman, 2000).

Not all organizations that violate audiences' identity expectations are penalized; some organizations may even be rewarded for their non-conformity. These may be highly innovative organizations or successful organizations with audiences which, because they are uncertain about how to evaluate organizational identity, turn to market performance as an indicator of the organization's value. Successful hedge funds, for example, that deviate from the central tendency in the industry regarding investment styles (e.g., event-driven funds, convertible arbitrage funds) may attract more investors than hedge funds that follow the industry norm in investment styles (Smith, 2011). There are also cases of organizations which are not penalized for juggling multiple identity categories because the categories are themselves still evolving. The emerging credit rating classification system in the late nineteenth-century United States is an example of an evolving environment that initially imposed few strict expectations on evaluated companies because the system was not yet institutionalized (Ruef and Patterson, 2009). At that time, there was no clear industrial taxonomy for classifying firms; training standards for evaluators were not yet developed; and the social legitimacy of evaluating businesses was not yet established. As a result, many businesses that straddled industry groups (e.g., barber shops that were also restaurants) were able to escape penalization from credit rating companies. Thus, the consequences of identity ambiguity depend on the preferences and ability of audiences to evaluate identity categories.

The contestability and fragility of organizational identity in evolving environments is most visible during the formation process of new organizations. Transaction cost economists tend to take the identity of an organization as given. The organization, as a distinct and recognizable entity, *exists* because it is considered the most efficient arrangement under given circumstances; the founding process and the construction of an organizational identity are not seen as a problem. Evolutionary theorists, by contrast, pay attention to the full array of experiences during the founding process, including any failed attempts at getting a nascent organization off the ground (Katz and Gartner, 1988). Setting up a new organization often involves a long gestation period, during which founders can make many mistakes and change direction several times. They may change their strategy, retrace past steps, and revitalize old connections. Only a small minority of all organizing attempts reach a stage where a recognizable organizational identity is established, and most organizations that do reach this stage don't survive for long because they have difficulty convincing suppliers and investors of their continued creditworthiness (Stuart et al., 1999). From an evolutionary perspective, failed attempts at establishing an organization contribute important variation to the environment. All organizing attempts, both successful and unsuccessful, provide the raw material for change and innovation, and by adding to competitive pressure, they keep environments fertile for the creation of new organizations. Successful foundings contribute new ideas, technologies, or organizational forms, and failures leave behind resources that can be recycled back into the environment (Aldrich and Martinez, 2001).

4. Environmental uncertainty and organizational adaptation

Environmental uncertainty is a problem for organizations in many areas, including strategic planning, human resource management, and stakeholder relations. Some environments pose extreme levels of uncertainty, as in the travel and leisure industry in countries where organizations are exposed to threats from political instability and terrorism (Sullivan-Taylor and Wilson, 2009). Uncertainty is not only a problem for organizations operating in global markets, where it is essential to adapt to the idiosyncratic conditions in different national environments (Jones, 2008). It is also a challenge for organizations at the local level, where the actions of competitors and institutions must be attended to because they have immediate effects.

Uncertainty can be problematic for organizations in ways related to states, effects, and responses (Milliken, 1987). *State uncertainty* refers to the lack of information about changes in environmental conditions, such as the inability to predict the introduction of a new industry regulation. *Effect uncertainty* refers to a perceived lack of knowledge about the anticipated effects of environmental conditions, such as whether the new regulation will raise production costs. And *response uncertainty* refers to ambiguity about the potential options for dealing with environmental demands and the likely consequences of organizational actions, such as whether the new regulation will entice competitors to innovate or leave the industry. The pop music industry is an example of an industry experiencing high uncertainty along all three dimensions. Global demand is highly variable and consumer tastes are largely unpredictable, leading to very short product cycles (Huygens et al., 2002). It is difficult in such markets to know how to respond efficiently to erratic changes in demand without triggering competitors to innovate in entirely new directions. Metaphorically speaking, this setting is similar to the situation experienced by people sitting in a small boat drifting in the middle of an ocean, exposed to shifting currents and changing weather conditions (see Exhibit 3.1). The way the individuals perceive uncertainty may be highly idiosyncratic to their personal backgrounds, their relations with others in the boat, and the boat's material condition. Just as the boat occupants may debate different strategic options for survival, within the constraints of technical skills and available tools, organizations cope with uncertainty in different

Exhibit 3.1

ways, leading to variations in organizational forms, even in the same industry (Beckman et al., 2004).

Organizations often use linkages to other organizations not only as means to reduce production or development costs but also as a buffering mechanism against unanticipated environmental change. The perceptions of individual boundary spanners are critical in this respect because of their role in interpreting the state of the environment and communicating with the relevant actors in the environment (Pfeffer and Salancik, 1978). Uncertainty reduction is a fundamental principle in human behavior, related to individuals' need to manage their existence in situations they perceive as ambiguous and risky. In keeping with the image shown in Exhibit 3.1, many people would interpret the prospect of being thrown out of a boat as threatening, even if remaining in the boat is no long-term solution because it is drifting without rudder and sail in the open sea and there is no prospect of getting rescued. Certainty-oriented people prefer to remain in the most familiar and predictable environment and they avoid threats to their understanding of current conditions. They seek certainty because it "renders existence meaningful and confers confidence in how to behave and what to expect from the physical and social environment" (Hogg and Terry, 2000: 133).

When interdependence between people is high and the need to coordinate their actions is greatest, they tend to look to others most familiar to them. This is one reason why organizations often enter into joint ventures and strategic alliances with partner organizations in which the key decision-makers know one another personally and share similar understandings (Klein Woolthuis et al., 2005). In the hotel industry in Sydney, for example, it is not uncommon that the managers of competing establishments are friends with each other (Ingram and Roberts, 2000). Close social connections provide information at a level of detail that is useful for investment decisions in highly uncertain environments. In the film industry, projects are often staffed with personnel who know each other from previous projects (Perretti and Negro, 2007), and in the travel and leisure industry, suppliers work closely with their clients to create reliable terrorist threat-management processes (Sullivan-Taylor and Wilson, 2009).

Transaction cost economists argue that an organization is itself a solution to environmental uncertainty in situations where transaction problems can be handled more efficiently through organizational arrangements than through contractual relations in the open market, as long as the problem of bounded rationality and opportunism can be addressed with cost-effective hierarchical governance structures. For institutional and evolutionary theorists, uncertainty is also a problem of perception and interpretation. From an institutional perspective, the uncertain aspects of organizational life reflect the inability of actors to attribute clear categories to events and relationships (Powell and Colyvas, 2008). When new information does not fit preconceived categories, many people will ignore it, relying instead on old routines, especially in threatening situations where decisions have to be made on the spot, as in fires or medical emergencies (Weick, 1993). From an evolutionary perspective, organizational routines help individuals to act on information that has been transmitted through a competitive selection process. Perceptual routines are themselves the outcome of a selection and retention process, rewarding those cognitive techniques that increase the survival prospects of their carriers (Dennett, 1995). New environments will lead to new distributions of elements in cognitive processes, such as ideas, beliefs, and learning styles. This is also a problem for organizations, because the outcomes of efforts to reduce uncertainty cannot be known until after the decisions have been made. Uncertainty reduction is more than a problem of collecting and interpreting information. The actions taken to reduce uncertainty are essentially blind with respect to their long-term consequences, and any short-term successes may be negated by new developments in the future.

Given human cognitive limitations and stable routines, it is possible that organizations exist in an environment that is relatively simple and stable but act as if uncertainty were high, or that they exist in a highly uncertain environment but act as if uncertainty were low. Organizational boundary spanners do not merely react to environmental forces as they exist objectively. Rather, they selectively attend to those conditions they believe are salient or require most attention, and then they try to make sense of what they attend to (Weick et al., 2005). Selective attention may lead boundary spanners to misperceive the level of uncertainty and to make wrong decisions with regard to the organizational adjustments deemed necessary (Zajac and Bazerman, 1991). For example, if the heads of an organization believe that the relevant market is shrinking, they may adopt a "lean and mean" strategy of cost-cutting in production, streamlining administrative structures, and outsourcing peripheral activities (Bozeman, 2010), in order to economize on transaction costs, when it may be more effective, in the long term, to nurture some redundancies to improve adaptability (Staber and Sydow, 2002). While institutional theorists would explain rationalization measures as a strategy to maintain social legitimacy by doing what everybody else in the industry is doing, evolutionary theorists would view rationalization as leading to a reduction in variation, narrowing the range of opportunities for improving the organization's adaptive capacity.

Studies have found a generally low correlation between managers' perceptions of environmental uncertainty and concurrent objective conditions of uncertainty (e.g., Lorenzi et al., 1981; Starbuck and Mezias, 1996). The implications of a mismatch between perceived and actual conditions for organizational performance are not clear without examining this question with comparative and longitudinal data on perceptions and performance outcomes. The problem is confounded by the fact that different studies often use different measures of uncertainty. We do know, however, that there are large variations across individuals, situations, and cultures regarding perceptions of risk, ambiguity, and so forth (Oishi et al., 2004). On the other hand, although perceptual accuracy improves decision-making, it does not guarantee success. Environmental changes can lead to organizational success or failure directly and without managerial intervention. For example, a terrorist attack may reduce the survival chances of organizations located in the neighborhood of the attack regardless of what managers do (Soofi et al., 2009). The obverse condition may exist as well, as when an organizational decision turns out correct because the environment has changed in a way that "rewards" this decision. For example, the success of Japanese cars in the US market immediately after the oil crisis in the 1970s was hardly the result of Japanese firms having predicted this crisis and then deciding to produce fuel-efficient vehicles. The foreign environment had changed radically and abruptly to a state where Japanese producers could find ready customers for the cars they had already been producing. Similarly, Honda's successful entry into the United States motorcycle market in the 1960s was not the result of deliberate and careful strategic planning, but the outcome of a fortunate combination of actions and events (Pascale, 1984). Honda executives had stumbled upon a market niche, and it was not motorcycle dealers but sporting goods stores that first sold the Honda cycles.

Such cases suggest that organizational success is not always the result of careful strategic planning and organizational design; trial and error, experimentation, and chance play a significant role as well. One needs to distinguish between organizational actions and outcomes. From an evolutionary perspective, it is not the actions of individuals that count in the long run, but the consequences of actions. The question of whether individuals perceive environments correctly and respond to them appropriately is one that can be answered only in retrospect, once the consequences are known. For evolutionary theorists, differences in individuals' cognitive and behavioral capacity are an important source of variation on which selection can operate. By contrast, transaction cost economists view human shortcomings, such as limited rationality and opportunistic tendencies, more as a problem, leading to inefficiencies in resource allocation and calling for elaborate organizational control structures. Combined with environmental uncertainty, human limitations create uncertainty in transactions, which requires higher investments in governance systems than would otherwise be necessary. To institutional theorists, cognitive limitations and social conflicts can make it difficult for organizations to secure legitimacy, requiring ongoing efforts at negotiation and clarification, potentially changing the institutional environment to which they then adapt. Different theories thus provide different explanations for the tenuous link between actions and outcomes.

5. Conclusion

The interest of organization theorists in organizational environments as something more than a set of contingencies to be controlled for in research designs stems from the impression that a basic shift has occurred in modern economies over the last few decades. The change from a materials-based to a knowledge-based economy (Powell and Snellman, 2004) has alerted scholars to fundamental reconfigurations in organizational forms, as organizations have developed forms to increase flexibility, both internally and externally (Child and McGrath, 2001). In line with these changes, theorists have begun to pay more attention to adaptability rather than merely adaptation.

The key challenge for organizations in highly uncertain environments is not to find a perfect match (i.e., adaptation) between environmental requirements and organizational capabilities, but to create organizational forms that are sufficiently malleable (i.e., adaptability) to permit adjustments *if* environmental conditions change. The goal of adaptable forms is not primarily to protect organizations from external uncertainties but to embrace them. This requires, from an evolutionary perspective, structures and processes that are able to create new variations, including variations that can fail, in task and institutional environments imposing competitive and social pressure. Organizational forms are adaptable if they can be adjusted to conditions as they emerge over time. Adaptability also requires some freedom to move in space, where space is not "something out there," like a building or a street, but is a medium through which actions are conceived and enacted. Spatial concepts, such as mobility, border crossing, domain shifting, and contact zones, figure prominently at all levels at which organizations are active, as will be discussed in the next chapter.

Recommended further reading

Carroll, W. (2010) *The Making of a Transnational Capitalist Class: Corporate Power in the 21st Century*. New York: Zed Books.
Using the techniques of social network analysis, the author examines the changing organization of corporate power in the global economy, arguing that the corporate elite has achieved a remarkable degree of connectivity.

Davis, G. (2009) *Managed by the Markets: How Finance Reshaped America*. Oxford: Oxford University Press.
An analysis of the growing importance of financial markets and the implications for the growth and decline of organizations.

Drori, G., Meyer, J., and Hwang, H. (eds) (2006) *Globalization and Organization: World Society and Organizational Change*. New York: Oxford University Press.
An analysis of global society creating an environment of institutions and economic interdependencies in which organizations can develop and expand into previously unstructured areas of social life.

Thompson, J. (1967) *Organizations in Action*. New York: McGraw-Hill.
This is considered one of the first theoretical analyses of organizations' interdependence with environments. Thompson argues that the central problem for organizations is coping with environmental uncertainty.

 ■ **Practice questions for Anecdote 3.1** ▬▬▬▬▬▬▬▬▬▬▬▬

1   If you were Tony, what would you do to support Kathleen making new contacts outside the firm, while ensuring that she doesn't give away the firm's trade secrets?

2   In what ways are advertising firms interdependent with others in this industry?

3   Think of some examples of how advertising firms enact their environment.

4

Space and Spatiality

| **Learning Objectives** |

This chapter will:

- Identify the various uses of the concept of space in organizational analysis

- Discuss organizations' embeddedness in agglomerations, niches, and fields

- Discuss the relational meaning of space

1. Introduction

When we meet strangers, it is common to ask them "What do you do?" if we want to learn something about "*where* they are coming from." When they tell us that they are a newly hired school teacher or a recently unemployed advertising specialist, we tend to "place" their response into a category, such as an occupation or employment status, and we infer outcomes, such as social status or missed career opportunities. By "emplacing" the information given to us, we fill the otherwise empty space of social relations, identity, or history with meaning. As a general rule, nothing of interest to people is nowhere; everything occurs in some space. Space is not just a backdrop for organizational behavior but a constituent element of organizational life. Space enables and constrains actions; it is itself organized by the actions through which resources are mobilized, success models are emulated, or conflicts are resolved. Organizations are constantly engaged in the construction of goals, plans, and blueprints, metaphorically calling them "roadmaps" or "building blocks," and using them to avoid getting "lost in space."

Some organizational scholars draw on concepts from cognitive science, such as schema or scripts, to examine how people spatially structure their understanding of events, roles, or persons (Elsbach et al., 2005). Others refer to economic concepts, such as utility or marginality, to explain spatial outcomes like neighborhood or spillover effects (Audretsch and Feldman, 1996). Sociologically inclined researchers focus more on the social relations underlying the contestability of space and the different meanings that space has for people in specific situations, referring to such markers as identity, security, community, or equality (Gieryn, 2000). Some social relations in organizations may be embedded in the "safe space" of friendship cliques; others may evolve in the "free space" of brainstorming meetings. The social space of a job may be assigned different meanings, as when newly hired workers experience employment as a "home," whereas senior employees may feel "out of place" when being moved to a different part of the organization. Researchers impose spatial meanings as well, for example when they speak of redundant workers getting "displaced" or drug-addicted workers being "spaced-out." In each case, space is given a meaning other than the materiality of physical location embodied in buildings, offices, or work stations. Place becomes a *spatial* matter when social, cultural, technological, or political meanings are assigned.

Relations are considered spatial when they give *meaningful* content to abstract geometries of distance, direction, shape, or size. For example, knowing the physical distance between a company's headquarters and a foreign subsidiary is useless for understanding resource flows or communication patterns if nothing more is said about the meaning attributed to distance and location. When a company invests in a foreign facility, the firm's financial officers may think of this as "moving closer" to new innovation possibilities, whereas the workers may interpret this as "moving further away" from their goal of job security. Sensitivity to distance requires more than using two locations merely to get a comparative handle on questions such as whether a firm's location near competitors has a positive or negative effect on the ability to hire qualified labor. When managers put physical distance between themselves and lower-level employees, for example by taking their meals in separate locations in the cafeteria, they may have several reasons for doing so. "Distanciated" behavior, such as Bernhard's behavior in the anecdote below (4.1), can have different meanings for different people, which must be *deduced* from the observation of physical distance. Bernhard's unwillingness to share his private parking space is interpreted by his colleagues as indicating his felt need for personal power and social status. Others might believe that access to private parking space is a normal requirement in a job that involves the person coming and going several times on a given day.

Bernhard Haller has always felt misunderstood as an employee of Working Comfort, a company that designs office furniture. He had supervised quite a few projects over the last two years. He had even attracted several new clients, even though customer relations were not in his job description. He felt good about his job and his commitment to the company, but he felt distraught by the idea that his colleagues did not pay him the respect he thought he deserved. When he was finally promoted to a managerial position, he saw this as a chance to get the kind of recognition he wanted from his colleagues. To make sure that everyone would acknowledge his new status as a manager, he insisted that no one be allowed to use his private parking space. He had a personal name plate attached to the sign indicating that this parking space was reserved for managers. He also sent memos and e-mails to all employees, advising them that his parking space should remain vacant even when he was absent from the company premises. His former colleagues considered Bernhard's behavior childish and wholly inappropriate for a person in a managerial position. People should not "blow their ego out of proportion just because they got promoted," they said. They made jokes about him. "He's one of those people who think they are a hen that not only lays eggs but gives milk as well."

Bernhard saw things very differently. To him, private parking space meant private *property*, not something to be shared. He viewed his parking space as something attached to his position as *manager*, and being a manager, he thought, was very different from being an employee. He expected that all employees, including those who were his former colleagues, should respect his wish to have his own parking space. After all, his new employment contract included a reserved parking space as one of the perks. His promotion to manager also implied new responsibilities. He was now required to be away from his office several times during the day. He therefore needed ready access to company premises, even if this meant that his parking space would be vacant frequently. "So what's their problem?" he thought to himself, as he wrote another e-mail to all employees, reminding them once again that he was now a manager and not a "regular employee," signing the e-mail with "Mr Haller, Manager."

Space is not an inert, neutral, and pre-existing given, but an ongoing project of meaning construction. Space is implicated in the organization's environment, but it *is not* environment. Space is not only the technical product of organization designers or architects who arrange physical spaces like parking lots, cafeterias, and offices. Rather, space is *experienced*, cognitively and relationally, and the social networks that are implicated in space have a cognitive (Janicik and Larrick, 2005) as well as structural foundation (Burt, 2005). This suggests that the geographical notion of space, the idea of here and there, and of near and far, may be infused with multiple, contradictory, and shifting meanings. These meanings become blurred when workers move between offices or learn a new trade, or when organizations become involved in different technology domains through merger or product innovation. Organizational spaces are empty until they are filled by actions through which organizations constitute themselves as spatial entities. This chapter explores three such spatial entities which have figured prominently in organization studies: economic agglomeration, ecological niche, and **organizational field**. They are sometimes used as metaphors (Mohr, 2012) to provide an entry point for scholars studying inter-organizational relations, but there is also a growing research literature on the construction of relations in agglomerations, niches, and fields, using arguments from economic, institutional, and evolutionary perspectives.

2. Spatial metaphors

The concept of space is used differently across academic disciplines, and even within disciplines. In geography, for example, researchers have different understandings of the "primitive" term *region*, depending on the disciplinary field from which they draw the arguments (Taylor, 1999). Economic geographers study locations (e.g., neighborhood), cultural geographers focus on landscapes (e.g., aesthetics), social geographers study interest domains (e.g., conflict, cooperation), and political geographers write about resource territories (e.g., domination, dependence). Organizational sociologists distinguish between historical, cultural, occupational, and institutional space (Scott, 2008), organizational psychologists study cognitive space (Gavetti, 2005), environmental sociologists study soundspace (Hopkins, 1994), and legal scholars worry about organizations exploiting cyberspace (Lemley, 2003). Many researchers in these fields treat space at an abstract and metaphoric level. Spatial metaphors like the organization being at a "crossroads" or investing in a "greenfield site" are useful if they motivate researchers to arrange phenomena in a way that enables systematic comparisons. However, they are not as concrete as one may like them to be in specific instances. It is only when scholars look into the details of spatial mechanisms that they find that a metaphor "may assume unexpected meanings and raise questions we have not thought to ask" (Tuan, 1977: 3).

In organization studies, the tendency has been to give space a geographical meaning and to infer consequences of "proximity" or "location" for competition and cooperation. Studies of **interlocking directorates**, for example, have found that corporations tend to forge strategically important linkages with economic and institutional actors in urban areas where the resource space is sufficiently diverse to generate competitive opportunities (Kono et al., 1998). Studies of cultural workers, like artists and fashion designers, have shown that they often cluster in locations rich in different technologies, ethnicities, and institutions, on the expectation that cultural diversity creates spaces of tolerance for new ideas (Evans, 2009). These and many other studies indicate that geography matters, but in ways that cannot be explained effectively if proximity is given only physical meaning. For example, the image of the bureaucratic organization as an "iron cage" suggests the idea of involuntary confinement and permanence, whereas the image of "golden cage" indicates enclosure that is constraining, but with a self-imposed quality and with pleasant consequences for the individual. For top managers, "golden cages" may be accompanied by "golden parachutes" or "golden handshakes" in employment contracts, opening up new spaces of opportunity for managers and organizations alike. For managers they may be a mechanism to exert political influence in the organization's strategic matters (Boivie et al., 2011), and for organizations they may be a mechanism to reduce planning uncertainty (Singh and Harianto, 1989). To the extent that top managers are linked across organizational boundaries via interlocking directorates, joint ventures, social networks, and the like, "golden parachute" clauses are also a mechanism to reproduce the dominant position of corporate elites in society (Davis et al., 2003).

Physical closeness needs to be interpreted in terms of what it means to the actors themselves. Material sites like buildings, rooms, and work stations can have a variety of meanings other than the abstract properties of size, height, and distance. Organization designers know this all too well when they hire architects and artists to turn physical facilities into signs and symbols, as when landmark skyscrapers, mega shopping malls, and urban entertainment centers are used to symbolize power, social progress, postmodern creativity, or whatever. A medieval cathedral (Exhibit 4.1) not only has great height (symbolizing worship) and is located in the center of town (symbolizing political significance), it can exist in various spaces simultaneously: as a religious organization in ecclesiastical space, as a historical monument in cultural space, as a musical stage in entertainment space, and as a tourist attraction in economic space. Different meanings are promoted by individuals and organizations in contexts that serve as arenas of action in their own right. For example, physical crowding in a well-established restaurant may be interpreted as the result of bad management, whereas in a newly opened restaurant long lines may be seen as a sign of good management. Or, whether a workplace at home is considered "free space" or "constrained space" may depend on the worker's social status in the family structure of society or on one's economic position in the labor market (Collinson and Collinson, 1997).

Each of the spatial entities discussed below is broadly associated with either the economic, evolutionary, or institutional framework, but there are also overlaps in some of the key arguments. Economists draw attention to the fact that in many industries production is geographically concentrated if firms find it easier to manage uncertainty in their transactions with suppliers, customers, and institutions when they are located in close vicinity. Niche space is typically examined from an evolutionary perspective with respect to the resource interdependence among a set of organizations, and with a view to the institutional rules with which organizations manage interdependence. And organizational field space is conceptualized in terms of the communicative

Exhibit 4.1

and interpretive relations connecting organizations to the broader institutional environment of which they are an integral and active part. Institutional theorists take an evolutionary perspective when they note the continuities and discontinuities in inter-organizational relations in a field, and they draw on transaction cost reasoning when they argue that untraded institutional relations based on trust and reciprocity are often accompanied by traded pecuniary interdependencies (Asheim et al., 2006).

2.1 The economics of agglomeration space

Economists have long noted the general tendency of production to be concentrated in geographic space (Norton, 1992). The agglomerated firms are functionally related in that they draw on the same or similar resource pools (e.g., in technological domains, labor markets), but they are not joined together by common ownership or management. Well-known agglomerations include the cluster of design agencies in London, the textile clusters in northern Italy, the Tuttlingen medical equipment cluster in southwest Germany, and the film cluster in Mumbai, India. Typical clusters include hundreds of specialized producers, each concentrating on a narrow range of outputs in comparatively limited quantities and in ever-changing shapes and forms. The standard economic explanation given for agglomeration emphasizes the efficiency of exchange between organizations specializing in production and services. In many studies, political and cultural reasons are advanced as well, but these are often treated more as contextual control variables, reflecting the specifics of the particular industrial or regional setting, rather than as variables in their own right (Benneworth and Henry, 2004). Agglomeration is a typical feature of production systems where transactions are small in scale and rich in information content, requiring close interaction between the actors (Malmberg and Maskell, 2006). Economists highlight three types of transaction-based advantages of agglomeration, commonly referred to as "external agglomeration economies": a pool of workers with specialized competencies, a population of organizations supplying specialized inputs, and technological spillovers.

2.1.1 Labor pool

A large local pool of qualified workers can offer efficiency gains for both firms and workers by improving job-matching capabilities and providing skill training opportunities (Sorenson and Audia, 2000). Firms benefit from access to a pool of qualified workers through the lower costs associated with identifying, recruiting, and retaining labor. Workers may accept lower wages in exchange for employment stability if they remain in the region. Workers also benefit from the ability to move between local employers. This reduces the risk of unemployment, while giving workers an incentive to invest in skill development, thus increasing the local accumulation of **human capital**. As agglomeration intensifies, individuals already working in firms within the cluster are especially well positioned to take up emerging employment opportunities, thus further stimulating economic development in the region.

The human capital advantages of agglomeration can be seen best in industries where knowledge is an essential resource and creativity is key to innovation, as in the multimedia sector (e.g., web design and image-processing used in advertising, publishing, and film production). Film production in the Hollywood film cluster, for example, involves networks of highly specialized small firms and self-employed subcontractors (Scott and Pope, 2007). Many activities are organized in the form of temporally limited projects, bringing together a variety of labor skills in areas such as location scouting, camera work, lighting, transportation, costume design, stunt training, visual effects, food catering, security, and editing. The typical film producer may have a permanent staff of no more than five persons but organizes project networks in which several hundred people collaborate at any given time (Sydow and Staber, 2002). Transaction costs derive from the qualitative attributes of the final product because detailed quality control is required at all stages in the production process. In the case of high-budget feature films, the transaction costs associated with labor coordination and quality control are lower when production is geographically concentrated. Agglomeration ensures that trained workers with frequently updated, industry-specific know-how are constantly supplied to various places of employment in the region. Agglomeration econo-mies keep the local labor market functioning as a dynamic and well-organized spatial unit.

Not all activities in film production are geographically concentrated. Labor outsourcing to far-away sites may occur if producers seek novelty benefits from location rather than from specific labor competencies, for example when location offers a unique scenery or cultural identity that cannot be compen-sated by lower transaction costs in centralized locations (Scott and Pope, 2007). Firms may also decentralize production to sites where production costs are lowest, for example because governments there provide institutional sup-port in the form of subsidies or tax relief, while new digital technologies reduce transaction costs in communication and coordination. It is especially routine film projects in highly competitive markets, such as television program series, which are more likely to be decentralized geographically. The history of declining clusters in mature and intensely competitive industries, such as textile machinery and cutlery, shows that agglomerations are not immune to pressures of disintegration (Staber, 2001).

2.1.2 Pool of specialized suppliers

Economic advantages of agglomeration also derive from the scale economies associated with locating near specialized input providers. The standard argument is that a geographically concentrated population of firms can support more suppliers, which leads to increased levels of specialization and, in turn, enhances the efficiency of supply provision, while also attracting more customers (Porter, 2000). For film production companies, for example, specialized inputs include a diverse set of services ranging from technology consulting to language translation. Geographic proximity between producers and service suppliers reduces transpor-tation and communication costs. Economizing on these costs is crucial in film production where project success depends on timely coordination and continu-ous adjustment, given high levels of uncertainty in the work process and the frequent demand for back-up support (Blair, 2003).

Firms in close vicinity can share a local infrastructure of specialized resource providers, with spin-off effects on consumer demand. In the hotel industry, for example, an agglomeration of hotels is likely to stimulate the provision of additional services in shopping, entertainment, dining, and trans-portation, which affects travelers' choice of hotels and locations (Tsang and Yip, 2009). These advantages, however, may not be distributed equally across all subsegments of a hotel cluster and related industries. For example, the pres-ence of a jewelry shop may be a shopping convenience for customers of lead-ing hotels but not for customers of lower-quality hotels. Whether the shared infrastructure provides benefits for all hotels also depends on the nature of exchange relations between the hotels. Hotel managers may cooperate with each other on a personal basis, as in the Sydney hotel industry (Ingram and Roberts, 2000), or they may compete head-on, as in the New York City hotel industry (Baum and Mezias, 1992). Local culture may explain such differences. The quality of inter-organizational relations may also be influenced by the nature of institutions in the region. For example, governments may invest in the local infrastructure as a public good available to everyone, and there may be strong business interest associations controlling access to infrastructural services.

2.1.3 Knowledge spillovers

The third advantage of agglomeration concerns the knowledge space in which the firms operate (Audretsch and Feldman, 1996). Especially in industries where innovation involves the creation of highly specialized knowledge, it is important that organizations can make novel associations and linkages. This requires an environment where "collective learning" can take place, where firms can readily observe and monitor each other's innovations and, thus, knowledge can "spill over" to benefit other firms. Communication is most important when knowledge is specific to the needs of the exchange partners, as in film projects with local content, where the producers must be sensitive to local traditions and institutional regulations (Sydow et al., 2010). Physical proximity between the project partners is important because it increases the availability of information and the incentive to attend to it. For this reason, innovative small firms are particularly likely to agglomerate because this provides them with a rich mixture of potential partners from which they can obtain the different types of knowledge they need in the development of innovative products (Simmie, 2002).

Knowledge spillover may also occur without direct interaction and coordination. In some cases, the actors can learn from simply "being there" (Gertler, 1995), because they are embedded in a local social milieu that is sufficiently open and transparent to enable observation and comparison (Malmberg and Maskell, 2006). Cultural-products industries are examples of settings where much creative learning occurs through the *ad hoc* contact between individuals in sites like workshops and arts festivals (Storper and Venables, 2004). On the downside, co-location also increases the risk of having one's own ideas copied by competitors (Aharonson et al., 2007). In regions with a local business culture emphasizing rivalry, firms will sometimes devise ingenious measures to protect their activities from being copied (Staber, 2009).

In cases where the search for new knowledge occurs primarily through local channels, and the institutional environment encourages close and trust-based inter-organizational relations, there is also the risk of self-reinforcing consequences, leading to lock-in (Asheim et al., 2006). Collective mindsets and behavioral routines may be useful for the efficient governance of inter-organizational relations, by speeding up communication and reinforcing reliability, but they may also cause the organizations to band together against common adversaries, leading to the cluster's social closure. Social closure discourages the entry of new firms with different competencies, thus reducing the richness of knowledge available for new innovations. To overcome these limitations, the more innovative firms may eventually leave the cluster, leading to the cluster's stagnation or even disintegration, as in the Black Forest clock-making cluster in Germany (Staber and Sautter, 2011). Or, firms may recruit workers from outside the cluster to import new knowledge, rather than invest in local labor training (Rosenkopf and Almeida, 2003). Thus, when firms locate near other firms, they make strategic decisions not only about how best to organize their activities in geographic space. Their location decisions also have implications for their performance in interconnected social, cultural, political, and technological spaces in which ideas, knowledge, and material resources circulate and keep the production system moving.

2.2 The evolutionary dynamics of niche space

The concept of niche, as used in organization studies, is informed by ideas from human ecology, a field of inquiry which imported the concept from biology, where it describes the ecological habitat within which organisms compete for life-sustaining resources (Gaziano, 1996). Human ecology is the study of the adaptive spatial and temporal relations of human beings in interaction within a population and with the environment (Hawley, 1986). The concept of space in human ecology has a relational meaning. An individual's position in ecological space does not denote location *per se* – that is, where individuals live – but refers to the spatial distribution of individuals *vis-à-vis* each other. The specific contribution of evolutionary theory is to conceptualize niche space in dynamic relational terms by asking how the actors come to occupy positions of power, status, reputation, and so forth in relation to one other.

The concern for "relatedness" represents a shift from geographic space to analytical space. The ecological conceptualization of "relatedness" leads to a characterization of niche as an abstract *n*-dimensional resource space, measuring along each dimension the presence or absence, or the quantity of a particular resource (McPherson, 2004). In the organizational world, niche space might consist of variations in worker characteristics like job experience and professionalism (Hannan et al., 2006), consumer attributes like cultural tastes for different types of restaurant services (Rao et al., 2005), or stakeholder attributes like the evaluative schemas used by film critics (Hsu et al., 2009). Not all niches are fully exploited at any given time. Some niches are empty, waiting to be filled by actors in their search for new resources. A "fundamental niche" is the niche that *could* be fully exploited by an organization if there were no competitors or institutional requirements (e.g., licensing, accreditation) setting limits on niche exploitation. The "realized niche" is the space that is actually occupied; it is limited by the extent of competition for available resources. The realized niche is usually smaller than the fundamental niche, given the displacement effect of competition or the constraining effects of institutions.

The concept of niche is intertwined with the concept of population, as used by population ecology theorists (Hannan and Freeman, 1989). In order to define a niche one needs to know what a population is, and to define a population requires the concept of niche. In evolutionary theory, populations are defined as groups of entities of the same species living together in the same environment and drawing on the same resources (Mayr, 2001). Environment is defined "naturally" in terms of the resources necessary for reproducing the population for many generations. The evolutionary definition of space is thus related to the characteristics and resource needs of the population. Artists, for example, are often found in specific areas of a city (e.g., "artistic quarters," "cultural districts") where they can closely observe competitors and interact with relevant cultural institutions and where they can carve out specialized niches for themselves (see Anecdote 2.1). By contrast, clustered high-tech firms may be spread over a larger geographic area (e.g., Silicon Valley) and may reach into a variety of domains in technological space (e.g., multimedia), whereas voluntary associations (e.g., internet chat groups, religious communities) may not be limited by any geographic boundaries. Populations of organizations exist in the same niche if they compete for the same resources available in that niche. For example, trade associations compete for member firms subject to the same government regulations (Aldrich et al., 1994); fast-food restaurants compete for consumers with a taste for ready-made foods and speedy service (Freeman and Hannan, 1983); and "high-culture" restaurants compete for consumers with a taste for *haute cuisine* (Rao et al., 2005).

The concept of niche space has found many applications in ecological studies of organizations and populations (Baum, 1996). Ecologists studying variations within organizations explore the evolving distribution of entities such as skills, rules, and routines (Galunic and Weeks, 2002). Ecologists working at the level of organizational populations study the conditions under which a population can flourish in niches of varying width, with implications for social change, technological innovation, employment careers, and so on (Hannan and Freeman, 1989). A broad and diverse niche can accommodate a larger number of different types of organizations and organizational forms than a narrow niche. Many markets are partitioned into segments, including broad segments with general appeal and narrow segments for audiences with special tastes. In the automobile industry, for instance, firms have historically specialized in product features such as engine capacity, luxury, and safety (Dobrev et al., 2001), and in the restaurant business, firms compete in narrow niches such as natural food restaurants, coffee shops, and ethnic restaurants (Freeman and Hannan, 1983). In some markets, consumers are highly discriminating in their evaluation of a product, using narrow criteria for sorting producers into distinct reference groups. In the feature film industry, for example, genre definitions have become an important precondition for the functioning of markets. Consumers tend to prefer films that fit into the content categories of a single genre over films that span several genres (e.g., action-documentary-comedy) (Hsu, 2006).

As organizations position themselves in markets, they contribute to the evolution of niches through changes in their composition in terms of organizational size, specialization, or any other attribute relevant to competition. The partitioning of environments into resource niches leads to variable opportunities for organizational specialists and generalists. In the newspaper industry, for example, organizations targeting narrow segments (e.g., neighborhood papers) have limited growth opportunities, but they may be able to survive in markets populated by generalists (e.g., newspapers with national coverage) (Carroll and Hannan, 1989). Generalist organizations do not always expand to occupy the entire "fundamental" resource space available to a population. Consumers may be spread too thinly in the marginal segments of markets, creating opportunities for small specialist organizations to flourish. Studies have shown that as market concentration rises and a small number of organizations cover an increasing share of a market, some of the resource space becomes vacant and the potential of specialist organizations to survive in niches increases. In the US beer brewing industry, for example, specialized microbrewers and brewpubs have become more popular over the years, in an environment that is receptive to "authentic" beer as distinct from mass-produced beer (Carroll and Swaminathan, 2000), whereas the German beer market has always been dominated by small, specialized breweries surviving in culturally differentiated local markets (Carroll et al., 1993).

The challenge for evolutionary theorists is to design studies that capture the spatial fluidity of population boundaries. For researchers, it is important to know the boundaries of the entity they are studying (Aldrich and McKelvey, 1983). In settings where organizational competencies are mobile and populations are not reproductively isolated from other similar populations, there is the possibility that research mis-specifies population boundaries. One may not be able to generalize the findings from a study of, say, organizational forms in car repair shops to populations of car dealerships, even though the organizations are all in the "car business." On the other hand, organizations in different populations may not be unique in all relevant attributes. To the extent that organizations share important competencies, essential for reproduction, they may be studied as members of the same population. It is unlikely that *all* attributes held by the organizations in a population are unique to that population. Competencies, routines, and identities may travel across organizations, for example when workers move between employers or when organizations merge with others. Visual artists often work with book writers; industrial firms sometimes recruit politicians as chief executives and sociologists occasionally collaborate with economists. In each case, competencies spread to other populations. Research shows that the mobility of top managers across firms and industries can provide organizations with additional diversity in the pool of competencies, which may increase organizational survival chances (Pennings and Wezel, 2010). Labor mobility that injects "new blood" and shakes up old routines can lead to changes in organizational and population boundaries, and create new variations in the composition of realized niches.

The boundaries of organizations and organizational populations are neither clear-cut nor fixed. Wine lovers, for example, do not usually limit their consumption of alcohol to one type of beverage, and their preferences may change over time, altering the composition of niches in which alcoholic beverage companies can survive. People obtain news from a variety of sources and they are open to new sources that may emerge. Many people participate in multiple organizations simultaneously, spreading their commitments of time, money, and energy across employers, neighborhood action groups, sports clubs, and so forth. In modern society, the organizational affiliations of individuals are variable and dynamic, affecting the ecology in which organizations struggle to survive, and forcing the most vulnerable organizations to constantly ask themselves the question, "What business are we really in?" In practice, it may be difficult to distinguish between a social movement organization and a labor union, or between a coffee shop serving snacks and a small restaurant serving a wide range of coffee.

The perceptions of internal and external audiences are critical in this respect. The members of a trade association may view the organization as a mechanism for enforcing common industry standards, whereas legislators may perceive it mostly as a political interest organization. Major differences in audience perceptions can be consequential for the developmental path of organizations which have to decide what identity to promote and in which niche to stake out their future (Hsu and Hannan, 2005). When audiences evaluate an organization's performance, they often focus not on the organization as a whole but on specific organizational attributes, particularly those they can observe easily. Airline passengers may care more about the quality of service on particular routes than the performance of the organization in general (Tyler and Abbott, 1998). In the film industry, consumers normally assess product quality at the level of specific features of a film project (e.g., film music, location aesthetics) rather than the film studio (Zuckerman and Kim, 2003). Variabilities in audience perceptions of organizational attributes, rather than organizations, can make it difficult to assign an organization unambiguously to a population with a distinct organizational form and boundary.

Many organizations exist in multi-dimensional identity space, linking them to stakeholders and audiences with potentially different understandings of the organization's *raison d'être*, although these understandings may also involve overlaps. Industrial mass beer brewers and small boutique brewpubs, for example, compete for different types of customers, but they both subscribe to a "beer culture" as distinct from, say, a "wine culture." To the extent that there are overlaps in cultural, technological, symbolic, or social spaces, organizations are in ecological competition. Sports clubs, for example, tend to overlap to some degree with youth service organizations on membership attributes related to age, education, occupation, and gender, whereas there is little identity overlap between professional associations and social clubs for the elderly (McPherson, 2004). Given that the resource commitments of individuals to any one organization are limited, one can examine how the position of organizations in multi-dimensional niche space evolves over time as the result of ongoing competitive interactions with other organizations sharing the niche. Organizations evolve together with the niches in which they exist and which they help to structure through their actions and interactions. In the French restaurant industry, for example, the gradual weakening of the boundary separating classical from nouvelle cuisine – two traditional rival categories competing for the attention of chefs, consumers, and restaurant critics – has made it easier for chefs to cross this boundary and to experiment with new menus (Rao et al., 2005). High-status chefs, who have previously worked within one category, have contributed to the weakening of the boundary by increasingly using techniques from the rival category, thus changing the competitive dynamics in this industry. Institutions have contributed to such changes as well, for example by accrediting new organizational forms or by setting new standards for critical reviews.

2.3 The institutional dynamics of field space

The evolution of identity spaces is framed by institutional norms and rules, evident, for example, in the names and labels organizations use to distinguish themselves from competitors. Institutional actors use labels as well, to sort organizations into reference groups within which their actions are evaluated and sanctioned. In the mental health field, for example, professional associations – often in interaction with pharmaceutical firms, insurance companies, and medical schools – assign patients to different types of treatment organizations based on the categorization of mental disorders (Shorter, 2009). Identity categorizations, and the labels used to reinforce them, may be subject to contestation, creating new variations and fueling the evolution of organizational forms.

Labels reflect the meanings that people assign to things like events, websites, and decisions. Some people label buildings like the one shown in Exhibit 4.1 as "grandiose" to celebrate their architectural grandeur; others might label them "monstrous" to denigrate their original purpose. Organizations often use labels to signal to relevant audiences that they are closely following institutional rules. Labeling can be an important part of the social legitimation of organizational forms, by emphasizing distinctions and similarities that help organizations to communicate more clearly on the basis of representations signaling economic power, cultural value, or some other criterion (Hsu and Hannan, 2005). Restaurants use the number of stars to indicate service quality and social status; universities use accreditation to signal academic excellence; and hotels participate in a chain organization to maximize their appeal to a particular set of customers. Research has found that hotels in the United States that name more of their units the same tend to survive longer, because a common-naming strategy signals conformity to a particular standard of service (Ingram, 1996), while also reducing transaction costs. The institutional effects of naming and labeling may be so strong that they diffuse beyond an organizational population to an entire organizational field. In the mental health field, for example, cultural definitions of mental illness have become the foundation for the evolution of a vast sector that includes professions, drug companies, clinics, insurance companies, interest associations, regulatory agencies, and licensing boards (Shorter, 2009).

The concept of organizational field was first introduced to theorize about organizational environments in terms of the connections between a set of organizations (Warren, 1967). It was later expanded to include the totality of organizations that are oriented to each other in their strategies and structures, without necessarily directly interacting with each other. An organizational field consists of "those organizations that, in the aggregate, constitute a recognized area of institutional life: key suppliers, resource and product consumers, regulatory agencies, and other organizations that produce similar services or products" (DiMaggio and Powell, 1983: 148). Field space identifies a potentially much broader domain than the niche space of competitively and cooperatively interrelated organizations, as studied by population ecologists. The organizational field of education, for example, includes organizations active in various social, economic, political, and cultural spaces related to such issues as teacher licensing and professionalization, student identity formation and social rehabilitation, classroom quality control, and informational and learning technology. The different purposes and logics underlying the actions of organizations in these field spaces have created a system of diverse classifications, categories, ranks, programs, and curricula, contested in the details of expectations, but sustained by broad social consensus regarding the necessity of education (Meyer, Scott, and Strang, 1994b). Organizations in fields that enjoy a taken-for-granted status in society, such as education and health, may have higher survival chances on average, but this status is not guaranteed forever. The dramatic decline of the state-based, central planning logic of economic production in Eastern Europe demonstrates how fast de-institutionalization can proceed, stretching into every corner of society (Grabher and Stark, 1997). The institutional field perspective motivates researchers to look for the origins of changes anywhere in the spatial system of a field.

Institutional theory views organizations not as entities that are separate from the field environment and that merely react to institutional demands, but as an integral part of the field whose structure they help shape through their actions and interactions. A field is not something "external" to organizational action; a field shapes organizational life, but it is not itself that shape. It exists through the adaptive actions of organizations, which is an insight shared by evolutionary theorists who study the co-evolution of organizations and environments. The structure of an organizational field is an outcome of actors struggling to reproduce or modify the institutions that provide coherence to the field. For instance, the structural changes in the American health care sector, stemming from the introduction of new organizational forms such as home-based health care delivery, private clinics, and walk-in health centers, went hand in hand with institutional changes in funding and in the meaning systems (e.g., market efficiency, social equity) used to interpret and guide these structural changes (Town et al., 2007).

Heterogeneous fields with actors who have divergent interests and resource capabilities are likely to evolve along different paths than more homogeneous fields. For example, the fields of law in the United Kingdom and in Germany show continuing differentiation in organizational forms despite global pressures towards common standards, as law firms adjust to the specific demands of different legal subfields, sometimes even going against the recommendations of their own professional associations (Morgan and Quack, 2005). In Japan, group-based norms and traditions in industry, reinforced through mutual stock-holding, interlocking corporate directorships, and close personal ties between individuals in the private and public domain, have created organizational fields that are more homogeneous and structured than fields in many other liberal democracies (Hollingsworth, 1997). Transformations of fields occur at a speed and in a direction that is shaped by the current structure of the field. A field is considered highly structured if information can flow freely between the actors who are connected through social networks and relational contracting, within an institutional system providing the rules for exchange. An example of a highly structured field is the cluster of advertising firms located along a single street in New York City (Arzaghi and Henderson, 2008). Co-location helps the firms to share ideas and to supplement their limited in-house capacity when preparing proposals and recruiting additional labor to meet their contractual obligations with clients. Many of the firms participate in tightly knit networks, which operate as formal (e.g., contracts) and informal mechanisms (e.g., social interaction in bars and golf clubs) for exchanging information and for keeping transaction costs to a minimum. Some of the firms are linked to individuals and organizations in other locations and industries, which they use as sources of new information. Globally extended networks ensure that the boundaries of organizations are not so rigidly fixed that no innovations can take place.

In sum, the spatial concepts of agglomeration, niche, and field share a common concern for geographic notions like location and distance, while incorporating other meanings of space as well. The idea of agglomeration stresses relational density and offers insights into the role of territorially concentrated labor and other input markets. The ecological concept of niche addresses organizational evolution with a view to shifting boundaries in identity space. And the concept of field adds the idea that organizations are an integral part of the environment, which they help shape through their actions and interactions. The notion of field widens the analytical lens considerably, addressing the transformation of spaces through changes in meaning systems and organizational forms, and at different spatial scales. While competition for material resources is generally more intense at the local level, broad cultural concerns (e.g., general issues like worker rights and environmental protection) prevail at more global levels. The inflow of general ideologies can be blocked less successfully at the local level than the inflow of material resources, with implications for the form and durability of local institutions.

3. Giving meaning to space

Our understanding of space calls for explanations that are sensitive to the ways in which people assign meaning to their actions and circumstances. Because people do not exist as social isolates, one needs to pay special attention to social relations as a mechanism through which meanings are constituted. The spaces in which people are embedded are not just an outcome of social relations but are part of the explanation of those relations. People create social relations through spaces as both a medium and outcome of relations (Giddens, 1984). Social relations are informed by rules of conduct, authority, standards, and so forth, which individuals draw on to accomplish their goals, at the same time that these rules and resources are given force and legitimacy through social relations. Spatial structure informs the nature of social interaction (Eliasoph and Lichterman, 2003) as well as the presentation of self in interactionist settings (Goffman, 1959). For example, individuals tend to stage different "performances" in public encounters, like taskforce meetings or employee-of-the-month award ceremonies, than in private encounters in the restroom or in one's office. Similar to performance differences between the front stage in a theater and the private space of a dressing room, the structuration of space proceeds differently in different parts of an organization, involving mechanisms such as conversation, imitation, and coercion.

Spatial metaphors like "global village" or "global city" have no meaning other than saying something about the presence and absence of entities like organizations, contracts, or networks, from which meanings must be *inferred*. Investigators are often limited in their interpretation of observations about agglomeration, ecological, and institutional effects on the basis of data that measure the presence of particular policies, organizational structures, or social conventions but give no insights into the mechanisms that generate the effects. Inferences about innovation in agglomerations are derived, for example, from the argument that new knowledge arises at the fringes of a cluster if peripheral organizations are linked to sources outside the cluster. Inferences about niche processes are taken from differences in the rates of growth of competing organizational populations. And inferences about field evolution are derived from knowledge of the presence of particular institutional actors at a given time. Likewise, the meanings of different institutional logics for the actors are often not tested directly, but are assumed. Some agglomeration theorists relegate meanings to an abstract, unmeasured space, privileging notions of distance over the meaning of resources or information that flow across distance. As a result, flows in geographic space are not analyzed in a way that enables meanings to be treated as constitutive of agglomeration itself. Similarly, ecologists often treat environments and niches as an unmeasured abstraction from which inferences are made about competition and cooperation. And many researchers working from the institutional perspective theorize about flows of ideas without inquiring into the meanings that ideas have for different actors in different contexts. This is not to say that the interpretive aspects of space are being ignored altogether. Many scholars do acknowledge the significance of meanings, but they often *infer* meanings from the data they have collected.

Opportunities to theorize meanings of space exist particularly in those areas of organization studies where relations are emphasized over substances, following John Dewey's views on the psychology of *How We Think*: "To grasp the meaning of a thing, an event, or a situation is to see it in its *relations* to other things" (Dewey, 1910: 137; emphasis mine). The fundamental unit of analysis is the relation between entities, seen as an unfolding process of events, decisions, or actions, rather than the entities themselves. Meanings are not contained in the object in question. For example, the meaning of a company uniform is not provided by the uniform itself, but arises out of the person's experience of wearing the uniform in social interaction with colleagues or people outside the company. From a relational perspective, people's identities are not fixed in space, but evolve in relation to their opposites, played out as reversals, antitheses, or antinomies (Roth, 1986). Managers may derive their location in identity space not so much from their formal position in the organization than from the conversational "back and forth" in discussion networks in which they meet their opposites (Gibson, 2005).

Individual actions can also be understood relationally in terms of their embeddedness in a "life space" (Lewin, 1951). Life space is defined as an ecology of social domains, each of which derives meaning from its location *vis-à-vis* the other domains. In this view, life spaces are relational systems in the sense that their members stand in a particular relation – close or far, concentrated or spread out – to one another. Life spaces exist as webs of relations rather than as substances, and meanings are implicated in the structure of relations rather than their content. Cultural spaces in the arts sector, for example, are places where individuals meet relationally, even though they may not meet physically. Lower-class individuals might be distant from upper-class individuals in terms of control over economic resources, but they might be close to upper-class individuals relationally in that they watch the same television news channel (Peterson and Kern, 1996). In this case, social class is given a relational meaning independent of conventional categories such as status or income.

Relational thinking has found its way into research on agglomerations mostly with a view to the agency aspects of inter-organizational relations (Bathelt and Glückler, 2003). Some studies inquire into the cognitive foundations of, for example, knowledge sharing in a network of scientists (Borgatti and Cross, 2003), or they investigate trust and mistrust in relations between business owners (Staber, 2009). Individuals may be located in close physical proximity and may have plenty of opportunity to engage in face-to-face interaction, but they may not exchange information because they do not value the knowledge the potential exchange partners have or because they do not trust them. In agglomerations of highly specialized firms with different production functions and learning competencies, some degree of mutual understanding is critical to communication and coordination. An organization may be structurally close to other firms, for example because it shares with them the same supplier, but it may not be able to interpret and apply the information it obtains through the network. Some studies (see Research Brief 4.1) have found that firms located at the fringes of a knowledge network are not necessarily at a disadvantage, as long as they have the capacity to absorb and apply the information they receive from firms having relevant knowledge (Giuliani and Bell, 2005). What matters is not only the pattern of connections but also the ability of the firms to interpret and process the information that is exchanged. Two organizations may be structurally similar in a network but may benefit differently from their participation in the network because they differ in the capacity to absorb information (Cohen and Levinthal, 1990). Therefore, to understand the outcomes of participation in a network, one needs to know how organizations acquire, assimilate, adapt, and apply new knowledge in specific contexts, as will be discussed in Chapter 7.

RESEARCH BRIEF 4.1

Recent research has examined the question of whether firms that are strongly embedded in geographic clusters outperform more isolated firms. One argument is that cluster firms have competitive advantages because information can circulate comparatively easily when firms are located in physical proximity. An opposing argument emphasizes the importance of linkages between cluster firms and firms located outside the cluster. Knowledge that is generated only within the boundaries of a tightly knit cluster may become obsolete over time if there are no opportunities to import new information from outside the cluster. To adjudicate these arguments, one needs to consider differences in firms' cognitive capacity to acquire, process, and apply information, rather than merely study the presence of linkages between organizations.

Giuliani and Bell (2005) studied interfirm networks with regard to firms' ability to access and process knowledge. They argued that for cluster relations to be useful, firms need to have the capacity to absorb and exploit the knowledge they obtain from various sources, both inside and outside the cluster. They hypothesized that this capacity is especially important in technologically lagging regions or industries. Using data on interfirm networks in an emerging wine cluster in Chile, they found that the best positioned firms in the cluster were those playing a "technological gatekeeper" role. Such firms constituted a small core in the cluster network. They were linked to other firms which did not produce knowledge themselves but were able to absorb knowledge from this core group or, in some cases, directly from sources outside the cluster. The innovativeness of the cluster as a whole was not the result of a high degree of connectedness among all firms in the cluster. The findings suggest that cluster firms may be successful not primarily because they are geographically close but because they have the capacity to identify, acquire, assimilate, adapt, and apply new knowledge, and are able to develop their own unique knowledge base.

As is typical in network research, the data were collected through structured interviews, using standardized measures of variables. Many of the variables were measured as proxy indicators. Although this study explored issues related to the "cognitive interconnectedness" of the cluster, the proxy measures used did not directly capture cognition. For example, the number of months a worker has been active in the wine industry is not necessarily a valid indicator of "accumulated knowledge," and the number of technically qualified personnel does not necessarily indicate the firm's capacity to "absorb" knowledge. Further information is needed on the mechanisms by which the firms assimilated, adapted, and applied knowledge in their specific contexts. The mechanisms may include deliberate learning, imitation, or trial-by-error improvisation.

(Continued)

Because the data used in this study were cross-sectional, the authors could not investigate the dynamics of knowledge. Knowledge is not a fixed feature of firms and clusters. In addition to understanding how the structure of interfirm networks shapes and is shaped by firms' knowledge bases, one would also like to know something about the dynamics of networks and the effects of network changes. For example, under what conditions do firms existing at the periphery of the cluster move towards the center? Do such movements lead to changes in the knowledge base of firms? Do they alter the absorptive capacity of firms? And do they then further integrate the cluster? Dynamic data are needed to investigate such questions. Such data would have to capture changes in variations over time and would have to identify the sources and outcomes of any disequilibrium in the cluster.

Recent studies in organizational ecology have revealed a growing interest in measuring meaning systems directly rather than by inference (Hsu and Hannan, 2005). New insights have come from research on the role of external organizational audiences in defining and evaluating organizational identities. Identities help to determine an organization's position relative to the other organizations with which it competes in technological, industrial, or social spaces. The practical problem for organizations interacting with multiple audiences with diverse interests is that they need to decide whether they should promote a single, distinct identity or whether they should juggle multiple, overlapping identities. The advantage of a single, narrow identity is that it helps organizations signal to audiences what is distinct and valuable about the organization. The advantage of a broad set of different identity categories is that it helps the organization address the demands of multiple audiences. Studies have shown that the way organizations manage the trade-offs between narrowly focused, robust identities and complex, multi-dimensional identities affects their performance in the niches in which they seek to survive and prosper. In the film industry, for instance, the outcomes of audience categorizations and evaluations in the identity space of film genre and actor roles have a direct impact on the life chances of films and producers (Hsu et al., 2009).

Research on the institutional elements of organizational fields has also moved in directions where scholars attempt to decipher the meanings of people's actions with a view to how social relationships are organized according to shared understandings of what goes on inside the field (Pachucki and Breiger, 2010). Relations exist not only between individuals but also between ideas and concepts. By exploring interconnections between concepts, researchers look for meaning systems (e.g., in the form of collective mindsets or ideologies) without having to study individuals. Concepts, ideas, beliefs, and so on can be studied with data from texts such as websites, company reports, newspaper accounts, or literature reviews (Franzosi, 1998). For example, one way to study organizational culture is to investigate what scientists write about culture, what the key concepts are that they work with, and whether there are any patterns in the way interrelated concepts converge to "schools of thought" or academic communities like "invisible colleges" (Hill and Carley, 1999).

Studies that investigate the evolutionary aspects of meaning systems show how organizational cultures and strategies are constructed out of a complex process of contestation over meanings. For example, Weber (2005) examined changes in the corporate identities of pharmaceutical companies in the United States and Germany, as reflected in strategic goals and forms of corporate governance. To investigate identity changes, he studied interconnections between statements and concepts (e.g., equity, service, tradition) in annual reports, which the companies used to define and promote their strategic mission *vis-à-vis* their audiences. Over a span of two decades, the companies had become very similar in their identities, which is indicative of an evolving international organizational field in which the actors learn to share a universally valid technical knowledge base (e.g., in biochemistry or genetics), a societal task orientation (e.g., to improve human health or to promote social equity), and a customer focus in service delivery (e.g., to contribute to an efficient health care delivery system or to support the medical profession). The significance of societal developments and institutions in this learning process is apparent from the fact that the organizations' identity categories evolved in line with changes in demography (e.g., age, ethnicity) and ideology (e.g., market orientation, individualism).

Other studies have examined evolving meaning systems by studying the relationship between ideas and the practices with which ideas are implemented. In a study of changes in the US social welfare system between 1880 and 1917, it was shown how organizations' (e.g., orphanages, soup kitchens, homes for the destitute) evolving position within this field was determined by their relationship to the ideas prevailing in society at that time regarding the meaning of poverty, homelessness, justice, need, and misfortune (Mohr and Duquenne, 1997). The meanings of different categories of poor people (e.g., distressed, indigent) were shaped by the various practices (e.g., giving money, offering shelter) through which the organizations offered relief. Through changes in the constellation of practices and meanings, the social welfare logic of the poorhouse system prevailing in the 1880s gradually gave way to the logic of professional social work and social investigation. Studies like these show that the cultural beliefs that make up institutions evolve together with the organizational actions through which they are reproduced and transformed. Economic motives are often important, but they are not the only rationale for such changes.

4. Conclusion

While it has long been known that organizations are not randomly distributed in geographic, cultural, social, and technological space, it is only recently that researchers have begun to examine in detail the origins and outcomes of spatial concentration or dispersion in agglomerations, niches, and fields. On the whole, studies have shown that the boundaries of different spaces may overlap, and that developments in one space are often shaped by conditions in another space. For example, differences in geographic space (such as the distinction between "core" and "peripheral" regional economies) may be produced by differences in economic space (through the unequal distribution of economic resources) and by differences in cultural space (through interpretations in different meaning systems). Organizations that are adjacent to one another in economic transactions may use very different organizational forms in terms of the social relations and cultural ideas that bind the actors to each other. The key insight from this research is that space can be thought of as a multi-dimensional relational system in which different spatial elements obtain meaning from their location *vis-à-vis* each other. The analytical benefit of this perspective is that it can incorporate multiple variables simultaneously in the same space of organizations and organizational populations, linking units from economic, social, and institutional domains. In this way, meaning can be given to "relatedness" as something other than the abstract geographic notions of location and distance. Knowing how organizations position themselves in different kinds of spaces helps understand how organizations deal with different entities in their environments.

The relational view on space also draws attention to the fact that meanings need to be constructed actively to obtain force. Space acquires meaning through the specific ways in which concrete individuals, work groups, and organizations make decisions, manipulate information, jockey for political power, and obtain privileged access to economic resources. Even the egalitarianism and professionalism of "high-end" knowledge-intensive organizations like law firms and museums are not devoid of "hard-wired" practices and structures involving material interests, hard-nosed rhetorics, and institutional logics (Brown et al., 2010). Institutions matter in the form of rules, beliefs, and conventions, regulating organizational actions and distributing rights and benefits, but not all institutions are created equal. Some institutions exercise causal power by undermining, dislodging, and replacing a previously dominant organizational form, while others persist only as long as they "fit" the interests of the most powerful actors.

The concern for the importance of interests, as opposed to ideas and preferences, raises the issue of power and domination. Who constructs meaning, and for what ends? Where do the resources and rules come from with which institutions are created and which then provide the framework for action? What are the contextual conditions that explain why power and domination in spaces are not always explicit? There is nothing natural about the way organizations fill economic, social, and cultural spaces. Local spaces are intertwined with global spaces in many different ways, sometimes reinforcing existing power relations, and sometimes opening up new opportunities for fundamental change. Globalization has not rendered localities irrelevant, but it has created new kinds of places and spatial meanings, as suggested by the image of "Global Cities" and "World Olympics," which combine traditional understandings of places with new understandings of economic and social relations. When resources are reassembled in new locations, they may acquire new meanings for some people, as when replicas of the Canal Grande in Venice are moved next to the Paris Eiffel Tower in Las Vegas, and when American Disneyland is recreated in Paris.

In some cases, internationalizing organizations work hard to embed themselves in distant localities, by building strong local ties and investing in assets that have meaning only in a particular locale. In other cases, internationalizing organizations adapt to local circumstances merely in the peripheral aspects of names, décors, and marketing strategies, while retaining centralized control and standard setting in their home base (Harzing and Sorge, 2003). Place-making and space-filling are not interest-free processes but involve the self-interested strategies and activities of organization designers, politicians, entrepreneurs, and interest group activists. The spaces in agglomerations, niches, and fields are not only arenas of mutual understanding and collective action, but are also arenas of conflict and strife. Individuals and groups struggle for advantageous locations within the spaces that then enable them to determine the meanings that come to be recognized as useful, progressive, legitimate, or whatever. In this way, conflicts and negotiations over spatial meanings add an important temporal aspect to organizations and organizational adaptation, as will be discussed in the next chapter.

Recommended further reading

Dale, K. and Burrell, G. (2008) *The Spaces of Organization and the Organization of Space: Power Identity and Materiality at Work*. Basingstoke: Palgrave Macmillan.
The authors argue that not only is work a spatially ordered activity, but space itself is organized. Space is an outcome of work and politics, at the same time that it is a medium of power.

Hernes, T. (2004) *The Spatial Construction of Organization*. Amsterdam: John Benjamins.

A discussion of organizations as a "composite of spaces," containing social, cognitive, and material processes that operate simultaneously and contribute to organizational change.

Lefebvre, H. (1991) *The Production of Space*. Oxford: Blackwell.
Space is viewed as an ongoing production of spatial relations. Spaces emerge as a result of the relation between spatial actions and symbolic representations of space.

Tilly, C. (2005) *Identities, Boundaries, and Social Ties*. Boulder, CO: Paradigm Publishers.
A discussion of the various mechanisms through which social relations in organizations, and society in general, are constituted in space.

 ■ **Practice questions for Anecdote 4.1** ▬▬▬▬▬▬▬

1　What are the features of the symbolic space in which Bernhard defines his identity?

2　If you were Bernhard, how would you restructure your social space to improve your relationship with your former colleagues?

3　When Bernhard was promoted to a managerial position, he switched to a new space. How would you characterize this spatial move?

5

Time and Temporality

Learning Objectives

This chapter will:

- Discuss organizations as temporal systems
- Discuss various meanings of time
- Discuss time as a social construct

---

1. Introduction

What makes a specific scene in a motion picture or story interesting is not always the scene's substance but its position in a sequence of events. A snapshot means nothing outside its context. Similarly, a single event becomes intelligible only when placed in a series of events in the preceding and following periods, allowing the observer to say that this event is rare, significant, or "old wine in new bottles." Events are not isolated occurrences; they are linked contingencies, marking beginnings, endings, and turning points in a temporal process. Temporality means more than simply coming out of the past and moving into the future. It also means that phenomena develop in a sequential order, but this order need not be linear and predictable; it may be fraught with disruptions, reversals, and new directions. Jobs, for example, are folded into careers, which rarely evolve as predictable sequences of positions, but are interrupted by transitions between new assignments and organizations.

Because organizations are structured entities involving some degree of continuity, much can be learned about them by studying how they came to be the way they are and how they structure options for the future. Routines, for example, are used to channel options for future actions, but they are themselves the outcome of actions in the past. They are part of an organizing process that includes remembering and forgetting. Routines function like a memory system by organizing past events so that they can be selectively recalled for coping with current and future events. Routines thus impose order on temporal processes in organizations, but they are themselves a temporal process composed of ordered sequences of options and decisions. Organizational actions occur in and through time; they are informed by occurrences in the past, and, metaphorically speaking, they cast a shadow to the future.

History matters, but it matters differently for people with different understandings of past events and expectations for the future. People often differ in their interpretation of temporal categories such as schedules, deadlines, and routines geared to the exigencies of specific situations. In the anecdote (5.1) below, Heather has difficulty adjusting to her situation because her orientation to time has led her to tightly schedule all of her activities in advance. She had invested a great deal of time in preparing for her lecture and organizing her journey, and she now feels that her time has been wasted, given the way the events unfolded. The temporality of her engagement has affected the engagement itself. Temporality provides a context not only for a single event (what happened) but also for the causal relations between events (when it happened). Temporality is linked to causality in that *how* things unfold over time influences *why* they have the effects they do. To explain Heather's decision to disengage herself in her dealings with Luciana in the future, one needs to know how the way the events unfolded led to Heather's decision. Heather *could* have arrived at a different decision if Luciana had not been sidetracked by the surprise visit of a colleague, if students had not left early to prepare for another class following immediately afterwards, or if the technician had arrived sooner. When viewed through a temporal lens, Heather's decision to disengage from Luciana reveals deeper insights than taking merely a "snapshot" view of her relationship with Luciana.

ANECDOTE 5.1

Heather, an assistant professor at an American university, felt very flattered when she was invited by Luciana, a well-known professor at a university in Italy, whom she had met at a conference the year before, to give a talk to one of her classes. At the time when she received the invitation she was in Austria with her husband on a brief vacation. "I am sure you have some paper or some project that you could present to my students," Luciana wrote in her e-mail. "I think it would be good for my students to actually see the author of an article on their reading list. And while you are here, we could also talk about doing a research project together."

Heather planned her trip to Luciana's university very carefully. To save money she traveled on the same day she was to give her lecture, rather than staying at a hotel the night before. It took her six hours by car to reach Luciana's town. And when, after a brisk walk from the parking lot in the early afternoon heat, she arrived at the seminar room five minutes before the lecture was to begin, she felt proud about her accomplishment to be on time. After all, she had never been to this city before and had never before driven a car in an Italian city. And she had kept to her record of never being late to a lecture since she had started her job as an assistant professor four years earlier.

She found only about ten students waiting outside the room, but Luciana was not present. Fifteen minutes later, Luciana was still not there. Nearly twenty students, including those who had arrived late, were now sitting in front of her, chatting and waiting for something to happen. A student told her that they had not been informed that this class session was to include a guest lecturer. Heather felt increasingly nervous because her presentation was carefully timed, with an introduction and a conclusion that were critical to making sense of the research findings she wanted to present for discussion. Luciana arrived nearly half an hour after the lecture was scheduled to begin. Several of the students had already left. "Sorry for being a little late," she said. "I had lunch with two of our PhD students in the department, and they wanted to chat a little." Heather was perplexed. "And then one of my colleagues came," Luciana continued. "He brought along a visitor from Sweden who insisted on having ice-cream. Swedes like our ice-cream, you know," she said with a smile. "And it's just so hot today, even for us." But you expect *me* to be on time, after spending six hours on the road in this heat, Heather thought to herself. "We are very late now, and I'm not sure I can present my entire lecture," she said in a tone that she hoped would signal to Luciana her concern about not being able to fully present the findings of her study. "Don't worry, we'll just finish a little later. Those students who have another class right after this one can just leave. No problem." But to Heather, this *was* a problem. "But then not everyone in your class will hear my presentation. Isn't that a problem for *you*?" "That's OK, I just won't test them on this material," Luciana smiled. So why did you invite me then, Heather thought to herself.

Luciana's laptop took some time to boot, and when it finally ran she discovered that the beamer was not working. "Oh, not again!" She called a technician on her cell phone and, while waiting for him, she introduced Heather to her class. By the time the technician arrived, about ten minutes later, nearly half of the students had already left the room. When Heather finally started her presentation, she knew that it would be a disaster. She didn't have enough time left to get through all of her material and to make her presentation a meaningful learning experience. Heather could hardly concentrate; she was boiling with anger. She had interrupted her only vacation this year to prepare a lecture, which she now considered useless, and she felt utterly embarrassed about this. She swore to herself that she would never accept an invitation from Luciana again, and she would certainly not work with her on a research project.

This chapter presents a temporal lens for exploring organizational phenomena, as opposed to studying variations in fixed organizational attributes. Temporality is discussed with a view to the sequencing, pacing, and discontinuities in the component elements of the phenomenon under investigation. Time itself is socially constructed, in ways involving economic, institutional, and evolutionary considerations.

2. The temporal lens

Organizational historians are among those theorists who are most directly interested in time as a concept in its own right. To understand organizations in their present form, they suggest looking for cues in the past. In some cases this may take them back to a period well before industrialization when the foundations were laid for current organizational forms. The European medieval guild system, for example, produced a lasting impact that is still evident in modern organizational cultures in the form of rituals and symbols related to honor codes, craft mentality, solidarity, and the like (Kieser, 1989). The differences between French and German corporate hierarchies have their historical roots in the educational systems of the early industrialization period (Lawrence and Edwards, 2000). And in Italy, the ancient putting-out system has survived as a reasonably efficient alternative to modern integrated mass-production (Lazerson, 1995). In many cases, organizational cultures are informed by local community cultures with a long history. For example, while many Japanese firms have adopted American-style shareholder-based organizational practices (e.g., related to downsizing and asset divestiture), the American influence has been weakest in firms that are most deeply embedded in local business cultures (Ahmadjian and Robbins, 2005). Luciana's lateness and Heather's promptness (Anecdote 5.1) may be a case of "historical embeddedness," reflecting the enduring influence of their **socialization** in different academic cultures, but this is only part of the story.

Many studies that refer to the historical origins of current organizational forms do not examine directly *how* past events have come to shape organizational development. Researchers often take a variable-based approach, measuring the entities under investigation at one point in time across a sample of individuals, organizations, or situational contexts. They examine variations in the attributes of entities, but ignore the temporal process by which variables and relationships between variables unfold. The (often implicit) assumption in this research is that the attributes are stable over time or have reached equilibrium at the point when they are observed. Managers, for instance, may be assumed to be either risk friendly or risk averse, but the possibility that they change their preferences over time is not normally investigated. Consider the influence of attributes like age, gender, or national background of the tourists shown in the photograph below (Exhibit 5.1). Researchers may assume that the causal role of these attributes in the behavior of these individuals will not change during the course of their crossing the bridge. They might hypothesize, for instance, that older people are more likely than younger people to stop mid-course and admire the architectural design of the bridge, but they would not expect that the effect of age *changes en route*. It might be that older people *become* more or less inclined

Exhibit 5.1

to "stop and look" as their engagement in this social situation evolves, just as the impact of employee age on creativity may increase or decline with tenure in an organization, holding everything else constant (Fineman, 2011). To the extent that human attributes are social constructions, in the sense that they involve interpretation and negotiation, their effects may change under changing circumstances. If, on the other hand, human attributes are assumed to be fixed, the past development of an entity can have no influence on its future development, nor can the causal importance of an attribute change over time (Abbott, 1995).

The assumption of temporal stability in the causal influence of human attributes is unrealistic in most social and organizational settings. One would think that at least some of the people shown in the photograph above will change their plan to visit a particular tourist site once they find themselves in a slow-moving crowd or discover that everyone else in this crowd intends to visit the same site at the same time. The causal importance of people's age – or some other attribute – may increase or decrease while crossing the bridge, in response to what they observe in their social surroundings or with whom they interact. In an evolving environment, people often adjust their attitudes and goals as they go along (Wilson and Hodges, 1992). People may accept their national identity as historical fate, but they also look for new ways to enact the conflicts stemming from fate. They learn from experience, improvise, or simply change their behavior to what the majority are doing. People working in organizations construct biographies and build careers, in line with regular performance evaluations and well-timed promotions, but they also respond innovatively to unexpected opportunities or disruptions (Docco et al., 2009). Variables do not behave, but people do, and it is through their actions and interactions that things change over time.

Consider the spread of the **matrix design** of organizational structure in hospitals in the United States since the 1960s (Burns and Wholey, 1993). An increasing number of hospitals adopted a structure featuring a horizontal overlay of project managers or some other specialized unit to coordinate functional personnel (e.g., nurses, technicians, dietary aides) across clinical areas (e.g., pediatrics, gynecology). Hospital organizations vary in attributes like employment size and financial assets. One can theorize about the relationship between these variables and the presence of the matrix design across a sample of hospitals, testing the argument that, for example, larger hospitals are more likely to use the matrix design, because the complexity of large organizations requires flexible coordination across functions and services. The finding that larger hospitals are indeed more likely to use matrix structures may be interesting at the descriptive level, but by itself it yields no insights into the concrete problems that organizations face when *developing* the matrix design and *changing* from a different structural design. Analytically more interesting are studies of hospitals conceived as structurally dynamic systems with a history of political conflict, both internally and externally, where the matrix structure is only one of several potential outcomes (Town et al., 2007). In most countries, the health care sector has changed significantly over the last few decades through organizational foundings, closures, mergers, and organizational transformations (Dent, 2003). Individual hospitals have experienced changes in size, technologies, and budgets, and strategic initiatives have come and gone, shaped by events like the introduction of new government regulations or privatization programs. The histories of hospitals have followed different paths, influenced by specific traditions and requirements in their local environments, which makes it difficult to generalize statements about hospitals to the industry as a whole.

When viewed through a temporal lens, organizational life appears as a sequence of events, individual actions, and social interactions, in an environment that changes as well. In many industries, markets and technologies are becoming more complex, new ones are emerging, and old ones are disappearing in a process involving relations among a diverse set of actors across organizational, social, cultural, and locational spaces. Some effects are immediate and short term; others are more distant in time. Things that may appear routine and repetitive, and thus fixed in the short term, may reveal significant changes when observed over a long time interval. Outcomes in one time period may impact on subsequent outcomes. The underlying processes may be slow or fast moving, or they may build slowly until some critical threshold is reached and then broad-sweeping changes are triggered, extending to neighboring domains. Some processes may lead to a change of direction; others may lock development on to a particular path from which it is impossible to break away.

Understanding these differences, and the conditions under which they occur, requires the incorporation of time – its meanings as well as the mechanisms driving temporal effects – into the analysis.

3. Meanings of time

The concern of organizational scholars for time and temporality has a history going back to the work of Frederick Taylor (1911) on time and motion, Max Weber's (1904/1958) ideas about social change, and Karl Marx's (1867/1954) arguments about economic "laws of development." Much writing since then has taken a metaphoric approach to time, referring to time as something that is costly ("Time is money"), treating time as another word for progress ("Time heals") or patience ("All in good time"), or thinking of time as simply meaning change ("The only thing constant is change"). A growing number of organizational scholars, however, have treated time as a distinct concept in its own right. Following insights from sociology (Zerubavel, 1976) and political science (Pierson, 2004), they have proposed a range of strategies to incorporate time into explanations of organizational phenomena (e.g., Ancona et al., 2001; Crossan et al., 2005; Martine and Jones, 2000; Zaheer et al., 1999). Others have developed new methods for studying temporal processes, such as event-history analysis (Tuma et al., 1979), sequence analysis (Abbott, 1995), and process tracing (George and McKeown, 1985). Some of the key debates have revolved around the usefulness of different conceptions of time and the ways these conceptions matter in the social construction of time.

3.1 Conceptions of time

There are many different ways to think about time, leading to distinct interpretations of time-based phenomena (Ancona et al., 2001). For example, one can conceptualize time as clock time, by treating time as a linear and infinitely divisible continuum of quantifiable units, like minute and hour. Clock time is used, for example, in the assessment of work performance. Shift workers in restaurants might be evaluated in four-week cycles, whereas academic faculty in universities might be evaluated in three- or six-year cycles. One can also distinguish between relative time (e.g., age) and absolute time (e.g., period). Descriptive meanings of time ("When did this happen?") are applied differently than normative understandings of time ("When should you do this?"). Differences in the conceptualization of time suggest that it may be more insightful to characterize organizational forms as orderings – rather than orders – of entities (e.g., rules, positions, policies), and to study the temporal process connecting the entities in terms of event sequences, rates of change, and continuity.

3.1.1 Events and sequences

Events are distinguishable occurrences taking place within a delimited amount of time, such as the merger of two departments or the signing of a supply contract. Many events occur as a normal aspect of organizational life and can be assimilated in the customs and routines of an organization quite easily, such as the Monday morning staff meetings in some organizations. Some events are small and their impact is locally limited, such as Luciana in the anecdote (5.1) above being held back by an unexpected visitor; other events are small but they can mushroom into big events, such as the recruitment of a new governing board member leading to a fundamental change in the organization's strategic direction. Some events occur only once in the life course of an organization, such as the closing of a production facility; other events recur regularly, such as the "morning tea" ritual in many British organizations. Some events originate outside an organization, such as a natural disaster causing the destruction of a factory; other events grow out of the structure of an organization, such as the replacement of a team member who refuses to collaborate with colleagues. Some events initiate a process; others complete a process. "Starting events" set a process in motion, such as organizational foundings triggering the development of a new industry. "Closing events," such as leaving a tip at a restaurant or signing a contract, bring a process to an end.

Events are always debatable since they cannot be abstracted from time. They are social constructions, produced and reproduced through action, negotiation, and conversation (Tilly, 2008). A labor strike, for example, means more than people's absence from work. It involves people issuing declarations, making claims, mobilizing supporters, staging ceremonies, and so forth. Signing an agreement at the level of the European Union is the outcome of actions in a series of events (e.g., negotiations, media presentations, parliamentary debates) and the beginning of institutional changes at the national level of each country. Even seemingly random and fortuitous events occur under circumstances that have their own history. An event like the fall of the Berlin Wall, which had a profound impact on economic development across Europe, did not occur in a vacuum. It was the result of a series of political developments, themselves the outcome of events that happened in a particular sequence, setting the stage for potential developments in the future. In the immediate aftermath of the collapse of the World Trade Center in New York, the rescue event became infused with a variety of meanings, as firefighters, spectators, police, politicians, and journalists struggled over an acceptable definition of rescue work, invoking symbols (e.g., flags, emblems, uniforms) and material artifacts (e.g., hard hats, cameras, cordons) to substantiate their viewpoints. Because events have no determinate character independent of the practices that produce them, they are always subject to interpretive modification.

The interpretation of temporal processes requires that events, the circumstances in which they occur, and the causal connections between them are clearly explicated. In product development projects, for example, the success of a new idea may depend on whether the project follows a particular sequence, from idea generation to idea screening, testing, and evaluation. Whether close collaboration among the project participants makes a difference for project performance may depend on *when* in this sequence the participants begin to work together, rather than merely *whether* they collaborate (Kijkuit and van den Ende, 2010). The temporality of group structure – whether the tasks are synchronized, how fast the group structure evolves, and so on – may be as important as the structure itself. The meaning of a given structural arrangement may change as the project unfolds. Initially, non-cooperation may be viewed as signaling individual creativity, whereas in later stages it may be interpreted as indicating status competition.

The same event may have a different meaning dependent on its location in a sequence of events. In restaurants, for example, whether a cheese dish is considered an appetizer or a dessert depends on the moment in the course of a dinner when it is served. E-mails sent by students to professors before an examination may be interpreted as a sign of academic studiousness; those sent to them after an examination may be interpreted as harassment. The sequential order of things may also influence their outcome. For example, an individual's decision to become self-employed may not so much depend on personal characteristics (e.g., gender, religious affiliation) than on the person's movement between previous episodes of labor market involvement (e.g., wage employment, out of the labor force) (Carroll and Mosakowski, 1987). Also, the factors that lead to self-employment early in one's career (e.g., having parents who were self-employed) may be very different than those leading to self-employment later in the career (e.g., accumulated experience as a wage employee). And the transitions between episodes of self-employment, wage-employment, or unemployment may be as important as the episodes themselves. One could ask, for example, why for some people there is a high probability that an episode is followed by another episode, of the same or a different type. Transition probabilities are the focus in studies of rates of change.

3.1.2 Rate of change

Activities in organizations are driven not only by events but also by tempo. In restaurant work, for example, it is essential that meals are prepared and served at a well-synchronized pace, in line with the flow of incoming and departing customers (Fine, 2009). Timing is critical to distinguishing between a steak that is medium rare and one that is charred, forcing the workflow participants to compete for temporal access to resources within the confines of lunch hours, holiday seasons, banking hours, or whatever markings may be relevant in a particular context. Events may be important too, as occurrences affecting rates of change. Events set the pace of activities occurring at specific times (e.g., film opening ceremonies) or at regular intervals (e.g., film award ceremonies). If one were to compare the experiences of locally known film directors with internationally known ones only at a single point in time, one would miss the fact that the latter reach the top through pathways that are paced very differently (e.g., involving more steps, shorter episodes of inactivity) than those of their local counterparts (De Vany and Walls, 1999).

The corollary of the duration of an entity's existence in a particular state is the rate at which the entity is transformed into a different state. This rate is the length of time it takes to change from one state to another, such as the transformation of a financial institution selling residential mortgages to an organization specializing in commercial real estate (Haveman, 1992). Rates of change differ widely between populations, for reasons related to population-level factors such as union rules or legal barriers limiting organizations' ability to enter or leave an industry (Aldrich and Fiol, 1994). Rates of change also vary between organizations in the same population, because of differences in the adaptability of organizational structures. "Strong" organizational structures, grounded in formal rules and standard procedures, make deviations difficult and potentially hazardous (Hannan and Freeman, 1984). Whether structural change enhances an organization's survival chances depends on the organizational features that change relative to the rate of environmental change. An organization may be able to alter some of its core features, such as changing its business model or replacing the top management team, but it may not achieve such changes quickly enough to keep pace with environmental change. In some environments, organizational change may even be detrimental, if investors, consumers, and suppliers expect the organization to be reliable and to reproduce routines that signal the organization's long-term commitments.

Rates of change are the focus of analysis in studies linking organizational transformation to environmental fluctuations, distinguishing between the amplitude and frequency of change in the environment (Wholey and Brittain, 1989). Amplitude measures the degree of difference in changes. In the restaurant industry, for example, sales (used as a measure of market fluctuations) may not vary much from month to month. Exceptions are changes in sales volume during major holidays, but this is not necessarily problematic for restaurants because this change is predictable. Frequency of change indicates the length of time between changes, that is, the interval in which some phenomenon exists in a steady state. Seasonal changes in the demand for hotel services in cities staging a major annual trade show are relatively coarse-grained, whereas day-to-day changes in demand for fast-food services are more fine-grained. Different organizations do not experience the amplitude and frequency of changes in the same way, depending, for example, on whether they aim at a broad market or a narrow niche market. One would expect large, generalist organizations with a broad market orientation to have higher survival chances in coarse-grained volatile environments because they can more easily ride out long periods of low demand, using their excess capacity in resources. Small specialists, by contrast, might perform comparatively well in stable environments. A specialist strategy of placing all bets on a narrow market segment and avoiding excess capacity can pay off only if demand is relatively stable (Freeman and Hannan, 1983). Small, specialized restaurants, like whole-food establishments located in college towns with a stable flow of customers, can do quite well in such environments. For theater companies, by contrast, specializing in the production of a particular genre aimed at low-income audiences would likely be an ineffective survival strategy.

Rates of change may themselves vary over time. In some cases, the environment may impose strong selection pressure, rewarding organizations that become structurally more inert by developing stable routines and strict hierarchies (Hannan et al., 2006). In other cases, organizations may become more adaptable, as they learn to cope with continually changing circumstances (Rerup and Feldman, 2011). Learning from experience is critical in situations where social capabilities are essential, as in joint ventures of organizations with different cultures (Gulati, 1995), or in work teams with members of different occupational background (Bunderson and Boumgarden, 2010). Learning to cooperate does not necessarily mean that the actors' interpretations of tasks converge. Research on project teams, for instance, has shown that the participants do not always develop similar mental models during the course of their project work (Research Brief 5.1). Projects are temporary arrangements and there may not be enough time for the participants to develop interaction structures and practices supportive of shared understandings (Levesque et al., 2001). The pressure of speed may motivate them to rely on familiar routines they have used in the past rather than develop new understandings.

RESEARCH BRIEF 5.1

Many scholars think of people's mindset as a time-varying construct that adapts itself to changing requirements from the environment. In research on team work, it is normally assumed that the mental models of individual members converge over time because shared mindsets facilitate coordination. To test this assumption, Levesque et al. (2001) studied a sample of 62 software development project teams composed of undergraduate students majoring in information systems

(Continued)

(Continued)

programming. The results of this study show that, contrary to the researchers' expectations, team members' mental models regarding task technology, working climate, authority relations, and client expectations did not become more similar over time; they actually became less similar. According to the researchers, a possible explanation for this finding is that group members' work roles became increasingly specialized over the course of the projects, which led to a corresponding decline in social interaction among the participants and thus limited opportunities to develop shared understandings.

This finding is directly relevant to the question of how the attributes of individual team members, such as their educational and skill background, influence coordination as a fundamental requirement of effective group work. Individuals' attitudes concerning collaboration may evolve together with the work context. Group members come and go, and work roles may become more or less specialized as the project evolves. Whether individual mindsets converge over time may depend on the expectation of members that they will interact repeatedly in the future. In the student project teams investigated in this study, there was no expectation that the groups would remain together indefinitely. The same may hold in other organizational settings. Many organizations accomplish tasks through temporary arrangements and limited-duration projects, where there is not enough time for shared mindsets to develop.

A main limitation of this study is the use of data in a setting that may be very different from the kind of work environment in "real-world" organizations. The sample of subjects consisted of undergraduate students at a university working on a course project. The full range of behaviors that is open to people in real organizations is not available to participants in this setting. Students may not have the level of commitment to each other and may not face the same kinds of challenges and requirements that employees face in actual organizations. Team members embedded in a firm, particularly if they expect to work together on further projects, may feel greater pressure to develop shared mindsets.

3.1.3 Continuity and discontinuity

Change may be continuous and incremental, or discontinuous and haphazard. A temporal process is discontinuous if there is a shift in some state with no intervening steps, moving a relationship in a new direction. The fall of the Berlin Wall, for example, marked a significant point of discontinuity in the development of organizations in the eastern part of Germany, but it also was the beginning of a continuous transition period during which political institutions there were replaced wholesale and companies were restructured from the ground up (Nilsson, 1996). In other Eastern European economies, historical legacies in the institutional domain were strong enough to keep many organizations on the existing developmental path, even though it was not the most efficient one relative to emerging alternative paths (Grabher and Stark, 1997). **Path dependence** is often used in the organizational literature as a

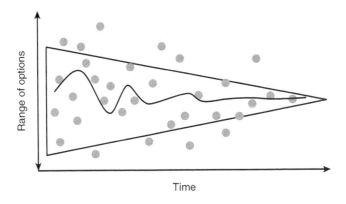

Exhibit 5.2 Stylistic representation of path dependence

metaphoric concept to describe situations where what happened in the past determines what will happen in the future. A more differentiated conception of path dependence identifies specific mechanisms of reproducing existing structures and practices. Path dependence without a specification of mechanisms of reproduction is nothing more than the suggestion that history matters.

The central idea of path dependence is that once a particular pattern of development is established, it can become cumulative and persist into the future, given a narrowing range of choice opportunities (Exhibit 5.2). Possible future developments are conditioned by both the past and the current state of the entity in question. The past determines the possibilities, while the present influences which of the possibilities are explored. The mechanisms that reinforce existing patterns include factors at the individual and organizational level. At the cognitive level, what has been known in the past influences what can be learned in the present, for reasons to do with people's need for cognitive consistency and their preference for routines that faithfully reproduce existing knowledge (Szulanski, 1996). Individuals often rely on mental models (e.g., reasoning by hindsight) they have applied in the past, especially in situations perceived as ambiguous. They often refrain from pursuing alternative courses of action, even if these alternatives appear potentially more effective (Heath et al., 1998). For example, supervisors may hold on to their first assessment of an employee's *potential* ability, ignoring new behaviors that they interpret as inconsistent with their original beliefs. If they codify their assessment (e.g., formal evaluation), it can lead to the institutionalization of their beliefs in the form of an official employment record that is used by others as evidence of the employee's "track record." At the organizational level, rules, routines, and formal control structures can create a dynamic favoring the continuation of existing pathways (Sydow et al., 2009). Once a particular structure is set in place, it can become a defining characteristic of the organization, giving the organization a distinct identity that stakeholders may use to evaluate the organization's course of action (Hannan et al., 2006). If, for example, an *haute cuisine* French restaurant were to introduce a cafeteria-style self-service food counter, many clients would consider this a serious violation of a long trail of identity-marking organizational practices (Rao et al., 2005).

Path-dependent developments are largely irreversible, with outcomes that may be non-optimal or even downright harmful, as in the case of a nuclear power plant where decisions made within highly constraining structures eventually lead to an accident (Ross and Staw, 1993). Decision-making may include cognitive processes in which people, when confronted with feedback suggesting that the chosen course of action is ineffective, are more likely to escalate their commitment to the existing course than to develop new commitments in a different direction. People may also be kept from switching to alternative courses of action because of social biases (e.g., conformity pressure) or institutional constraints (e.g., regulation, accreditation). Law schools in the United States, for example, are subject to an external ranking mechanism that leads faculties to conform closely to standards and expectations to the point where they internalize them and do whatever they can to improve on the attributes that the ranking criteria are intended to capture (Sauder and Espeland, 2009).

While organizational processes may be geared towards producing consistent outcomes and preserving past achievements, they are not always path-dependent in the sense that deviations from the selected path are impossible. What is already known does not always prevent learning new things in the future. For example, the concept of the organizational life cycle (Exhibit 5.3) describes a situation where organizations experience during their life course a series of crises, triggered by internal organizational and external environmental

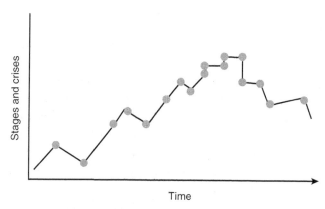

Exhibit 5.3 Stylistic representation of organizational life cycle

changes. If the crises are resolved, the organization moves to a higher level of development, with new capabilities, but also facing new challenges (Greiner, 1998). While the concept of the organizational life cycle – as well as the life cycle of industries, clusters, and technologies – suggests a rhythmic and predictable pattern, the mechanisms of change may differ across life-cycle stages, indicating possibilities for organizations to create new forms. For example, the organizational identity threat from academic ranking systems may be perceived as serious enough to induce the faculty leadership to redefine the school's goals and missions in line with rankings (Elsbach and Kramer, 1996). Alternatively, the leadership may more forcefully embrace the school's current position in the ranking as a testament to its identity commitment. Which organizational response is chosen in a crisis situation depends on such contingencies as the age of the organization, the credibility and resource significance of the external audience, and the way the boundary spanners and key decision-makers in the organization interpret the crisis (Sauder and Espeland, 2009).

The temporal lens draws attention to the possibility that organizations adopt a particular structure depending on their location along a timeline, such as their position in the organizational or industrial life cycle. For example, firms participating in the formation of a business cluster are often more forward looking with respect to developing a new market and creating a joint strategy, whereas in the maturity stage of cluster development they tend to be more backward looking, trying to protect their turf or defend a common identity (Staber and Sautter, 2011). Competitive conditions can vary greatly across stages of industry development. Firms that enter an industry before and after a particular stage in the industry's life cycle face different challenges, with differential effects on organizational performance (Agarwal et al., 2002). Firms entering an industry during its growth phase tend to face fewer resource barriers and are less likely to fail than maturity-phase entrants.

Understanding resource constraints across different stages in the development of an entity is crucial to understanding the very nature of the entity itself. Differences in the way organizations respond to a crisis situation during the industry's early growth compared to their response in a mature industry can provide important clues to the effectiveness of the particular structure an organization has developed over time. Some organizations erect tight control structures to buffer themselves from disruptions, such as nightclubs, which use strict rules to filter the inflow of new members, or the organization of the Vatican, which relies heavily on secrecy and mysticism to stabilize the flow of resources. Other organizations create structures that actively encourage disruptions, but at different stages in the workflow. Universities, for instance, often design large standardized introductory lectures to minimize interruptions from students, whereas at upper levels in the program of study they use small seminar courses to provoke interruptions and critical questioning.

Organizations also use feedback mechanisms to regulate temporal processes. Some feedback may have spiraling consequences, triggering feedback cycles that accelerate change. For example, a creativity project may initially attract few participants, given vague goals and uncertain outcomes. Over time, as the success of the project becomes more apparent, more people begin to join, hoping to benefit from their active participation, such as improving their career prospects or gaining social status. There is then an accelerating feedback among participation, motivation, and results. As the number of participants in the project increases, the force attracting even more people accelerates and the perceived impact on the results of the project increases. The nature of the entire project thus changes as it evolves, but the transformations do not necessarily occur in a linear fashion. The effects of an increase in the number of participants at high levels of participation may be much stronger or more visible than the same increase at low levels of participation.

Rather than accelerating change, feedback cycles may also slow down change. Research in cognitive psychology and sociology shows that many people who operate in a situation of high complexity and uncertainty tend to draw on knowledge they already have, filtering new information so that it confirms rather than challenges existing beliefs (Zerubavel, 1997). As a result, mistaken beliefs do not get corrected, with sub-optimal consequences, for example for people going through career transitions, which are moments when they should be most open to feedback (Ibarra, 1999). Some people use feedback to reinforce their existing beliefs, or they avoid feedback altogether; others view feedback as an opportunity to learn new things, aggregating feedback cycles into episodes for exploration and reflection. In most cases, however, feedback is a deeply personal experience, which is affected by the quality of social relations.

3.2 Social constructions of time

Time and timing are experienced subjectively, and temporal concepts, like shift work or overtime work, can have strictly personal interpretations, independent of measures of absolute time. Workers may recall how they felt as members of the organization for the first time when their supervisor invited them for a cup of coffee "four staff meetings ago," or managers may define organizational success in terms of having signed a major client contract "during the last Olympics." Subjective differences in the way people use time as a reference point make it difficult to predict exactly how temporal categories (e.g., timeframes, milestones) are constructed in a particular social situation.

Although time has a subjective dimension, it is also an intersubjective experience that is given meaning through social interaction. Team members may date their last successful project with reference to "the days when we hired Jack," using a collectively meaningful event as a temporal marker. And team members who insist on their personal understanding of being "on time" will eventually be asked by their colleagues to reconsider their standing in the group. Organizations depend on people's willingness to accept standard definitions of time as a basis for communication and coordination. Even simple tasks, such as scheduling group meetings, would not be possible if there were no shared understanding of "punctuality." The organization's definition of "workweek" or "overtime" has a structuring effect on the workflow and on workers' sense of accessibility. Innovations such as round-the-clock e-mail technology may enlarge the scope of communication, but the actual *use* of this technology is affected by the organizational structure within which interpersonal synchronization is required (Flaherty and Seipp-Williams, 2005). An employee who calls in sick in order to sleep during the day and use e-mail at night is normally in conflict with the needs of the organization.

The social construction of time often involves disagreement over the meaning of time. People may disagree about the meaning of "a full day's work" or of "being late" in an organizational context where those in power determine the scheduling and pacing of work activities. Max Weber (1904/1958) referred to the moral value of time when he called wasting time the "deadliest of sins." The designers of workplaces during the early industrialization period put most weight on the economic value of time in mass production systems (Piore and Sabel, 1984). Contemporary understandings of time also include psychological considerations of emotional well-being, which has stimulated the growth of entire new industries, such as the leisure and fitness industry (Frew and McGillivray, 2005). Meanings of time can also differ systematically within a given organization, reflecting differences in technology or occupation. In a classic study of organizational structure in American firms, it was found that the time horizons used in production units differed significantly from those used in research and development and in marketing units (Lawrence and Lorsch, 1967). It is easy to imagine that the orientation to time is quite different in organizations in different parts of the world (Levine, 1997).

The study of geographic-spatial differences in time orientations has a long tradition in cross-cultural management research (Hofstede, 1980). The idea of "missing my flight home" has a different meaning for Pakistani people than it has for the Swiss, and the concept of a "relaxed" atmosphere at work is interpreted differently in New Zealand than in Sweden. Austrian business negotiators tend to interpret the concept of day as meaning 24 hours in clock time, whereas their Jordanian counterpart will likely think of it as meaning "a while" in event time. Because time has cultural content, it operates as a "silent language" (Hall, 1959), existing in the background but strong enough to shape action and social interaction. In societies where people view the world more in terms of objects, which can be separated from their context, time is treated monochronically and measured quantitatively in clock time (e.g., "time is short," "time is money"). People come to organizational meetings prepared with a formal agenda of tasks and deadlines for accomplishing them, because they believe that the forward-oriented scheduling of one activity at a time is the most efficient and effective approach. By contrast, in societies where people see the world more holistically and as a collection of ongoing and inter-weaving processes, time is treated polychronically in event time (e.g., "time is what you make of it"). They come to meetings with an open agenda because they expect new tasks to emerge as discussions evolve. Luciana's and Heather's behaviors (Anecdote 5.1) may reflect a polychronic and monochronic approach to time, respectively. Luciana, the Italian, may be more inclined to live for the moment and to appreciate events as they happen, whereas for Heather, the American, time is a commodity that should not be wasted.

From a temporal perspective, however, the main issue is not whether individuals and organizations are more monochronically or more polychronically oriented. Rather, the question concerns the way the actors adjust behaviorally as they pursue their goals over time and space. What makes Heather in the above anecdote analytically interesting is not her cultural background *per se*, but what she makes of it behaviorally. For example, does she engage in actions that reinforce or alter existing conventions? Do her decisions open up new opportunities for redefining the situation so that the social exchange is mutually beneficial for the actors? While Heather and Luciana may not be consciously aware of the role that time plays in their everyday lives, they do construct their reality as agents. Individually, they use the past as a resource for interpreting the here-and-now and for constructing a future for themselves. Collectively, they assemble their interpretations to create a future for further interaction.

Social construction thus involves not only interaction but also cognition, in the form of sense-making and performative techniques such as counting, recalling, reporting, and conversing. People use *speech acts* to declare a temporal reality when, for example, they "promise" that something will happen or when they "apologize" for something that happened in the past. Speech acts represent reality and function as a medium through which this reality is created (Searle, 1976). In Heather's view, Luciana's promise of an opportunity for Heather to present a lecture was broken by Luciana's inability or refusal to provide the necessary infrastructure (e.g., technology, audience). As a result, the organization – of the classroom, in this case – lacked the logical structure that is created when a speech act is connected to social rights and obligations.

Story-telling is another key mechanism in the social construction of time (Franzosi, 1998). For example, when people tell stories about their personal experiences, which is what Heather undoubtedly did when she returned home to her husband, they order the relevant events in a temporal sequence and around a purpose. They construct stories to integrate what is present with what is absent. Stories normally have a beginning and an end, and in-between there may be turning points, reversals, or repetitions. Stories unify a set of otherwise unrelated events and actions into a coherent relational whole, thus giving it some meaning. Temporal coherence can be provided by goals, plans, plots, or some other form of constraint. Heather will likely tell a story that is motivated by her main goal: to deliver an effective lecture as efficiently as possible. Her story will appear coherent to her husband, not necessarily because he shares Heather's cultural background and orientation to time, but because the sequence of reported events adds up consistently to her final decision regarding her future engagement with Luciana. Narratives offer useful insights by detailing the sequential connections between the elements in a text (e.g., words, data, signs), but they are theoretically empty if they leave open the *interpretation* of what is said in a text. Heather may have decided against further collaboration with Luciana because she thought of the high economic costs of her engagement with Luciana or because she saw Luciana's lateness as a display of social status. Explaining the construction of time requires more than simply mapping actors, interests, decisions, or events.

4. Theorizing time

When viewing organizations through a temporal len, the intention is not to use a separate perspective the way one would employ, say, a psychological perspective as opposed to a sociological perspective. Rather than treating the temporal lens as an approach with its own independent and dependent variables, it is more insightful to weave it into the various perspectives with which scholars study organizations. The point of this integrative strategy is to highlight the differences and similarities in the way temporality is treated in different theories, such as organizational economics, institutionalism, and evolutionary theory. Studying the temporality of organizational phenomena thus contributes to the dialogue between these literatures, with a view to the role of time in economic relations, institutional rules, and evolutionary processes.

4.1 Time and economics

There is no single economic understanding of the role of time in organizational matters. Many economists take a static approach to organizational behavior, studying phenomena as if they are frozen in time or have reached a state of equilibrium. They might examine, for example, differences in the efficiency of matrix structures without asking how these structures arose in the first place, assuming that all variables have worked themselves out at the point of observation. Other economists study prices, budgets, or organizational turnover as things that fluctuate endlessly, but they evaluate these fluctuations from a single point in time, such as the time when an organization was founded. Or, if the moment of observation is the present, it is understood in terms of actors' decisions about the future, which is discounted because of uncertainty about the future. The underlying assumption here is that people are relatively fixed in incorporating assumptions about the future, because they are seen as being decoupled from social structure. This view is in contrast to the approach taken by institutional and evolutionary theorists who emphasize the social embeddedness of individuals and organizations and who view the dynamics of social structures as a source of change in the actors' evaluation of future possibilities.

Transaction cost economists include variations in social and institutional contexts in their explanation of reasons why organizations adopt a particular form of governance, but they generally do not examine how *changes* in the context *lead* to adaptations in governance forms. Organizations are viewed as a form of governance constructed in response to contextual conditions (e.g., laws, ideologies), but these conditions are generally taken as given and the processes and mechanisms by which actors' interpretations of conditions are translated into organizational forms are not problematized. Adaptation is viewed statically, either as the starting condition from which future consequences emerge, or as the result of previous decisions, rather than as a process of learning, imitating, improvising, and so on. For example, organizations operating in highly uncertain markets are hypothesized to internalize some of the exchanges and to manage them through hierarchical structures, but the temporal process by which internalization happens is generally ignored. Questions related to the length of time it takes to set up appropriate control structures, the sequence of steps that are involved, the interruptions that are caused by social resistance, or the iterations in bargaining with external subcontractors are typically not at the center of attention. Transaction cost economists identify areas *where* adjustments should be made (e.g., incentive systems), but not *how* the adjustments unfold over time.

The lack of concern in organizational economics for processes is related to the assumption that people's interests are largely fixed. Given the premise of individuals as being basically opportunistic, there is little room for theorizing about the adjustment of interests and preferences to changing circumstances, and in social interaction with a dynamic set of exchange partners. Much research in cognitive sociology suggests that behavioral dispositions, including the tendency to behave opportunistically, is conditioned by individuals' past experiences and anticipations of the future, and in light of the social group of which they are a member (Zerubavel, 1997). For example, studies of organizational forms in which close coordination is essential, such as strategic alliances between firms in newly emerging industries (Gulati, 1995) and projects in dynamic high-technology fields (Levesque et al., 2001), have shown that a person's ongoing experience in social interaction is critical to the way interaction unfolds. This suggests that investigators should pay attention to the way constructs related to social interaction, such as opportunism and information asymmetry, evolve over time. The analytical question is not merely *that* people are conditioned by their past experiences but *how* they learn from experience and how learning feeds into their interactions with others.

Some economists, particularly those working in the field of strategic management and entrepreneurship, are more explicit about the temporality of organizational forms. They tend to take an actor-centered view of organizations as entities building "dynamic capabilities" to explore and exploit emerging opportunities in uncertain environments (Ambrosini and Bowman, 2009). However, they often do not distinguish between intentions and results, or they deal with temporality only indirectly, incorporating in their analysis notions of change through the use of proxy variables, such as the age of an organization as an indicator of time-based factors like organizational memory or experience. Organizational age, however, mixes a range of competencies that evolve differently over time, responding to changes in the context in which they are applied.

Economic historians are most keenly interested in the way organizations create the conditions to which they then respond (North, 2005). By studying the influence of past events on present institutions and economic relations, they come close to a central question addressed by evolutionary economists: how do organizational actions produce variations, which then provide choice opportunities for adaptation? Organizations' search for new solutions to gain **competitive advantages** over rivals keeps the system in motion (Nelson, 2006), producing successes but also many failures. Many industries with high founding rates of organizations also have high failure rates, as in the restaurant industry in New York City where about two-thirds of the 3,000 restaurants that open each year are closed within a year (Fine, 2009). It is likely that at least some learning takes place in such populations, thus changing the terms of competition, however slightly. In some industries (e.g., performing arts), organizational failure is immediate if products do not attract a sufficient number of customers and investors. In other industries (e.g., schooling), organizations may linger on for many years before one can speak of failure. For some organizations, performance does not improve with age; in a sense, they are "permanently failing" (Meyer and Zucker, 1989). They underperform continuously but are kept alive, for example, by the owner's supportive family or with help from the local community, based on perceptions regarding their social value. The educational sector is an example of an environment where institutional norms are particularly strong and consumers are prepared to accept a high level of economic inefficiency because schools, counseling centers, daycare centers, and other organizations meet important societal expectations or because it is difficult to obtain reliable evidence of their performance. In strongly institutionalized organizations, such as religious schools, continued economic underperformance creates the paradoxical situation where the solution – closing down those programs that cost more than the value they generate – would violate the very mission of the organization.

4.2 Time and institutions

For institutional theorists, temporality is an issue at all levels of analysis. At the level of ideas, beliefs regarding, say, the scarcity of time or the significance of history are reproduced through institutions that either reinforce or reframe understandings (Campbell, 1998). For example, the ideas which police officers in East Berlin held regarding their role in a politically divided city changed radically after the fall of the Berlin Wall, leading to conflicts in their relations with their new colleagues from the western part of the city and creating mental confusion regarding the separation between work time and private time (Glaeser, 2000). The confrontation with a different ideology (e.g., regarding the importance of self-initiative and personal responsibility), exposure to a different bureaucratic regime, and participation in unfamiliar organizational rituals all had an impact on the formation process of new police officer identities. Ideas do not simply appear and diffuse; they are initiated, translated, and promoted by individuals and groups. People do not simply replicate old ideas but engage with them reflexively, adapt them to current circumstances, and combine them with different ideas from other domains (Czarniawska, 2004). The result of translation may be a radical break from the familiar "pace of life" and from the accustomed meaning of temporal categories like work holidays or commemoration days. After German reunification, for example, East German workers had to learn to construct new meanings for traditional holidays, such as International Labor Day, from a day of political speeches and massive military parades to a day for leisure and the family (Glaeser, 2000).

At the organizational level, ideas may be firmly embedded in routines, such as the student registration system of college residences (Feldman, 2000), or in innovations like security installations in schools (Gill et al., 1998), but the long-term outcomes of routines and innovations are difficult to predict in changing environments. If the introduction of weapon detectors in schools is the product of idiosyncratic understandings and motives of school principals or school board members, the rules of maintaining safety and security will likely be subject to change in organizations with personnel turnover and volatile stakeholder involvement. Alternatively, routines and innovations may become a taken-for-granted feature of organizational structure, removed in time from the individuals who first introduced them, if they are interpreted as "best practice" or part of the organization's culture. Studying the temporal process by which rules and routines are reproduced can reveal a range of possible outcomes, including the roads *not* taken. Temporally sensitive research designs can also show how organizations produce the context to which they then react. For example, law firms create for themselves a homogeneous and stable resource environment when they recruit new employees from the same law school that the older associates attended. Given this environment, they then use less elaborate control systems, subjecting the new recruits to fewer performance evaluations and training interventions during the first few years than they otherwise would (Tolbert, 1988).

At the level of organizational fields, institutional variations in logics and value systems are most visible when studied over periods of time long enough to show an evolutionary pattern. Fundamental changes in the health care system in many countries over the last few decades provide an example of the impact of both long-term societal-level transformations in the constellation of different institutional logics (e.g., quality of health care, equity in access to health care, cost containment) and short-term local variations in the implementation of innovations with respect to the delivery and evaluation of health care (Dent, 2003). The timing of institutional changes, such as governments introducing public health insurance schemes before or after a large portion of the public is enrolled in private insurance plans, may be more important for the path of future development than the substance of these changes (Hacker, 1998). Given the staggering costs of delivering high-quality health care, institutional arrangements regarding insurance schemes and universal access are difficult to change once they are in place. On the other hand, institutional structures and logics are not givens, but are the result of negotiations between actors with different interests and power. For example, the rise of "nouvelle cuisine" in France since the 1970s has been accompanied by changes in institutional logics related to work rules (e.g., preparing and presenting food dishes) and organizational strategies (e.g., promoting authenticity and originality) (Rao et al., 2005). Institutional changes were pushed by powerful and publicly visible chefs, endorsed by culinary magazines and journalists, and enforced by a governance system composed of interest associations and training schools. A temporal perspective highlights the variabilities and discontinuities in the evolution of institutions and institutional logics.

4.3 Time and evolution

The central goal of theorists working within an evolutionary framework is to investigate the processes and mechanisms of organizational change, in environments characterized by more or less diversity in resource requirements and competitive pressure. The most insightful studies take the long view, exploring the origins and outcomes of current phenomena, as well as all the steps, turns, and interruptions that lie on the path between origin and result. In cases where causal processes connect events in different periods, one could not explain, for example, why a particular organizational form persists despite changes in the environment, if one were to study only the current context. For instance, government policies in France towards the Paris Opera, as well as the organizational design of the Paris Opera, have been influenced for over three hundred years by organizational models of 17th-century French society (Johnson, 2007). Organizations may retain the structures created at the time they were founded but not because these structures maximize efficiency. Technically or economically inferior forms may survive over extended periods because they are reproduced by social traditions or are reinforced by powerful individuals with an interest in their maintenance. The history of the funeral services industry in the United States, for example, shows how the owners of funeral establishments referred to professionalism as a set of standards regarding expertise and self-regulation to ward off government regulation. This helped them pre-empt environmental selection and contributed to the maintenance of a rather homogeneous and stable organizational population (Torres, 1988).

Historical legacies can have an enormous influence on the character of an organization long after the organization was founded. However, there can be large differences in timescales in the evolution of different organizational phenomena or populations at different levels, which constitutes a problem for comparative analysis. At the level of ideas (e.g., in brainstorming projects), the timescale may be as short as a few hours for the composition of idea populations to undergo significant change (Paulus and Yang, 2000). By contrast, populations of organizations (e.g., interest associations) evolve along timescales involving years and decades (Aldrich et al., 1994). In cases where entities (e.g., rules) are embedded in higher-level entities that act as carriers (e.g., work groups), one needs to decide if one should trace the evolution of individual units independent from or together with the evolution of their carriers. At the level of organizations and populations, the relevant timescale is a function of the interplay between organizational form and environmental conditions, as well as the mechanisms connecting organization and environment. It makes a difference if organizational transformations occur, for instance, through change in actions, meanings, or the demography of actors. Actions may take less time to evolve than meanings, and changes in the demographic distribution of actors may accelerate changes in actions more than they affect changes in meanings. The state of the environment makes a difference as well. Institutionally highly regulated environments produce greater constraints on organizations' ability to change course quickly than more open environments.

From a research perspective, it may be difficult to define the temporal boundary of events – or decisions, crises, or some other unit driving evolution. What constitutes an event is an important definitional issue for evolutionary analysis which cannot be taken for granted, given that events may be interpreted differently by the subjects being studied. In the absence of fine-grained historical data, empirical studies often work with the assumption of time-invariant effects of events on transition rates in the organizational phenomenon in question. Investigators incorporate in their models "period effects" or annual "time series," but it is a heroic assumption to believe that what happens between "periods" or "years" is clearly distinct from what happens within them, or that the periods defined for research purposes are of equal duration in terms of the actual processes and causal effects. Events occurring in one period may flow into the next period, and overlapping events may be connected through sequences that move at different speeds. One cannot really assume, for instance, that the causal relationship between fiscal policy in Greece and economic growth in that country was the same in 1995 and 2005 without simultaneously assuming that there has been no change in the institutional and macro-economic context between these years, or that contextual changes had no effect on the causal relationship (Spanou, 2008). New exogenous events, fluid membership in decision-making bodies, different feedback cycles, and so on can dramatically alter the pace and direction of evolutionary change in the system under investigation.

Some events and conditions are important only in the early history of an organizational population, while others have relevance only in later phases of population evolution. One might expect, for example, that the number of competitors in a population matters for the social acceptability of a given organizational form more during the early development of the population, when market needs are poorly defined and resources are limited (Zucker, 1989). During the early history of an industry, competitors not only pose threats to newly founded organizations; they also provide role models for successful organizing and reputation building. Population expansion in a new industry may be interpreted by potential organizational founders as a sign that the organizational form used in the population is effective, so they will be more inclined to establish an organization with that form. At later stages, however, when there are many direct competitors, further population growth may signal that the population is reaching the environment's capacity limits (Hannan and Freeman, 1989). The nature and effects of competition thus change over the course of a population's evolution. The early growth of the automobile industry, for example, was heavily dependent on the development of intricate networks of automobile dealers, parts suppliers, and insurance companies (Hannan, 1997). The structure of these networks affected the terms on which resources were available to automobile producers, also helping them gain institutional standing. Once these networks were institutionalized and consumers and investors had accepted the industry as a legitimate player in society, they lost importance for the social standing of the industry. Changes in environmental conditions thus determine not only the terms on which material resources are available for exploitation; they can also affect the meaning of organization–environment relations. A joint venture between two firms may be a "marriage of convenience" at the time of initiation. Several years after successful cooperation it may be a "marriage of love" – based on the evolutionary principle of reinforcement: whatever is successful is likely to be repeated – but, even happy marriages can end in disaster further down the road. The high failure rates of joint ventures are testament to the fact that even successful collaborations can end in an acrimonious divorce, given changes in organizational actors and external circumstances. The challenge for evolutionary analysis is to identify the relevant temporal window of observation to uncover the causal mechanisms involved in such developments.

5. Conclusion

Time and timing are obviously important considerations for managers who want to make effective decisions in fast-paced environments. In competitive environments, "survival of the fittest" often means "survival of the fastest." Aided by new technologies in communication, and symbolized by popular buzzwords (e.g., "just-in-time," "quick-fix"), organizations are devising strategies and structures that they hope will help them compete on the basis of speed. Temporally sensitive organizational forms include short-term employment arrangements, fixed-term supply contracts, and flexible work assignments, with implications for the careers of individuals, the social capital of organizations, and the integration of organizations into the wider social community, as will be discussed in Chapter 8. Temporality is experienced in organizations in that current events have a history which conditions how they are interpreted in the present and how they shape expectations for the future. The concept of temporality draws attention to the fact that many organizational phenomena arise not because they were planned intentionally, but because they *emerged* out of pre-existing conditions. The outcomes of actions depend not only on their substance but also on the way they unfold over time.

However, temporality means more than the idea that history matters. "Taking time seriously" requires that scholars embrace the messiness of temporal processes, with all the nuances in the sequencing of events, the pacing of steps, and the discontinuities in cycles, phases, and rhythms. Researchers using a temporal lens on organizational phenomena know this all too well when devising dynamic research designs to capture these nuances. The problem in many cases is that the fine-grained data necessary for exploring temporal processes are simply not available. Arguments about path dependence, for example, require data not just about associations between variables (e.g., new actors, problems, and choice opportunities) but also about associations between events (e.g., sequence). Adopting a temporal lens raises a number of thorny issues regarding methodological questions such as the determination of the appropriate time frame for analysis. Different social processes unfold at different speeds, for example because they occur on different scales or are driven by different mechanisms. Strategic change in a university may take a decade, involving quarrels over scarce resources, whereas a change in faculty recruitment procedures in a university department may be accomplished within a single year. The problem, from a methodological perspective, is that the question of what constitutes the correct time frame for analysis may depend on how temporal processes actually unfold in a particular instance, which cannot always be determined *a priori* but requires historical *hindsight*. This is then an ontological as well as an epistemological problem. It is an ontological problem because researchers need to decide what exists out there that they want to know about. It is an epistemological problem because they need to consider how to go about acquiring that knowledge. This makes it all the more important to develop strong theoretical arguments about what kinds of temporal processes are to be expected in different organizational settings. Once we agree that all behavior is affected by the temporal context in which it is embedded, studying the sequencing, pacing, and duration of events becomes central to our understanding of organizations as a whole, in all aspects of organizational economics, institutions, and evolution.

Recommended further reading

Abbott, A. (2001) *Time Matters: On Theory and Method.* Chicago, IL: University of Chicago Press.
A critical review of methodological approaches that do and do not capture the temporal processes in concepts fundamental to social systems.

Flaherty, M. (2011) *The Textures of Time: Agency and Temporal Experience.* Philadelphia, PA: Temple University Press.
Using agency theory, the author discusses how individuals perceive and adjust their perceptions and use of time, to purposefully regulate an event's passage through time.

Greif, A. (2006) *Institutions and the Path to the Modern Economy: Lessons from Medieval Trade*. Cambridge: Cambridge University Press.

An analysis of institutions as the fundamental drivers of economic history, restricting the range of options within which organizations construct forms of governance.

Kern, S. (2004) *A Cultural History of Causality*. Princeton, NJ: Princeton University Press.

An insightful analysis of the way novelists, from the Victorian era to modern times, have placed causality in a temporal process to explain how complexity, specificity, uncertainty, and probability unfold.

 ■ **Practice questions for Anecdote 5.1**

1   What explains Luciana's apparently relaxed attitude in this situation?

2   What could Luciana do to solve her problematic relationship with Heather?

3   If you were one of the students in this class, how would you act?

6

Structure and Structuring

┌───┐
Learning Objectives

This chapter will:

- Discuss differentiation and integration as joint principles of organizational structure
- Distinguish between formal and informal mechanisms of coordination
- Discuss the key contingency factors of organizational design
└───┘

1. Introduction

Organizations are structured activity systems composed of interdependent individuals whose competencies and preferences normally differ significantly enough to render workflow coordination and social integration problematic. Coordination is a challenge in any situation where there is a division of labor. Without coordination, specialized producers cannot be certain that their activities are properly aligned, that work is not duplicated, or that individuals do not make false claims about their contributions. If there were complete consensus among the actors regarding organizational matters, coordination would occur implicitly simply by virtue of the fact that the individuals view themselves as members of the same entity. The organization's social structure limits participants' choices, but it does not uniquely determine their actions. Full agreement is normally lacking because of differences in people's personality, social background, and cognitive styles. Even when people are highly motivated to align their goals with those of others, they might still fail to understand that coordination is important or might fail to take the necessary steps to minimize coordination problems (Heath and Staudenmayer, 2000).

Structurally speaking, one can characterize an organization as a combination of blocking action and getting action (White, 1992), using structure to achieve coherence and to enable change. A structure exists when three conditions prevail. First, structure involves temporal continuity. An organization is structured if the properties of structure (e.g., rules, policies, positions) endure long enough to be observable. Second, the structural features are independent of the individuals who occupy positions in the structure. For example, the decision-making power of individuals depends on the role they play in relation to other roles in the organization, not on the characteristics of the role occupants. Third, a structure exists if the individuals feel constrained by it in some way. Structural constraints may be perceived as coercive and regulative, or as supportive and enabling.

This chapter discusses organizational structure as both a problem of coordination and a solution to this problem. The problem concerns the rational ordering of actions and beliefs according to specified criteria, following Max Weber's (1924/1947) classic argument that administrative rationality is obtained through specialization, hierarchy, and formalization. The proposition that the social order of organizations is "the best known method of realizing some goal" (Gouldner, 1954: 23) leaves open the questions how is order to be achieved in a particular instance, and who benefits from the existing order? The structure provided by roles, rules, and authority is expected to enhance control and predictability, but it can create its own problems if people use the existing structure to resist change, push their personal interests, or sabotage leadership initiatives. The functional and social integration of an organization is not to be taken for granted but is a problem to be solved (Merton, 1940). Structure does not normally guarantee coordination because the mechanisms of coordination are also situated in people's minds regarding their interpretations of structurally relevant criteria such as reciprocity, commitment, and solidarity in social relations. For structure to enable coordination there must be a shared identity among organization members that is sufficiently strong to channel specialized activities and communication towards collective purposes (Kogut and Zander, 1996).

The next section of this chapter will identify division of labor as a basic principle of social organization at the level of job, organization, and industry. Division of labor creates a need for coordination, which can take various forms, contingent on factors such as the nature of individuals, environments, and tasks. Formal coordination can be enhanced through informal mechanisms, but the effectiveness of informal mechanisms also depends on the strength of shared identity in the organization. Shared identity requires socialization because the goals, meanings, and conventions of an organization are never adopted wholesale when people join the organization. Organizational economists, institutional theorists, and evolutionary theorists address different aspects of these issues.

2. Division of labor

The idea of division of labor has a history going back most prominently to Adam Smith who identified over 200 years ago in *The Wealth of Nations* the advantages of specialization. He argued that the division of labor is limited by the extent of the market, as stages in the production process are spun off into smaller, more specialized units. The reason for this is the increasing returns to specialization, which stem from the efficiency of focusing on narrow tasks rather than entire projects. Later social theorists like Max Weber (1924/1947) and industrial engineers like Frederick Taylor (1911) advocated narrowing the scope of people's jobs so that efficiency could be increased. Emile Durkheim (1893/1949) viewed division of labor as a basis for **organic solidarity** in society, while Georg Simmel (1908/1922/1955) saw in differentiated social structure a source of social identity. Organizational theorists have taken up various aspects of these ideas, viewing division of labor as a general principle at the level of jobs, organizations, industries, and economies.

2.1 Task specialization

Individuals may complete an entire job or specialize in parts of a job. A busboy working in a restaurant clears tables but does not normally also serve at tables. The work of cooks is far less specialized than that of busboys. Cooks prepare meals, supervise assistants, communicate with the serving staff, order supplies, and often participate in managerial decisions concerning the purchase of equipment (Fine, 2009). To the extent that generalists contribute to a wider variety of decisions and communicate with more people in other work domains, they face coordination demands at a higher level in the organization than specialists do at a lower level. The broad scope of generalist work may be useful for accomplishing tasks that require flexibility, as in a dance school where it is difficult to predict demand on any given day, but it may also create inefficiencies if the worker cannot fully attend to the unique demands of specialized activities. Specialization reduces the problem of bounded rationality because individuals can concentrate their attention on a limited range of task components, consistent with their particular abilities and preferences. Time saved comes from specialized training and from not having to change equipment or tasks because of repetition, and work projects benefit from the ability of specialists to contribute their unique skills to the collective effort.

High levels of specialization are normally found in complex jobs requiring different types of difficult-to-learn competencies, as in engineering or film making. Specialization is also a key characteristic of highly structured bureaucratic organizations where the boundaries of authority and responsibility are clearly demarcated. In hospitals, for example, there is differentiation between occupational specialists like orthopedists, pediatricians, X-ray technicians, dieticians, therapists, surgeons, and intensive care nurses. Each job requires focused training and is sanctioned with occupation-specific credentials (e.g., certificates, awards, licenses). Much of this training is acquired prior to the individual entering the organization, while further skill adjustments are made during the individual's tenure in the organization. Medical physicians, for example, go through a period of "residency" in hospitals during which they acquire competencies in various areas before they specialize in a particular area for the remainder of their career (Ku, 2011). Academic workers, by contrast, normally specialize in a particular field long before they begin their first job at a university, where they then further concentrate their research and teaching in line with their specific interests, as opposed to academically trained university administrators who become generalists during the tenure in the organization (Collinson, 2006). Academic researchers may switch to new subject areas during the course of their career, but they rarely move away from the disciplinary area in which they have obtained their basic training.

2.2 Organizational specialization

Above the level of jobs, organizations can be subdivided horizontally into distinct, specialized units at the same level, and vertically into levels of super- and subordination. The degree of horizontal differentiation represents a strategic decision regarding the grouping of related activities, such that efficiencies result from people working together who need to exchange information and resources on a day-to-day basis. Small restaurants have a simple horizontal structure, with the basic horizontal division being between cooking and serving food. Simple structures with low horizontal differentiation can be managed efficiently if the workers are capable of taking on a variety of jobs. In a coffee shop, those who prepare coffee may also staff the cash register and do all of the paperwork on weekends, and those who wait on tables may also take care of cleaning and decorating. Employees are able to switch jobs if necessary because the small size of the organization allows them to communicate directly and learn from each other. On the other hand, physical closeness in a small organization can also lead to disruptions if there is conflict between the employees. In a large and differentiated organization, the people located in different units can work more independently from those in other units, which is efficient as long as the units are coordinated.

The decision to differentiate horizontally may follow different logics, based, for example, on functional, product, or spatial considerations. The functional logic is to differentiate units on the basis of individuals' expertise. In a large art museum, for instance, employees may be grouped by functional skills related to the conservation (e.g., acquisition, restoration) and exhibition (e.g., art shows, special displays) of pieces of art (Lazzeretti, 2004). Product divisions may be based on differences between types of art (e.g., modern, classical), age group of visitors (e.g., children, adults), or service distinctions (e.g., book shop, cafeteria). Art museums may also be differentiated geographically, maintaining facilities in different cities, where program offerings are geared to specific local needs (e.g., reflecting local history or population demography). Large organizations often use several logics of specialization simultaneously. The air force unit in a military organization, for example, differentiates functionally between communications, research and development, logistics, and training. Within the training section, differentiation is between units on a service basis, such as technical services and staff support services. And the geographic distinction is between national operations and overseas "theaters."

2.3 Industrial specialization

A "fundamental principle of economic organization" (Stigler, 1951: 193) refers to the relationship between the size of a market and the distribution of firms of varying sizes in that market. The expansion of output creates scale economies for some firms, reducing the per-unit cost of production, while new specialized firms can emerge to take over the production of intermediate goods and services. Because a growing market means that it becomes profitable for the increasing-returns activities to be spun off to specialist firms, industry expansion creates incentives for larger firms to disintegrate across the value chain of production. The printing industry, for example, has evolved into a system of firms specializing in printing and firms specializing in the production of various inputs (e.g., paper, ink, printing presses). Other industries, such as the early automobile industry, became more rather than less integrated, as output expanded to exploit an expanding market. The problem with the classical argument of industrial division of labor being limited by the extent of the market is that it is essentially an argument about production costs, which says nothing about the costs of managing transactions (Langlois and Robertson, 1989). Whether a growing industry exhibits increasing division of labor depends much on the costs of negotiating and monitoring exchange relations between the interdependent specialized firms. The reason why firms with increasing returns do not grow indefinitely large in their respective product markets is that the production activities are held back by other activities which exhibit decreasing returns. For example, the transaction costs with suppliers of specialized inputs may be so high that it is more efficient to internalize the production of these inputs under one organizational roof. The answer to the "make-or-buy" question turns on the costs of coordination within an organization relative to the costs of coordination in a disintegrated production system.

2.4 The problem of coordination

Coordination needs are especially high in uncertain task environments, placing extra demands on cognition and communication, but people are limited in their ability to collect and process information (March and Simon, 1958). As an alternative to systematic reasoning, they tend to use simple, heuristic rules when drawing inferences from the information available to them, but these rules can lead to serious cognitive distortions (Kahneman, 2011). For example, people are more likely to judge an event as significant if it is easy to recall or if it is the most recent one they have encountered. They are also inclined to evaluate events by hindsight, reconstructing the past as if it caused the things observed in the present. For example, employees may not be surprised when learning that a colleague was dismissed, once they recall that he was "constantly late" at work, even though they cannot remember a single instance when the supervisor made a critical remark about the individual's lateness. People also tend to make decisions based on information drawn from small samples or even a single case. A single observation of a single organization's wrongdoing may be seen as evidence that the entire industry is problematic. By ignoring sampling variability, one may mistake chance events for typical events. People also have a tendency to look for information that confirms rather than challenges what they think they know, relying more on their own private information than new input from others. When looking backwards, the preference is to make prior decisions appear optimal, given the observable outcome. On the whole, people limit their search for information because they find it easier to construct coherent stories when they know little. The use of heuristic judgmental rules, such as those mentioned above, can lead to strong biases in decision-making (Barnes, 1984), with sub-optimal consequences for coordination in situations requiring clarity of analysis (Heath et al., 1998).

A related coordination problem concerns the specificity of information available to individuals with highly specialized skills. A hallmark of specialists is that they are well trained in their own specialty but they know much less about the specialties of others. Specialists are trained to communicate efficiently with their immediate colleagues who have the same technical competencies, understandings of career paths, interpretations of client demands, and so on. Family lawyers may communicate more frequently with family lawyers in other law firms than with their colleagues in their own firm who are specialized in different areas of law. However, even if people who work in the same specialized unit share the same knowledge, they may not *want* to communicate. The reason why organizational designers normally locate people with the same expertise in close physical proximity is to give them an opportunity to observe their colleagues and to minimize the probability of misattributions of goals and motivations (Brown et al., 2005). Organizational economists tend to view arrangements such as shared office space and meeting facilities as a means to minimize agency problems, predicting that people who work in close vicinity are less likely to assume that their exchange partner is motivated to behave opportunistically and to manipulate information. Institutional theorists interpret such arrangements more as an attempt to create spaces in which shared meanings can develop. And evolutionary theorists are interested in the conditions under which shared understandings are reproduced over time. In the situation described in the anecdote below (6.1), there is the possibility that the employees did not communicate with each other because they are rotated between offices and don't spend enough time together to be able to develop a shared understanding of unique customer problems.

ANECDOTE 6.1

When Kathleen started her sightseeing tour of Rome in a subway station, she could not imagine that a minor incident there would lead her to decide to never use that city's public transport system again. She had inserted a 50 euro bill into one of the six ticket machines to purchase a single-fare ticket. The machine did not print the ticket, nor did it return the money. When she explained the situation to the two clerks sitting in the nearby ticket office, and requested a refund of the money she lost, she was greeted with indifference. Despite language difficulties, she was certain that the staff understood her request. They first suggested that she was making a false claim because, as they said, "All machines were in working order this morning." Kathleen protested, insisting that the machine was not in working order when she used it. Shrugging their shoulders, the clerks said that they were responsible for tickets, not ticket machines, but she could come back after three o'clock on that day, when someone would be there to help her. When she returned, a different person sat in the booth, claiming ignorance of what to do with Kathleen's predicament. He said that she should have resolved the problem with his colleagues in the morning, when the incident happened. All that Kathleen could do now is report the problem to the transit authority's office. Kathleen was furious, demanding that she be helped now. After all, this is a ticket office, she said, and what else would staff there do but help people buy tickets. After ten minutes of heated exchange, with Kathleen demanding her

(Continued)

(Continued)

rights as a customer, and the staff person insisting that he was not responsible for ticket machines, he suggested that she come back the following day, at nine o'clock, when he would bring a form for her to fill out.

When Kathleen returned to the ticket booth the next day at the agreed time, a different clerk was present. She explained the situation to the man in the booth as best as she could, but the clerk seemed not to care. "We don't have forms for things like that," he said. Kathleen insisted on being taken seriously, threatening to call the police, but the clerk did not budge. He refused to phone the main office or, as Kathleen pleaded, "anyone who can help me." Finally, the clerk told her that a colleague of his would be there in the afternoon at four o'clock. He might know what to do, he said. Kathleen couldn't believe what she heard, but, once again, she returned to the ticket booth at the specified time but found the office closed.

The following day she went to the ticket booth again, this time more as a matter of principle than in the hope of getting anything accomplished. The two individuals in the booth, new to Kathleen, insisted that all ticket machines had been working and that, as far as they knew, no repairs had been ordered during the last few weeks. Kathleen was speechless and decided to go to the head office in the central train station. There she was asked why she didn't resolve the problem directly at the ticket booth at the station where the incident had occurred. "That's the proper procedure," they told her. All she could do now was to fill out a form, indicating the address of her hotel in Rome. She would then be contacted in due time. Kathleen was furious, yelling at the person that this made "absolutely no sense," as she was obviously a tourist and would be in this city only for three more days before returning home to Australia. The clerk smiled and, shrugging his shoulders, suggested that she "enjoy the ruins" during her last few days "in our ancient city."

Coordination problems can also arise from difficulties in translating the available information. For example, organizations often use strategic plans and public websites as occasions to explain their objectives and missions, but they don't realize that such sites are often understood differently by members and external audiences (Hwang and Suarez, 2005). Marketing specialists may think of websites as places with ceremonial purpose; public relations specialists may see them as platforms for signaling social legitimacy and customers may perceive them as sites providing information about products and services.

Translation requires interpretation, and this involves some difference between the information in the originator's and the translator's heads, if the source and recipient exist in different contexts. For example, the public media in France and the United States report differently about cases of sexual harassment at the workplace because they take their cues from different cultural frameworks (Benson and Saguy, 2005). In the United States media, sexual harassment is generally framed with reference to the importance of equal employment opportunities mediated by a "rational" job market. The French media, by contrast, put more emphasis on the idea of civic solidarity, condemning sexual harassment because it is seen as an abuse of power over dependent workers, violating cultural norms of personal integrity.

When ideas travel across organizational boundaries, their translation may lead to new variation in the application of the ideas. Evolutionary theorists see this as an instance of mutation, which is more likely to occur when ideas are carried by people who have difficulty adapting their perceptions, learning approaches, and communication styles to different environments because they work with highly specialized knowledge. When tasks are subdivided and assigned to specialized units, each group may develop a specialized language, including technical jargon, acronyms, and blueprints, for communicating knowledge. Real estate specialists, for example, may adopt a language denoting optimism and exaggeration, and may then wonder why some home buyers make bad decisions, calling them "emotional," while the disappointed buyers may call the agents "pushy" and "impossible to work with." When problems of translation arise, specialists often escalate their commitment to their own interpretations by increasing the level of abstraction and documentation in their own language, rather than learning a different language (Heath and Staudenmayer, 2000).

Specialists often live in different thought worlds. When looking from the outside in, one may conclude that technical people in an organization never agree on a design, field people cannot look to the long term, and planning people cannot be practical. But looking from the inside out, people think of themselves as being truly concerned with the quality of the product they are dealing with (Dougherty, 1992). From the external perspective of university students, it may appear that professors care more about their research than their students, but from the internal perspective of professors, it may seem that all they ever do is develop teaching objectives and research projects that will enhance student learning. Perceptions can vary greatly, depending on where one stands in relation to the specialized knowledge one has (Dearborn and Simon, 1958), as will be discussed in more detail in Chapter 7.

Coordination problems often arise in situations where power is unequally distributed and there is a chance that people feel misunderstood or manipulated. The problem in such situations is not necessarily that people find it difficult to translate what their discussion partner is saying, but that they think the other person is not trustworthy and purposively distorts information. This may be the case in the anecdote above (6.1), where Kathleen, after several attempts to obtain assistance, eventually stops trusting the clerks. Sensing her helplessness as an outsider to this organization, she becomes suspicious and emotional, which eventually leads to a complete breakdown of the interaction. Agency theorists would interpret this problem as one of agency misattribution, in the sense that individuals stop communicating because they believe that the information they receive is distorted by the other person's attempt to act opportunistically. Organizational specialization may exacerbate the problem, causing the actors to falsely attribute coordination failures to the negative motives of others. When people experience agency misattribution, it is unlikely that they invest much effort in correcting the problem because they believe that the others are not motivated to cooperate.

In summary, division of labor is a fundamental principle in organizational design. All forms of organization involve some degree of specialization because of the efficiency gains of dividing a large job into smaller parts, but specialization also involves costs. The communication problems discussed above relate to differentiation at all levels of action: jobs and projects, organizational groups and units, and industries and production systems. Highly differentiated systems in which tasks are performed by well-trained specialists working in specialized units are not necessarily as efficient as is commonly believed because of the resource investments required to coordinate the different activities in the workflow. The more the system subdivides its work horizontally, the more it must adopt mechanisms to integrate the specialized activities. The discussion below focuses on the integration of organizations, where jobs, projects, and groups must be coordinated, although many of the arguments also apply to larger production systems in which the specialized activities of organizations as a whole need to be coordinated, such as regional production systems and business clusters. The difference between coordination within organizations and between organizations is that it is generally easier to apply hierarchical control structures within organizations than between legally autonomous organizations.

3. Organizational integration

Mirroring social structure in society in general (Dahrendorf, 1959), organizational structure has two faces, differentiation and integration, reflecting the interweaving of division and cohesion, change and stability, and conflict and order. The two faces are mutually constitutive. The idea of integration makes little sense unless it presupposes the existence of different elements, and there can be no conflict between different elements unless this conflict occurs within the context of a coherent system. The concept of organizational integration includes the active aspects of social interaction (social integration) and the institutional side of system relations (system integration) (Lockwood, 1964). Social integration refers to the interactionist process of creating structures for the organization to be able to function as a coherent entity. In universities, for example, administrators, professors, student representatives, and governors are continuously engaged in negotiations regarding the roles in which particular activities should be placed, with consequences for faculty hiring routines, program accreditation, student evaluation, and so forth. Whereas social integration concerns integration *within* systems of interaction, system integration concerns the integration *of* systems of interaction. When we analyze, say, the structure of a work group, we are not only interested in the pattern of social integration, studying who pays attention to whom, who gives advice to whom, and so on. We are also interested in the form of system integration, examining the institutional rules that govern exchange relations and hold the organization together, in an external environment posing diverse constraints. To understand the system integration of a university, one might study, for example, the consequences of particular role distributions (e.g., the inclusion of local community representatives on the governing board) for the social legitimacy of the organization.

While social and system integration are interdependent in construction and consequence, it is possible that in a given organization there is more of one type of integration than of the other. In highly complex social systems, for example, where specialized knowledge is widely distributed among a large number of interdependent actors, systemic elements at the institutional level may become decoupled from social interactionist relations "on the ground." What are seen as system principles (e.g., "market needs," "organizational imperatives") may come to diminish the power of individuals to "make a difference," causing them to reduce their commitment to formal structures and to seek relief in informal social relations instead.

3.1 Formal structure

Formal techniques, such as codified regulations and hierarchical authority relations, are considered structural because their impact on human behavior stems from features of the organization rather than the individual. Weber's (1924/1947) insight was that the formal rationality of modern organizations depends less on the characteristics of any specific individual than on the structural mechanisms by which individuals are tied to the organization. In the Weberian bureaucratic organization, the purpose of formal rules is to limit the superior's scope of authority and to minimize decision arbitrariness in areas where personal discretion can be practiced. Of course, Weber realized that the personal characteristics of people (e.g., charisma, physical appearance) can make a difference even in the most bureaucratically rigid organization. For example, research shows that the governors of companies that have lost a chief executive officer often seek a replacement that is similar to themselves in their personal goals for the organization (Zajac and Westphal, 1996). This effect is greater the more power the governors have relative to the outgoing executive. In some cases it is the desire to get along well with a new executive or board member; in other cases it is the person's connections with other organizations that makes him or her an attractive candidate (Davis et al., 2003).

The impact of structural mechanisms on behavior may be direct and obtrusive, as when people are punished for violating the "women and children first" rule in wartime or natural disaster situations (Carpenter, 2003). Structural mechanisms may also work unobtrusively. People may comply with bureaucratic procedures because they have internalized them and no longer contemplate their origins or functional utility, as when employees choose attire in line with the implicit schemata constituting the organization's culture (Rafaeli et al., 1997). People have private beliefs, feelings, and preferences, but if we want to know how they will behave in a particular situation we need to know what choices are available to them within the formalized and hierarchical structure of an organization.

3.1.1 Formalization

Formalization indicates the degree to which actions and procedures are standardized. An organization is formalized if employees are expected to follow procedures that specify in detail (e.g., written job descriptions or training manuals) how work is to be done. The work performed by hospital cleaning staff, for example, is highly formalized with regard to hygiene. Their working hours are closely controlled as well, so that their activities don't interfere with the work of nursing and medical staff. By contrast, the day-to-day interactions of counselors, social workers, and architects with clients are not highly formalized, although there may be government or insurance regulations (e.g., regarding billing or safety) requiring formal compliance procedures.

Formalization makes organizational behavior more predictable and reduces the need for direct supervision, which enhances efficiency in the execution of jobs. The members of an auto racing pit stop team, for instance, can apply their specialized competencies swiftly, without standing around and arguing about who is supposed to do what. Mutual adjustment in the work process is achieved through extended skill training, aided by team members' sense of collegiality. In the case of professional workers, most of the formal training is obtained before entering the organization. Engineers, architects, physicians, university professors, and psychological counselors spend many years in professional training programs in which they learn about task requirements and techniques for solving them, to the point where they do not need to be supervised closely at the workplace and, instead, are subjected to "output control," for example in the form of commissions or achievement awards. "Process control" measures, which sanction the way workers execute their tasks, are used more often in situations where tasks involve high risk. The work of airline pilots, for example, includes both routine and non-routine activities, and both process and output controls. Pilots obtain much of their ongoing training on the job, using methods (e.g., simulator testing, in-flight evaluations) that are tailored to the specific requirements of the aircraft. The work setting of pilots is an example of extreme organizational calculability and accountability, although there are differences between airline companies and between military and commercial settings in terms of the degree of job autonomy granted to pilots (Rosenbach and Gregory, 1982).

In the airline industry, training and evaluation normally produce the intended results, but there are many other organizational settings where this is not the case, as in the situation described in the above anecdote (6.1). The behavior of the subway station staff does not necessarily indicate that they have not been properly trained. What it does show is that organizational structures are not always so tight that they leave no room for personal discretion, for example in the way employees choose to interact with customers. A subway station is part of a large functionally and spatially differentiated organization, with many spaces in which employees can exercise autonomy (Heath et al., 1999). Larger organizations tend to have higher levels of formalization than small organizations because of the coordination requirements of differentiated structures and because it is problematic to rely on direct supervisory controls across all vertical levels (Blau and Schoenherr, 1971). Still, formalization cannot prevent employees from circumventing rules and policies at least some of the time. Whether employees use the autonomy they have within formal structures "responsibly" (e.g., acting flexibly and innovatively, dealing ethically with clients in emotional distress) and whether they use their discretion to support the organization's goals – these are empirical questions, which cannot be answered *a priori* without knowledge of the subtle interplay of dispositional, behavioral, and structural variables in particular instances.

3.1.2 Hierarchy

The simplest, but not always most effective, mechanism of coordination is direct supervision. In small and non-differentiated organizations it is relatively easy for a single owner or manager to monitor the work of employees personally. The superior is sufficiently close to the employee so that direct communication can take place, and it is likely that the superior has sufficient understanding of the employee's job to be able to evaluate performance. By contrast, in large organizations with a complex division of labor, it is cognitively and physically not possible for a single manager to achieve control through direct oversight. Large organizations, therefore, have hierarchical systems of super- and subordination where different kinds of decisions are made at different levels of authority and responsibility. Hierarchy specifies the lines of authority, detailing who reports to whom and who is accountable for what. General policies are set by the occupants of top-level positions and are communicated to lower-level individuals, following a specified chain of command. In principle, information is made available to individuals at a higher rank before those at a lower rank, and decision-making is decentralized to the level where the appropriate competence exists. In practice, however, those in a subordinate position often feel the need to argue for more transparency in the criteria used by superiors in delegating certain powers – but not others – while those in a superior position often demand more engagement on the part of subordinates within the decision rights given to them.

Hierarchy is commonplace in both human and non-human societies, although human societies tend to prefer more fluid hierarchies, in line with individual differences in ability, disposition, and so on (Nicholson, 2010). Hierarchy is a natural consequence of leadership and it reflects people's need for recognition, status, and power. To the extent that hierarchy rewards abilities and achievements and allows some people to feel more important than others, it has motivating consequences for people who want to rise upwards. Hierarchy has also proven to be an efficient mechanism for coordinating the work of large numbers of people in situations where communication technology is under-developed or physical infrastructure does not allow face-to-face communication, as in the empire-building systems of ancient China and Rome. Hierarchy is considered a basic principle of human organization, despite the potential for political abuse and economic exploitation. Many of the innovations in organizational structure over the years have been aimed at improving the effectiveness of hierarchical structures rather than eliminating hierarchy altogether.

Adding layers of management to better control the flow of information does not solve communication problems between specialists if the managers themselves adopt the language and working style of specialists (Heath and Staudenmayer, 2000). Managers sometimes attempt to improve communication by meeting personally with as many people as possible (e.g., through spot visits in people's offices, or accompanying them to customers), only to discover that this behavior is interpreted by subordinates as interference in activities where managers are seen as having no competence. The result may be the opposite of what managers intended; subordinates may ignore managerial directives, hoard information, or manipulate communication upwards. Restrictions in the flow of information can have serious consequences in highly differentiated organizations, especially under conditions of uncertainty. The fall of the Berlin Wall in a matter of two hours is a classic example of lack of coordination due to miscommunication between people in key positions (government officials, news reporters, border control guards) and in physically separate organizational units (government, press conference, border control facility) (Hertle, 1996). In a politically charged situation, when emotions run high, it is unlikely that individuals exercise personal judgment and initiative fully in line with the formal rules of a bureaucratic organization.

From an economic perspective, hierarchy may be justified when there are task-related reasons to reward people who are willing to take on additional responsibility and to acquire the necessary skills. From an institutional perspective, however, it is not unusual that organizational designers conflate task-related reasons with non-task considerations (Perrow, 1986). People may want to move into higher-level positions for social or political reasons, for example to demonstrate social status or to exercise greater influence. The result is more layers in the hierarchy than are justified by the work to be done or the responsibility to be taken on. Organizations may then end up with an inefficient administrative superstructure that greatly exceeds what is required to coordinate the productive workforce (Freeman, 1973). Too many levels of authority may lead to overlapping responsibilities, causing people to move problems up and down the hierarchy rather than solving them at the level where they arise. However, while this may be resource-inefficient, it may be effective in institutional terms, if overlapping responsibilities are a by-product of satisfying the social demands of important stakeholders with divergent interests. It may also produce evolutionary benefits, if resource redundancy improves adaptability in volatile environments. A central idea in democratic societies is that the different logics, expectations, and functions of organizations in different domains "naturally" lead to differentiated structures. To the extent that economic problems cannot be solved only economically, scientific problems cannot be managed only on the basis of scientific criteria, and political problems reach for solutions into other domains as well, the integration of differentiated structures will lead to decision areas that include redundancies and overlapping responsibilities. Many school systems have a bloated administrative structure for exactly these institutional reasons (Meyer, Scott, and Strang, 1994b).

Hierarchical structures are often supplemented by temporary arrangements to achieve more flexibility in coordination, such as special liaison positions for "integrating managers" or temporary taskforces to handle coordination needs as they arise. The intention is to improve cross-functional or cross-product communication, speed up decision-making, identify customized responses to problems as they emerge, and build competence to translate the specialized understandings of people in different units. In practice, however, integrating mechanisms are often the first to be dismantled when organizations experience a crisis and adaptability is required (Yu et al., 2005). In crisis situations, organizations often increase rather than decrease the level of formalization and centralization (Staber and Sydow, 2002), tightening resource belts and behaving "as if complex, volatile, and interrelated environments are in fact simple, static and unrelated" (Bozeman and Slusher, 1979: 346). Integrating structures are often considered more expendable because they are positioned between rather than within organizational units. The paradox is that the individuals who occupy integrating roles have precisely the broad, overarching knowledge that is valuable for organizations in need of new solutions to problems that cannot be managed within different units in a differentiated structure. The study reported below (Research Brief 6.1) suggests that "lean and mean" strategies can seriously upset an organization's social fabric, if the individuals who hold a central, overarching position in the organization's social structure leave the organization and take with them not only information about tasks but also knowledge about how to connect people with specialized skills (Shaw et al., 2005). Rationalizing strategies, which are intended to increase organizational efficiency, may end up destroying any short-term efficiency gains.

RESEARCH BRIEF 6.1

Labor turnover has long been an important subject in organizational research. Some studies address the economic costs to an organization of losing human capital owing to labor turnover; others investigate the impact on the social structure of the organization. One argument is that turnover has negative consequences for organizational performance because it upsets the organization's social fabric. The study by Shaw et al. (2005) found that declines in organizational performance can be significant, depending on the structure of social relations through which information flows.

The authors of this study examined the relationships between employee turnover, organizational performance, and social relations in a population of organizations in an upscale restaurant chain in the United States. Using data from employee questionnaire surveys, company turnover records, restaurant sales, and supervisor performance evaluations, the researchers examined the effects of losses in "social capital," which they defined as the collective benefits produced by a dense social structure. Individuals who are embedded in a dense social structure communicate with each other frequently and intensely, to exchange information and resources, as needed. The findings of this study indicate that the loss of employees had disruptive consequences for the organizations' social structure, with implications for organizational performance. Performance declines were especially serious in those cases where the employees who left the organization occupied a "bridging" position in the communication network. These individuals functioned as boundary spanners, connecting individuals in different organizational units who would otherwise not be connected.

While these findings are strong and statistically robust, they are limited by the fact that the investigators examined only a single population of organizations. Without comparative data it is not possible to generalize the findings to organizations in other industries using different technologies, employing different skills, and dealing with different institutional requirements. One may surmise, however, that the estimated effects of social capital loss will likely be even stronger in organizations that process highly complex and variable knowledge, such as engineering firms or law firms. To the extent that such organizations place a premium on efficient communication and close coordination between all employees, labor turnover may have highly disruptive consequences. A further limitation of this study is that the researchers were not able to study all of the employees in the sampled organizations. If one is interested in examining the effects of social relations, one needs to know as much as possible about all members of the network. The exclusion of even a small number of participants can seriously bias the results of a study, especially if these individuals hold a critical position in the network.

3.1.3 Structural contingencies

A basic principle of organizational design is that activities should be grouped into units so as to optimize the trade-offs between the need to specialize and the need to coordinate. The appropriate balance of differentiation and integration is not to be determined as if the organization were an immutable object which "does this" or "does that." Rather, the trade-offs need to be approached with a view to the organization conceptualized as a precarious set of relations entered into by individuals who differ in competencies, dispositions, and interests. The organization is an evolving organism whose form varies according to the prevailing circumstances, referred to as "structural contingencies" (Donaldson, 1996). Contingency factors create uncertainty for the organization by imposing situation-specific demands on people to collect, interpret, and process information (Daft and Lengel, 1986). A long stream of research has identified three contingency factors considered important in most situations: the nature of individuals, the state of the environment, and the complexity and volatility of tasks. The implications of these contingencies for organizational structure are summarized in Table 6.1.

Human nature. The decisions of organization designers regarding organizational structure are informed, albeit often implicitly, by their assumptions about human nature. For example, if designers believe that people are by nature irresponsible, lazy, and unwilling to take initiative, they are more inclined to develop stringent rules, standard operating procedures, and tall hierarchies than if they believe that people are capable of making wise decisions and are willing to act in the best interest of the organization. Many of the innovations in human resource management regarding job enrichment, employee empowerment, and teamwork can be traced back to the recommendation coming out of the **Human Relations** movement in the 1960s that jobs should be designed on the premise that most people are ambitious and responsible

Table 6.1 Contingency situations and structure

Contingency	Defining characteristics	Structural implications
Professionalism Conceptual work Extensive training	Self-regulation High level of responsibility and accountability	Few formal rules Decision-making discretion Coordination by mutual adjustment
Environmental uncertainty	Variable stakeholder demands Volatile, difficult-to-predict markets	Specialization and fragmentation Decentralized decision-making Variable boundary-spanning roles
Task complexity Task volatility	Unique, non-recurring problems Many exceptions Low problem analyzability	Decentralized decision-making Information sharing across functions Face-to-face communication

(McGregor, 1960). Research, however, shows that there are many organizational situations where it is unrealistic to assume that people will show "due diligence" in handling their own responsibilities (Griffin and O'Leary-Kelly, 2004). People differ in their preferences for intrinsic and extrinsic rewards, their predisposition to behave altruistically or self-interestedly, and their appreciation of job structures granting them decision-making autonomy. Different subway station staff members than those described in the above anecdote (6.1) might have displayed different behaviors towards this customer.

While personal preferences and dispositions are important, human behavior is also affected by the existing opportunity structure. When university lecturers are dissatisfied with their work situation, they may be able to choose between protest and leaving the organization, whereas disgruntled sailors on ships at sea can only remain silent or engage in mutiny. The interplay of variations in human psychology and in opportunity structure is manifested, for instance, in the culture of an organization. The web of values, personalities, and orientations shapes and is shaped by organizational structure in ways that can lead to highly idiosyncratic evolutionary paths for organizations. Culture does not exist in the abstract; rather, it is created, maintained, and transformed by human agents who interpret and apply meanings to the ever-changing circumstances in their work lives. The structural consequences of turnover in the workforce (see Research Brief 6.1) can thus have consequences for the organization's culture as well, rather than only for the individual participants.

Environmental uncertainty. Environmental uncertainty puts a premium on organizational flexibility, calling for decentralized structures and low formalization to facilitate quick decision-making and mutual adjustment within and between organizational units. Most restaurants, for example, operate in highly volatile and intensely competitive market environments, requiring high levels of organizational adaptability (Fine, 2009). They depend on a steady flow of customers, many of whom have fickle tastes, don't leave tips, or display negative behavior towards the serving staff. Perfect timing is essential when hiring labor, serving food, and ordering supplies, which require structures that permit social relations to evolve in line with emerging needs. Organizational procedures are more standardized in industries with more certain environments. In the airline industry, for example, government regulations concerning safety change infrequently and slowly, forcing airlines to maintain an extensive catalogue of formal procedures regarding flight operations, aircraft refueling, and so on. In a military environment, organizations reduce uncertainties (e.g., risk of combat) through stringent monitoring structures. Air force organizations use detailed post-flight reviews and performance evaluations to detect errors and identify potential remedies; and rule infractions are followed by formal disciplinary action (Ron et al., 2006). For commercial airlines, intense international competition necessitates structural responses which may include close controls over the work process of lower-level employees. Flight attendants are normally subject to stringent formal rules regarding passenger service. If they have any discretion in their work behavior, for example in their dealings with passengers with special needs, it is only within the framework of rules set by management regarding physical appearance, behavioral demeanor, and safety (Tyler and Abbott, 1998).

The nature of tasks. Work tasks vary in complexity, even in a small organization, like a fitness center, where clients with special needs demand personalized attention, whereas routine procedures are used to maintain the exercise equipment. Task complexity can be characterized along two dimensions: whether there are *exceptions* to task requirements, and whether it is difficult to *analyze* the problems inherent in tasks (Perrow, 1967). Some jobs involve many exceptions and novel challenges related to, for example, changes in technology or customer preferences. Most of the activities in a takeaway pizza shop are routine because the same requirements repeat themselves with each customer, such as taking phone orders and preparing pizzas according to a fixed menu. Independent of exceptions, tasks also vary in the analyzability of requirements. Cleaning the facilities in a pizza shop and delivery to customers are activities that can be learned easily, whereas the development of new business strategies in this competitive industry involves problem solving with limited information about market opportunities.

The more task exceptions there are, and the more difficult it is to analyze task requirements, the more structural flexibility is called for. University lecturers, for example, insist on organizational structures that give them a great deal of personal freedom in their interactions with colleagues and students (Ogbonna and Harris, 2004). Artists and craftspeople want to create their own structures that allow them to work with tools and along timelines they control personally (Sennett, 2008). People are considered creative if they are able to make the most with limited resources, and this normally requires autonomy in decision-making. The vehicle shown in Exhibit 6.1 may appear to the external observer as utterly chaotic and largely non-operational, but the builder of this vehicle may insist on its functionality for purposes and road conditions for which he or she assembled this contraption, given limited resources. Building a vehicle constitutes a complex task for individuals working on their own, requiring personal judgment, initiative, and the acceptance of responsibility. Similarly, when seeing a student, a university lecturer needs personal discretion to explain the evaluation of a complex assignment. When seeing a patient, a psychiatrist needs discretion to determine what treatment should be applied. There is, however, also a larger institutional context which the employing organization needs to observe and which delimits job autonomy on the shop floor. Universities need to comply with human rights and employment legislation, and mental clinics need to follow insurance and workplace safety legislation.

Exhibit 6.1

3.2 Informal structure

The purpose of structural mechanisms of coordination is to minimize behavioral variations through standardization. Structural techniques are more effective in relatively simple and stable environments, when tasks are clear and performance outcomes are measurable, and when it is unlikely that employees will sabotage the organization's control system. When these conditions do not exist, social and cultural controls in the form of shared values, norms, and beliefs become more important. Studies such as the one reported in the research brief above (6.1) highlight the role of informal structures, not only for the flow of information but also for diffusing group norms and values. Social controls emerge from the everyday social interactions of organizational members; they include peer pressure, the application of shame, and the threat of ostracism. Social control is most powerful when individuals' self-concept is closely aligned with the collective identity of the group to which they belong.

3.2.1 Shared identity

The identity of individuals reflects their personal values and beliefs, but it is also implicated in how they believe they are seen by salient *others* (people whose expectations they value most), thus turning their self-concept into a *social* identity (Jenkins, 2004). To the extent that organizational participants are embedded in different kinds of social structures (Granovetter, 1985), such as workplace, residential neighborhood, or professional community, they have multiple identities, which may complement or conflict with one other, with implications for organizational integration and coordination. Identities are multiple and changing, and products of psychological dispositions and structural circumstances. An employee may have an occupational (e.g., chemist) and a psychological identity (e.g., competitive) at the same time that she may have a social (e.g., working mother) and national identity (e.g., Argentinian). Perceptions matter as well. Salespeople, for example, may be labeled by customers as something (e.g., extroverted, pushy) other than what they are or are expected to be by their organization's management (Schweingruber and Berns, 2005). Inconsistent identity perceptions have to be reconciled if the individual is to achieve a coherent social identity in an organizational context. That such reconciliation is deeply problematic in any social setting is the stuff of many novels in which actors, words, events, emotions, and contexts are thrown up against their opposites in the same story (Roth, 1986).

Social identity is constructed through processes of categorization, comparison, and identification (Jenkins, 2004). Social categories are divisions of the social world into distinct perceptual classes which provide individuals with a systematic means of defining themselves and others. For example, some employees of a marketing organization may think of themselves as artists pursuing "art for art's sake," whereas others see themselves as business entrepreneurs with a view mainly to profitability. Individuals give meaning to identity by highlighting the similarities within categories and the differences between them. They use identity distinctions as a basis for comparison with others, when developing expertise, establishing authority, identifying career opportunities, and so on. Categorical distinctions are activated in some situations, as when managers are challenged by subordinates asking for more decision-making power. In other situations, distinctions are taken for granted, as in the case of film actors retaining familiar role characters. "Typecasting" helps performers in film and theater build a robust reputation with which they can survive in the labor market (Zuckerman et al., 2003). Identity comparisons also provide status-enhancement benefits. For professional workers, for example, it is important to be perceived by clients as individuals who "deserve" employment in jobs with high levels of responsibility and remuneration because they have survived lengthy training programs and highly competitive selection processes (Thomas and Hewitt, 2011). When people use identity comparisons to enhance their self-esteem, they tend to identify most strongly with the group that is regarded favorably by outsiders. Some may identify so closely with a particular organization that they take on its identity wholesale, as in religious sects where shared identity is reinforced through secrecy and esotericism as a basis for distinction (Bennett, 2006).

Identity diversity at the individual level translates into identity diversity at the organizational level, but not perfectly so (Montgomery and Oliver, 2007).

Even small organizations are rarely homogeneous entities to the point where one can say that all members share the same single identity. Individuals differ, for example, in their attachment to groups outside the organization and in their preferences with respect to the incentives to commit themselves to the organization. People have a felt need to belong to a group, but they also have a need for autonomy. Some organizations, such as prisons and mental asylums, may act like "total institutions" (Goffman, 1961) by exercising control over their members' identification, but even these organizations leave some areas vacant where individuals can maintain some measure of personal identity. While some degree of shared identity is essential to the social and system integration of an organization, it can never guarantee integration. It can guide people's behavior, but it cannot control it (Kogut and Zander, 1996). As people are socialized into an organization, they learn more and more of the organization's expectations, but they never learn them all and they rarely comply with everything they have learned (Griffin and O'Leary-Kelly, 2004). The implicit control provided by shared identity is not a perfect substitute for the more obtrusive controls achieved through formalization and hierarchy.

3.2.2 Socialization

Shared identity is not a given, not even in a team of similar and like-minded individuals. Common understandings evolve over time and they must be nurtured continually to retain their strength. Socialization is a mechanism organizations use to standardize behavior by instructing their members what is expected of them and what is likely to happen if they deviate from expectations. It is also a mechanism to maintain an integrated culture in the face of membership turnover (Carroll and Harrison, 1991) by increasing mutual awareness of each other and by enhancing a sense of **sociality**. Successful socialization can bring substantial rewards to newcomers, co-workers, and the organization at large, but it rarely leads to a single shared identity (Slaughter and Zickar, 2006).

Some of the socialization may occur unobtrusively, as individuals observe and imitate what others are saying and doing. Other socialization techniques are more obtrusive, in the form of explicit mentoring, initiation rites, or some other means of orientation. Socialization is usually most visible and powerful when new members enter an organization. Organizations that expect their members to strongly identify with organizational goals, such as the army or police, often put their newly recruited employees through formal induction programs. When socialization occurs more informally, effectiveness is often a matter of luck and chance, dependent on the personal characteristics of the colleagues with whom the individual happens to work.

Evolutionary theorists draw attention to the adaptive value of variation caused by incomplete or faulty socialization techniques. Socialization creates the possibility of identity transformations, as people move between organizations and become exposed to different challenges and constraints. Even professional workers who have undergone lengthy training in a specific area of expertise and have a strong commitment to their job may experience identity changes during career transitions (Ibarra, 1999). Socialization is normally not a unilateral process by which the organization simply imposes standards on the individual. Rather, it is a long period of experimentation, as the individuals devise and test new images of themselves in light of organizational expectations and feedback from superiors and colleagues. The outcome may not be the reproduction of existing "old boy networks" but the creation of new opportunity structures. The question in evolutionary analysis is: What are the selective pressures which enhanced the relative "fitness" of socialization practices?

Organizational economists explain socialization as a process during which individuals incorporate identity in their utility set, which they then use to evaluate various incentives as a basis for committing to the organization (Akerlof and Kranton, 2005). For example, a well-socialized worker who identifies closely with the employer will accept a smaller wage differential to expend more effort at work. It may be relatively inexpensive for an organization to influence a person's identity in support of the organization's goals if the person has chosen membership in the organization for intrinsic reasons, as when college students join a fraternity or sorority club. When intrinsic motivations are lacking, socialization can turn into a major cost factor for the organization, as in prison organizations and authoritarian political regimes.

For institutional theorists, the economic costs of different socialization techniques are related to the meanings that organizational participants assign to them, and these may vary widely across contexts. For example, the traditions and rituals of the "dining experience" at Cambridge University serve to reinforce meanings that are connected to social class and social mobility (Dacin et al., 2010). "Orientation week" at state universities in the United States may be seen more as a mechanism to enhance academic achievement than to develop a sustainable "college identity" (Sanchez et al., 2006). Evolutionary theorists interpret such rituals and programs as a mechanism by which organizations retain selected cultural variants and reproduce existing meanings.

4. Theoretical perspectives on organizational structure

A central question in organizational theory concerns the origins and performance outcomes of differences in organizational structure. Theorists working from different perspectives emphasize different features of structure, examine different processes of structuring, and offer distinct insights into the conditions under which structural arrangements produce intended outcomes.

4.1 Organizational economics

Organizational economists view structure as an important element of calculative rationality. For agency theorists, the central question turns on the problem of safeguarding the interests of owners who are not directly involved in the management of the organization. A hierarchical distribution of authority, legitimated on the basis of property rights and combined with an incentive structure that rewards managers (and other employees) for acting in the best interest of owners, is considered the main mechanism for ensuring efficient control. Transaction cost economists add the argument that costs are involved in constructing and maintaining a hierarchy, creating and adapting the incentive system to changing circumstances, and negotiating and enforcing contracts. Organizations that outsource peripheral activities and retain core functions can achieve greater operational flexibility only if the transaction costs within the organization and with external input providers are held in check. Opportunism, to the extent that it exists, is not automatically eliminated through hierarchical controls. At best, an incentive system can be designed to minimize the associated transaction costs and to ensure that it is ultimately the agents who bear the agency costs – but this requires sufficient competition in labor and capital markets (Jensen and Meckling, 1976). Narrow rules and standard operating procedures will rarely be sufficient to create a sense of organizational commitment among the employees, and it may do nothing to instill sociality. Extensive formalization may even trigger employees to voice complaints or to sabotage operations, especially in a situation of asset specificity, when their individual contributions to the organization are indispensiable.

The coordination of exchanges between organizations involves costs, even if the organizations are located in close vicinity and can benefit from agglomeration economies. Territorial proximity may reduce information search costs, but contracts have to be negotiated and supervised, and social relations have to be nurtured with actors in local institutional organizations. Embeddedness in local social structures and traditions may be helpful in this regard, but there is a risk that this creates resource and institutional dependencies which lock the organizations into exchange relations they find difficult to terminate. Long-term commitments, vested interests, and resource investments in mutual exchange reduce organizational flexibility. Transaction cost economists view this as a problem of asset specificity, which requires organizations to adopt safeguarding measures to minimize the likelihood that their exchange partners exploit the lock-in condition (Bell et al., 2009). To the extent that safeguarding measures include formal rules, incentive structures, and legal recourse options, they are themselves subject to transaction and agency costs. Institutions supporting common understandings and creating convergence on expectations help to minimize the costs of safeguarding, but such institutions may take a long time to develop, especially in those cases where they are needed most.

4.2 Institutional theory

From an institutional perspective, the tendency of organizations to become more formalized and structured as they grow older and larger stems partly from the need to comply with legitimation requirements in societies in which particularistic notions of privilege and prejudice are frowned upon. The purpose of hierarchical controls, formal rules, and transparent sanctioning devices is to promote universalistic values (e.g., liberty, free speech, human rights) and to reduce the impact of particularistic values (e.g., extending special favors to one's friends and relatives). Organizational structure is seen as a mechanism to safeguard the universalistic logic of a bureaucratic organization by standardizing and making comparable the value of activities in a given context, while the proliferation of organizations with elaborate formal structures is seen as reflecting and contributing to the rationalization of society (Weber, 1924/1947). Organizations are expected to have structures that are consistent with a modern society's legal order, rules for governing markets, bookkeeping standards, and regulations for protecting private property. Any deviations from such requirements that may arise at the local level of individuals, organizations, or geographic sites are to remain within the broader cultural frame of the society in question (Meyer, Boli, and Thomas, 1994a). Lawyers, for example, may differ in technical specialty and communication style, but they are all expected to comply with universalistic notions of justice and to act within the rational logic of the law. From an institutional perspective, organizations that have formal training programs, comply with official licensing requirements, and hire people based on their technical contributions will be taken more seriously by external constituents, while organizations with an informal and particularistic structure that is inconsistent with the rational order of society are considered suspect.

Building elaborate structures to signal formal rationality may enhance the organization's social legitimacy, but it does not guarantee that scarce resources are allocated efficiently. Organizations that give preferential treatment in hiring and promotion to members of particular social groups may claim to act on the basis of universalistic criteria, by arguing, for example, that hiring like-minded or "familiar" people enhances organizational efficiency and reduces transaction costs in supervision and contract enforcement. This may well be the case in particular instances, but when viewed from a societal perspective, structures and practices intended to maximize organizational efficiency may be in conflict with public goals, such as supporting firms that create employment opportunities for visible minorities or that purchase inputs from economically peripheral regions. Also, even if organizational structures promote universalistic criteria, they may not be accepted by all internal constituents. For example, professional workers in social fields like medicine and education often complain about increasingly rationalized structures undermining their ability to provide social services flexibly and in line with cultural values of fairness and democracy (Ritzer and Walczak, 1988). Many physicians argue that they are controlled by structures that substitute non-human technology for human intervention. In highly rationalized health care systems, they say, the important decisions are made by managers and administrators who have no understanding of the requirements of "good" medical practice. In higher education as well, a frequent argument is that the proliferation of rules and regulations has led to greater organizational inefficiencies, while also creating a factory-like atmosphere in teaching and research (Ogbonna and Harris, 2004).

4.3 Evolutionary theory

From an evolutionary perspective, there is no one best organizational structure. At any given moment in time, there are a variety of organizational forms with a different mix of mechanistic and organic elements, and universalistic and particularistic features. In an open society, the causes of variation in organizational structure are diverse, including planned and unplanned interventions, but they cannot by themselves provide the explanation for what turn out to be their consequences. The success and failure of different structures depend not only on how they came about and who exactly was responsible for the outcome. Ultimately, they depend on the features of the relevant environment, rewarding one or the other structure. The structural variations that help organizations acquire vital resources are selected in a competitive environment and are reproduced through learning, imitation, institutional coercion, social convention, or by some other means. If environmental selection criteria favor, say, rule formalization because there is pressure from labor unions, then adaptable organizations will adopt bureaucratic forms and introduce human resource management systems that include clearly specified job descriptions, classification criteria for compensation, rules for evaluation and promotion, and regulations for dispute resolution (Baron et al., 1988).

The emphasis on environmental selection does not deny the existence of human choice and the power of human agency. Evolutionary theory suggests that variations in organizational structure are induced by human action, but much of this action is blind with respect to consequences (Campbell, 1969). For example, organizations actively and purposively create rules for hiring workers, allocating resources, and interacting with stakeholders, but the number and scope of rules is limited by the needs of the environment. Rules may breed new rules, especially in situations perceived as highly uncertain (Zhou, 1993), but the catalog of rules tends to grow only up to a point beyond which further rules no longer add to efficient problem solution (Schulz, 1998). Evolutionary thinking suggests that rule formalization has adaptive consequences if it helps the organization retain those practices that have turned out to be useful innovations, given conditions in the environment and given organizational goals. If the actual goal of, say, a men's social club were to provide good fellowship and offer leisure, then the rule to discriminate against women applicants for membership would be unjustified, from a social perspective. But if the goal were to promote specific men's interests and build male camaraderie, then the discriminatory rule is effective, from the organization's point of view. In evolutionary language, the membership rule has adaptive consequences for the organization, but not necessarily for society.

5. Conclusion

Despite attempts to "humanize" bureaucratic organizations through "quality of work life" schemes, such as job enrichment designs, employee empowerment programs, quality circles, and participative management initiatives, there is the continued belief that bureaucratic structures are the most efficient form of organization, under most circumstances. Employees often accept bureaucratic structures as long as they are appropriately designed and implemented to facilitate task performance and to reduce work stress and role ambiguity (Adler and Borys, 1996). In the political-administrative domain, bureaucratic structures are often seen as an effective means to ensure transparency, security, and dependability. Yet, organizations face a fundamental structural dilemma. On the one hand, in a changing environment they need to innovate and create new competencies, and this requires opportunities to specialize. On the other hand, specialization can lead to disruptive fragmentation in the workflow, and this necessitates additional investments in coordination. To improve coordination, organizations may employ socialization techniques that support a shared identity among the members, but such techniques can be expensive and they rarely succeed to the point where shared identity is fully consistent with the goals of the organization. The idea of "connectivity" (Kolb, 2008) characterizes this dilemma metaphorically as a conflict between the "hard-wiring" of formal rules, regulations, and hierarchy, and the "soft" elements of relational trust and informal control.

The uneasy relationship between formal and informal structure also speaks to an issue that is fundamental to our understanding of organizations. Regardless of how well designed organizations are, organizational structures will rarely produce all the intended outcomes, for reasons related to human psychology and unpredictable contingencies. People behave emotionally, interpret things differently, and make choices that are constrained by limited information about the future. For organizational economists this is primarily a question of finding the right governance structure, to minimize the costs associated with bounded rationality. Institutional theorists interpret the potential mismatch between intentions and outcomes as evidence that organizations have an "underlife" that is not always consistent with the values of society at large. And evolutionary theorists see differences in intentions and the resulting conflicts as an important source of variation

with potential adaptive value in changing environments. Knowledge plays a central role in each of these arguments because it is both a source and result of structures that function as the context for and medium through which ideas, beliefs, assumptions, and so on are reproduced. The creation and diffusion of knowledge is an area where structures contribute significantly to an organization's adaptive capacity, as will be discussed in the next chapter.

Recommended further reading

Kilduff, M. and Krackhardt, D. (2008) *Interpersonal Networks in Organizations: Cognition, Personality, Dynamics, and Culture*. New York: Cambridge University Press.
The authors argue that one key to organizational performance lies in the dynamic interplay between the psychology of individuals and the structure of the social networks in which they are embedded.

Kramer, R. and Cook, K. (eds) (2004) *Trust and Distrust in Organizations: Dilemmas and Approaches*. New York: Russell Sage Foundation.
Drawing on arguments from an array of social science disciplines, this collection of papers examines the relationship between trust and hierarchy, and the challenges of building trust.

Ritzer, G. (2008) *The McDonaldization of Society 5*. Los Angeles: Pine Forge Press.
An analysis of the bureaucratic organizational form of fast-food restaurants as representing rationalization, a process impacting deeply on human interaction and identity.

Sennett, R. (2012) *Together: The Rituals, Pleasures and Politics of Cooperation*. New Haven, CT: Yale University Press.
A study of the psychological and social mechanisms of cooperation in societies that value tribalism and competition.

Practice questions for Anecdote 6.1

1 Formulate some rules that would enhance the efficiency and effectiveness of customer relations.

2 Identify the elements that distinguish between formal and informal organizational structure.

3 Describe the relevant task contingencies in this case and discuss how they are reflected in the organization's formal and informal structure.

7

Knowledge and Understanding

Learning Objectives

This chapter will:

- Define knowledge and knowledge-intensive organizations
- Distinguish between different kinds of knowledge and knowledge bases
- Discuss the embeddedness of "knowledge work" in organizational structure

1. Introduction

The academic interest in organizations as "knowledge systems" (Tsoukas and Mylonopoulos, 2003) and sites of "knowledge work" (Blackler, 1995) derives from the insight that knowledge is central to value creation in society. Organizational designers are often advised to treat knowledge as "capital" (Dean and Kretschmer, 2007) and to create structures in which all participants can contribute in some way to knowledge creation (Adler, 2001). Different theoretical perspectives have added useful insights to a knowledge-based view of organizations, by exploring questions related to human cognition, knowledge structures, and resource contexts (Grant, 1996). Interpretivist theorists, for example, note the cognitive biases in people's perceptions, while social identity theorists emphasize the social categorization of perceptions. Learning theorists study the process by which individuals acquire, retain, and transmit knowledge, while resource dependence theorists draw attention to the political implications of unequal distributions of knowledge. The plurality of theoretical perspectives in use has made the study of organizations as knowledge systems a thriving field of inquiry, driven by debates about the nature of knowledge, the location of knowledge, and the conditions under which knowledge promotes or constrains goal achievement (Swidler and Arditi, 1994).

Knowledge is a deeply problematic concept, with the main debates concerning the relationship between information, understanding, and context, as well as the relationship between individual and collective knowledge. If, for example, knowledge consists of distinct pieces of information, it can be disassembled and reconnected in different contexts. People can take the various bits of information they have about a specific job in an organization and apply them to the same job in a different organization. It then does not matter to the quality of the work of an organ player if he or she performs in a circus or in a church. If, however, knowledge is a complex of related pieces of information with different meanings outside the context in which the complex is represented, it requires senders and receivers of information to have a deep understanding also of the context to be able to claim that they possess knowledge. Jobs are then not transferable to other contexts without understanding the situatedness of information and the contextual embeddedness of knowledge.

Scholars also debate the level in the organization at which one should study knowledge. On the one hand, knowledge is constructed from the sense impressions of individuals and is shaped by their idiosyncratic experiences. Understanding knowledge creation in organizations requires that we study the cognitive processes in learning related to perception, attribution, and interpretation. On the other hand, differences in perceptions and learning styles make it difficult to talk about the knowledge of an aggregate, such as an organization, without examining how organizational knowledge emerges out of social interaction. Knowledge is not something one *possesses*. It is not a static entity, and having knowledge says nothing about its *usage*.

This chapter begins with the characterization of knowledge as an entity basic to understanding, with particular reference to what this means in "knowledge-intensive" organizations. This discussion is followed by an analysis of different types of knowledge and their relationship to different knowledge bases in organizations and inter-organizational systems. Next, organizational structure is examined as both enabling and constraining the creation and diffusion of knowledge. Finally, organizational knowledge is explored from an economic, institutional, and evolutionary perspective, noting those areas where scholars offer distinct but also complementary insights.

2. Knowledge-intensive organizations

The concept of knowledge is broader than the information that it contains. Knowledge is the result both of a creative process in the human mind, which includes mental searching, categorizing, and exploring to arrive at new understanding (Hampton, 1998), and of a social interaction process, in which individuals observe and communicate (Gibson, 2005). Individuals are considered "knowledgeable" (Giddens, 1984: 3–5) if they are capable of reflecting on their condition and the actions they take to cope with their condition. Whatever goes on in an organization, it does not happen "behind the backs" of its participants. Although knowledge creation occurs within the structure of the organization, it is not contingent on that structure but constitutive of it. Organizations that want to produce new knowledge require structures with open spaces for individuals to self-reflect and criticize, including reflecting on the structures themselves.

Organizational research has long moved away from the standard economic characterization of knowledge as the end result of a straightforward process of accumulating information (Felin and Hesterly, 2007). For standard neo-classical economists, the idea of a "knowledge competence" is mostly irrelevant. Investors, households, workers, and organizations are assumed to acquire information where they can find it and to absorb new information at virtually no cost, but this characterization avoids the complexities of knowledge production in differentiated social collectivities (Amin and Cohendet, 2004; Argote and Miron-Spektor, 2011). Knowledge is *produced*, not merely replicated or accumulated, in a process involving cognitive as well as social competencies. Organizations are best described as heterogeneous knowledge systems in which individuals with different capacities and motives search for, retrieve, interpret, combine, convert, and store bits of information, transform information into knowledge by applying their own cognitive processes and learning styles, and in the process – typically in interaction with others who have different cognitive capacities and motivations – acquire new learning competencies, which are potentially useful in different temporal and spatial contexts as well. Knowledge is a contestable category, both at the level of individuals and at the collective level of groups and organizations.

Although there has been much talk about "knowledge-intensive" organizations, it is not always clear what is meant by this concept. Do knowledge-intensive organizations consider knowledge their main asset, rather than, say, material facilities or financial capital? Is an organization knowledge-intensive only if every member possesses substantial knowledge, or if the individuals who have knowledge share it with everyone else in the organization? Is knowledge in a knowledge-intensive organization grounded in organizational properties such as rules and job descriptions, as opposed to residing only in people's minds? Do knowledge-intensive organizations work on non-routine tasks requiring knowledge, as opposed to routine task settings requiring merely information? Interviews with members of organizations that are normally considered knowledge-intensive, such as architectural firms, museums, and consulting agencies, often turn up vastly different understandings in this regard (Starbuck, 1992). Some see their organization as being in the business of creating new knowledge, whereas others emphasize the preservation of existing knowledge or focus on the transfer of knowledge to clients who have difficulty interpreting information.

A useful way to conceptualize knowledge intensity is to consider the trade-off between accuracy and generality of knowledge. Some organizations possess highly specialized knowledge that is accurately geared to the demands of a narrow niche environment. Speech therapy clinics, for example, may specialize in the diagnosis and therapy of particular client problems (Bahr and Rosenfeld-Johnson, 2010). In evolutionary terms, their knowledge "fits" specific environmental conditions, and such organizations would probably not do well if they suddenly had to change their client base to one requiring different competencies. Other organizations pursue knowledge with more general applicability. Multimedia firms, for example, may use learning mechanisms that generate adaptive behavior in a wide range of environments composed of different clients and technologies (Grabher, 2004). They may organize production using a transient structure, involving temporary projects staffed with teams that are dissolved upon task completion and are reassembled, in different form, for new tasks. They may acquire new knowledge quickly, but they may also forget it quickly. They may perform well in diverse and volatile environments, but may be outcompeted by rival organizations that have specialized knowledge for the current environment. While the specialized learning regime of a speech clinic maximizes accuracy by economizing on recurring task demands, the learning regime of a multimedia firm maximizes generality by reconfiguring competencies for new environments.

The trade-off between knowledge accuracy and generality suggests a definition of knowledge-intensive organizations as entities with learning competencies required for *cumulative* knowledge adaptation in evolving environments. Their competencies facilitate the co-evolution of knowledge specialized to the demands of a specific environment and of more general knowledge necessary for adapting to new demands in different contexts. This requires an organizational structure that preserves knowledge about which cues predict a new state of the environment and which actions are appropriate in different environments. It also requires that the receivers of knowledge in different contexts can apply it because they understand what the knowledge means in these contexts. For this, they must already be in possession of some knowledge that tells them how to make sense of new information (Jablonka and Lamb, 2005).

The knowledge provided by senders has no meaning outside the context in which it is represented. This suggests that, without an understanding of that context, receivers cannot act appropriately towards the source of knowledge. A Canadian salesperson who is told by his superior to take a polychronic approach in his negotiations with Turkish buyers cannot react in a knowledgeable way unless he has knowledge that corresponds to the superior's understanding of this recommendation, plus the knowledge necessary to accommodate variations in his response required by the specific circumstances in which the sales negotiations may take place. This context-based and relational definition of knowledge-intensity thus includes cognitive as well as social elements, and permits consideration of any organization as potentially knowledge-intensive, independent of goals and technologies.

3. Types of knowledge and knowledge bases

Researchers have generally found it useful to distinguish between types of knowledge, in recognition of the fact that what people know is distinct from the process by which they acquire and pass on their knowledge. Knowledge derived from personal experience, for example, is often more difficult to share with others than knowledge contained in formal rules or procedures, not because it is *inherently* more complex – which it is not – but because it requires different forms of articulation. Some knowledge involves more analytical or ethical reasoning, whereas other knowledge derives more from the collection of indisputable facts. Some knowledge is intangible and has affective use-value (e.g., how to get along with "difficult" people); other knowledge is tangible and has instrumental use-value (e.g., how to operate a database management program). Different types of knowledge have different effects, depending on situational circumstances (Galunic and Rodan, 1998). Factual knowledge, for example, may be all that is needed for an employee performing a routine task, such as demonstrating the correct use of exercise machines in a fitness center. Analytical knowledge, by contrast, is most important in non-routine task settings, such as explaining to a person why his or her application for membership in an elite fitness club has been denied.

3.1 Explicit and tacit knowledge

A popular distinction running through the literature on organizational knowledge is that between explicit and tacit knowledge (Polanyi, 1966). Knowledge is considered explicit if it is codified in some form. People can acquire explicit knowledge from rulebooks and job manuals, or they can learn such knowledge through formal training programs and personal instruction. Explicit knowledge can be expressed in words, numbers, and procedures, such as the knowledge necessary to process customer payments in a restaurant. By contrast, the knowledge required to deal with "difficult" restaurant customers may be impossible to quantify or put in words. Such knowledge is more tacit, idiosyncratic, and context-dependent, embedded in personal experience and accumulated through long-time practice. Individuals who have tacit knowledge may sense that they possess unique skills for solving particular problems but may find it difficult to explain to others what exactly it takes to solve them. In the language of transaction cost economics, tacit knowledge can lead to asset-specificity in social interaction, by requiring the shared understandings of individuals working in close contact. This is one reason why restaurants at the upper end of the market prefer to recruit staff on a more permanent basis, given that the acquisition of tacit knowledge – necessary for satisfying the idiosyncratic demands of many customers in that market – requires continuous training and social interaction among colleagues. Organizations may use socialization programs to build the shared identity necessary for sustained social interaction, but socialization can be very costly and time demanding relative to arm's-length exchange in the open market.

There are many situations where it is difficult to distinguish between explicit and tacit knowledge. Restaurant cooks, for example, often improvise in the preparation of meals, mixing implicit understandings of task requirements with standard solutions. Improvisation involves both explicit and tacit knowledge, as in the "tricks of the trade" that cooks often employ to accelerate the production process (Fine, 2009). Also, knowledge acquired through personal experience is not necessarily tacit; it may merely be unarticulated. A teacher may have learned how to recognize a specific learning disability from interaction with a particular pupil, but may not want to share that knowledge with colleagues. Tacit knowledge that is not codified does not mean that it can never be codified. There is much medical knowledge that was long considered tacit (e.g., spiritual, magic) until scientific techniques were developed that enabled its codification for broad-based applications. A large self-help industry has emerged in many areas, based on the premise that even experiential knowledge can be converted into explicit categories. The proliferation of self-help books in management ("The no-nonsense manager"), psychological counseling ("How to become yourself"), and dating ("Five steps to finding your mate") suggests that the codification of tacit knowledge is an important element in its commodification for mass reproduction (Benjamin, 1973).

Knowledge may be codifiable, but there may still be some room for tacitness, for example in the way knowledge is applied in a new context. This is one reason why formal assessment techniques in personnel selection often fail to achieve their objectives. Assessment is difficult to carry out if there is disagreement on the meaning of qualifications such as "competency" and "commitment," and if skills are difficult to measure because they involve implicit categories such as emotions and values (Chen and Naquin, 2006). The problem is more serious when attempting to measure a person's potential performance compared to measuring actual achievement. Errors in employment decisions stemming from a faulty assessment of *potential* ability can be personally more devastating, with long-term consequences for the job applicant or promotional candidate, than wrongly concluding in an achievement test that "you were just not good enough." Job designers may misapply "best-practice" approaches to non-routine task situations perceived as routine, and job interviewers may be swayed by their personal impressions of applicants, even if they follow legal requirements meticulously and use standardized interview guides (Liden et al., 1993). In empirical research as well, the problem of understanding what study subjects say or don't say to the investigator is all too familiar to social scientists who regard the interview as an essential tool in knowledge production (Alvesson, 2003).

Just because some knowledge is expressed through language, written texts, or graphical displays does not imply that it is in fact codifiable. The photographs shown in this book present information about images, but the understanding of what the information means is not codifiable, at least not without much additional text and discourse. The proposition that "if you want to be a good leader, you should first obtain a business degree" is not very useful to the person who has been newly promoted to a managerial position. The possession of a university degree as an indicator of knowledge may not be an effective substitute for the experience-based learning by which leadership skills are acquired and put to use (DeRue and Ashford, 2010). The codification of "soft skills" (e.g., in team leadership and job counseling) in the form of publications and training workshops may mask much of the tacit knowledge required for surviving in the "trenches" of an organization and in situations that involve so much ambiguity that people don't even understand that a problem exists. Real learning is unlikely when people are not given the opportunity to engage in trial-and-error search and to admit mistakes because there is an overemphasis on codification. The anecdote below (7.1) describes a medical specialist trained to use standard routines in his area of expertise, without realizing that his detailed knowledge of gastroenterology is ineffective with patients suffering from a psychological disorder. What Dr Springfield needs in his interaction with Sally is an appreciation of not only "knowing *what*" (knowledge that can be broken down into bits of data) and "knowing *why*" (an understanding of scientific principles), but also of "knowing *how*" (an appreciation of situational specifics and the ability to transfer insights from one domain to another domain). He needs to understand that Sally's sense of reality is outside the formal knowledge that constitutes his specialized profession. Sally's condition is such that she is not well served by someone who slices her reality into categories and abstracts from the complexity of her situation, much of which may be unknown, even to herself. Her experience at this doctor's office may not be too dissimilar from the situation of organizational managers who don't understand why their well-intended efforts at leadership are rejected by the employees (Carsten et al., 2010). Such managers may follow a view of knowledge that is tied to the assumption that there is an external reality about which one can acquire information (e.g., by surveying employees about their job concerns) and then testing it (e.g., by changing work conditions and measuring the results) to see whether the knowledge gained from this information corresponds to reality and predicts the intended outcomes of managerial intervention.

ANECDOTE 7.1

Sally finally went to see Dr Springfield, a gastroenterologist, who had been recommended to her as someone "who doesn't take forever to figure out what's wrong with you." Everyone she had talked to, who claimed to know something about Dr Springfield, thought that he was most knowledgeable in his field. He was young and seemed to be up to date on the newest technologies. He also had a reputation of being efficient in his dealings with patients. Even though he normally had a long list of patients, many of whom were walk-ins rather than referrals, it was fairly easy for people to get an appointment for a consultation. Once in the office, no one had to wait longer than fifteen minutes.

Sally was desperate. For over a year now she had suffered from serious constipation, interrupted by bouts of diarrhea. During the last few months she had been experiencing abdominal pain that was so incapacitating that she had to take time off from work several times a month. She was afraid of losing her job if this continued. She explained to Dr Springfield that the painful "cramp attacks" would come on "all the time" and that the episodes of constipation often lasted for an entire week, even though she took laxatives daily and made sure that she consumed only food that was high in fibre content. "I don't eat anything but pure fibre," she told him. "I keep a diary and I take notes on everything that I eat. I mean, *everything*." He nodded impatiently when she informed him that she possessed an "entire library" of diet books and books on nutrition, and that she planned on starting a "discussion group" for people with dieting problems.

Dr Springfield wrote brief comments on his checklist, while Sally answered his questions. As far as she was concerned, he knew what he was doing. His questions were precise, allowing her to answer in a "yes-no" format, and were presented in a sequence indicating a well-structured order. After about ten minutes he concluded the consultation with a diagnosis of "irritable bowel syndrome." This, he said, was quite common in the population and could be treated easily with medication that had become "standard" in recent years. Sally was happy to hear that her condition was not unusual and that a well-tried therapy was available.

Unfortunately, Sally's expectations did not materialize. Her condition did not improve, and she felt as desperate as before. To make matters worse, her relations with colleagues at work, most of whom she had never liked, deteriorated to the point where she hated coming to work. More than once she overheard some of them say that she had "personal issues" and that she was "material for a psychiatrist."

Knowledge that is articulated, as when Sally tells Dr Springfield about her library of diet books, implies nothing about the truth value of what is being said. Dr Springfield may or may not believe what she says, and Sally may have sought his medical advice not because she trusted the recommendations of others but because she felt the need to do *something*. Dr Springfield's actions may follow "rationalized myths" (Meyer and Rowan, 1977) in that they reflect common assumptions about what he considers appropriate. He may decide on a diagnosis not because of the information his patient gives him but because he holds certain assumptions about the "kind of people" who come to his office. Or, he may adopt medical procedures ceremonially, not because he considers them technically necessary in Sally's case, but because he feels the need to comply with the standards in his profession. The modern, highly specialized physician may be as much subject to mythical interpretations as the traditional family doctor who is assumed to have an emotionally close relationship with his or her patients and their families. Myths are stories whose truth content may be unknown or may not even be relevant. What matters more is that everyone believes in the myth. A myth is what people say; "It is not something of which one can acquire the direct experience which can be called knowledge" (Lienhardt, 1954: 104).

The photograph in Exhibit 7.1 shows a representation of what is often considered mythical about ancient Greece. When observers look at the ruins of temples and other ceremonial sites, they deduce knowledge of cults, political institutions, and civic life from what they see. That this understanding may be partial, distorted, wholly wrong, or highly context-specific is the stuff from which myths are made. No one *really* knows for certain what happened over 2000 years ago. Yet, museum exhibits and archeological presentations project a state of knowledge from which mystical understandings of ancient Greek phenomena (e.g., cults, pagan rites) emerge. Elaborate television documentaries are produced to reconstruct ancient Chinese conceptions of government and to explain the meaning of the Son of Heaven and the mediation between the human and the natural worlds. Cultural sites in many parts of the world are rebuilt with devotion to detail to convey ancient meanings to modern-day tourists. And ancient mythologies may be sustained to modern times by incorporating them in national identity-building events like the Olympic opening and closing ceremonies (Traganou, 2010). Information about ancient places and traditions is, at best, incomplete, but incomplete information is not enough to raise doubts about the truth content of myths or to make people value them any less; ambiguities may even strengthen the myths. The study of organizations is full of half-truths and partial understandings, yet few would argue that this makes the subject matter any less relevant or credible. Even in the natural sciences, where one normally assumes a high degree of paradigmatic agreement on the essential concepts, the normal state

Exhibit 7.1

of knowing is not based on complete consensus but on uncertainty and controversy (Webster and Starbuck, 1988). Many people would argue that the debates that arise out of this uncertainty are more fruitful than harmful, to the extent that they keep scholars from dismissing criticism and rejecting alternative explanations for their empirical observations, while at the same time reminding them that scientific activities themselves are often infused with tacit notions like hidden agendas and wishful thinking.

All of this leads to the conclusion that the relationship between explicit and tacit knowledge is far more complex than is presumed in studies that treat them as dichotomous categories. In many organizational settings, it is more realistic to view explicit and tacit knowledge as dynamic and complementary than as static opposites (Amin and Cohendet, 2004). In some cases, tacit understandings are required for making codified knowledge operational. Newly hired employees, for instance, may need to learn the implicit rules of the organization without being given explicit knowledge of who is *really* in charge or what is *really* going on, before they can relax into the routines of the workplace. In other situations, as in organizational projects where initially implicitly held vague ideas eventually become codified in the form of new product applications, new understandings can emerge. The application of explicit knowledge may lead to new tacit understandings, which may run so deep that they even change the identity of the organization. Consulting firms are an example of settings where the inherent ambiguity of "knowledge work" is mediated by an ever-changing organizational identity, to the point where shared identity grounded in tacit interpretations – rather than, say, formal performance measures – serves as the main screening device for new recruits (Alvesson and Robertson, 2006).

The dynamic relationship between explicit and implicit knowledge can create situations where it is impossible to conclude that one type of knowledge is always privileged over the other type. For example, working on the flight deck of an aircraft carrier requires both codified knowledge (e.g., regarding the mechanics of take-off and landing operations) and tacit knowledge (e.g., understanding how to act in a crisis situation) (Weick and Roberts, 1993). When incoming planes are "recovered," people with distinct competencies working in different sites on the ship need to collaborate in a multitude of ways. They communicate by radio as well as visually, continually testing whether the representations of knowledge in the form of explicit regulations and implicit perceptions are correct, while the pilots ask themselves questions like, "Does this feel right?" The question of "feeling" is not limited to individuals but relates to the entire knowledge base in the organization, comprising co-evolving sets of actors, understandings, and situational demands.

3.2 Knowledge bases

Organizations operate within a knowledge base, which includes actors, actions, structures, meanings, and processes for creating and applying different types of knowledge. Knowledge bases contain variable combinations of explicit and tacit knowledge, learning possibilities, and routines at the level of organizations (Yang et al., 2010), industries (Laestadius, 1998), geographic regions (Asheim et al., 2007), and entire nations (Lundvall, 1998). A distinction that has proven useful, especially in research on entrepreneurship and innovation, is that between analytical, synthetic, and symbolic knowledge bases (Asheim et al., 2007), roughly corresponding to Aristotle's distinction between epistemic, technical, and phronetic knowledge, respectively (Lundvall and Johnson, 1994).

3.2.1 Analytical knowledge

An analytical knowledge base has deep theoretical content, embodied in principles, laws, and mechanisms. Organizations that work from an analytical knowledge base take a scientific approach to problem-solving. They seek solutions by applying rational, deductive processes, and by using formal models of knowledge building, involving abstraction and hypothesis testing. Prototypical examples of organizations with an analytical knowledge base are firms in the field of genetics and biotechnology. Their core competence lies in scientific research, both basic and applied, and aimed at understanding natural relationships through the discovery and application of scientific laws. Non-science-based organizations may employ analytical tools as well, such as models to scan the external environment for strategic planning, or models to assess the internal allocation of resources to improve cost control. Many larger organizations use the value-chain approach as an analytical device for explaining how new value can be created. By dividing the value chain into sequential activities, identifying the required resources, and systematically examining the activities along each stage, analysts search for areas where costs can be reduced and utilities increased. Much of the knowledge obtained analytically involves extensive codification, as in the pharmaceutical industry, where scientific facts and laws are documented in research reports, electronic files, and patent descriptions. Tacit knowledge and implicit understandings are important as well, especially in those areas where the goals and outcomes of innovative efforts are uncertain and deep social investments in trust and dependability are required to maintain the actors' commitment (Johnson et al., 2002). To achieve this goal, organizations may create structures that provide secure positions for scientists and decentralize decision-making to the level where the requisite competencies exist.

3.2.2 Synthetic knowledge

A synthetic knowledge base exists when problem-solving involves the recombination of elements of existing knowledge. A synthetic approach is typically used by organizations that deal with problems emerging in their interaction with customers and suppliers, as in the field of law and consulting, where the demand for service is driven by specialized client needs. Problem-solving activities are cyclical and iterative rather than sequential, and are adjusted to the outcomes of actions. In a mental health clinic, for example, employees would be expected to redefine a problem and to change their approach to client needs after learning that the chosen therapy has not been working (Nijsmans, 1991). This may require them to seek input from different specialists and to engage in several trials, which is what Dr Springfield in the anecdote above (7.1) did not do, given his insistence on following standard routines. Synthetic knowledge is created not so much deductively than through an inductive process of experimentation, improvisation, testing, simulation, and practical experience. Much of the knowledge gained this way is tacit, acquired through learning by doing and interacting. Compared to the "know-what" and "know-why" in the analytical knowledge base, the synthetic knowledge domain requires more concrete "know-how" and practical skill.

3.2.3 Symbolic knowledge

Some organizations operate mainly from a symbolic knowledge base, in which cultural understandings are at the center of innovation. Symbolic knowledge work is often heavily laden with value content and emotion, as in the cultural-products sector where explicit knowledge contained in films, designs, or theater performances combines with the subjective interpretations of images and impressions. In industries such as music, literature, and performing arts, knowledge evolves not so much through the analytical search for scientific principles and the synthetic combination of facts, than through association with particular individuals and organizations as a mechanism by which "know-who" is created. Films, for example, are produced in project teams with temporary structures, which are continually reconfigured with the input from a diverse set of individuals (e.g., actors, directors, and other creative and non-creative personnel) with unique skills, personal values, artistic tastes, and professional identities (Perretti and Negro, 2007), in a social milieu of extensive face-to-face interaction. Symbolic knowledge workers often describe the social climate in which meanings can freely circulate (e.g., through gossip, trade folklore, and random encounters) as "buzz" (Asheim et al., 2007). Creative artists, for example, normally prefer to work in culturally diverse urban settings, where they can learn through observation and by just "being there" (Pratt, 2002) and where they can meet people from various cultural and professional backgrounds (Evans, 2009), as described in Anecdote 2.1. Physical proximity may be important for new knowledge creation in geographically bounded "cultural districts," but this does not mean that the consumption of cultural output cannot spread well beyond the location of their production. Interpretations of cultural artifacts, such as football stadiums, world exhibitions, or those shown in Exhibit 7.1, may be carried swiftly and over long distances in the form of websites, tourist brochures, ethnology books, and museum guides.

The analytical, synthetic, and symbolic knowledge bases should be seen as "ideal types" in Weber's (1949: 90) sense of a "conceptual pattern [that] brings together certain relationships and events of historical life into a complex, which is conceived as an internally consistent system." Ideal types draw attention to the most distinctive features of a given phenomenon, not all of which may exist empirically in a particular instance, but enough of them exist to allow the researcher to conduct a comparative analysis. Organizations may be grounded in all three knowledge bases simultaneously, although the precise combination varies in particular instances. Automobile producers, for example, are often cited as examples of organizations embedded in a synthetic knowledge base (e.g., engine development), but they also do much science-based analytical work (e.g., regarding pollution control or chemical waste disposal) and process symbolic knowledge (e.g., power, status). The textbook publishing industry also combines elements from analytical (e.g., manuscript reviewing), synthetic (e.g., marketing), and symbolic (e.g., aesthetics) knowledge bases.

Product innovation in the life-science industry and in associated industries (e.g., agriculture and food production) illustrates the dynamic interplay of the main features of these three knowledge bases (Moodysson et al., 2008). The firms engage in analytical work (e.g., production of antibody-based drugs) in exploratory experimentation in laboratories, to uncover the causal mechanisms in chemical processes and to test the theories behind the mechanisms. Brainstorming in groups of scientists is most important in the initial phases of a new project, with results codified in the form of publications in journals, presentations at conferences, and documentation in patents and electronic databases. Linkages with other organizations (e.g., research institutes, hospitals), often located in other countries, are important for further developing and testing new knowledge. Much of this communication takes place in codified form by e-mail, backed up by occasional face-to-face meetings between scientists. Synthetic knowledge creation in functional product applications is carried out more within the boundaries of a given firm. When firms do collaborate with others in synthetic knowledge creation, they rely more on local linkages, supported by local institutions (e.g., public media, consultants, universities). Synthetic knowledge spillovers occur first and fastest within local social networks of scientists and entrepreneurs (Powell et al., 1996). Symbolic elements in the life-science industry are important in so far as they link the activities of firms, researchers, and public relations specialists at various stages in the development and production process to the interests of concerned consumers regarding culturally sensitive issues such as product safety and lifestyle (Weber et al., 2008). Much of the knowledge exchanged with social movement organizations and the public media has symbolic (e.g., regarding progress and innovation) and value content (e.g., regarding morality and authenticity).

In sum, the distinction between different types of knowledge and knowledge bases offers insights into the idiosyncrasies of organizational knowledge production. There typically are no singular and coherent knowledge systems. People may use vastly different criteria, even in the same organization, for evaluating knowledge and the conditions under which new forms of knowledge are necessary to achieve their goals. Scholars working from different theoretical perspectives propose different interpretations of these criteria and focus on different processes by which criteria are enacted. Institutional theorists, for example, draw attention to logics of action that, depending on the distribution of power, may lead either to organizational convergence or to fragmentation. Evolutionary theorists note that the selection criteria embedded in different institutions contain the seeds for the creation of new variations in knowledge bases as sources of innovation. And organizational economists see in these variations an important source of economic rents for organizations. Whether organizations have an efficiency advantage over open markets in the creation and diffusion of knowledge depends, among other things, on how flows of knowledge are structured.

4. Structuring the flow of knowledge

It is not clear *a priori* that organizations are always the best mechanism to generate new knowledge (Spender, 1998). Population ecology theorists, for example, note the tendency of organizations to evolve towards structural inertia, developing strict hierarchies and procedures that retard new learning (Hannan and Freeman, 1984). Organizations may prefer to create structures to exploit the knowledge that they already have, rather than seek new knowledge, if exploring new opportunities would consume more resources or lead into wholly unknown terrain. Change at the margins may be beneficial, but organizations that stray too far from existing structures may risk failure (Haveman, 1992). The study of engineering firms reported in the research brief (7.1) below examines the disruptive impact of deep changes in the organizations' employment structure, such as managing workers bureaucratically along strict hierarchical principles, or professionally with an emphasis on employee autonomy (Hannan et al., 2006). In this sample, employment structures are considered central to organizational identity. Firms which deviated from the employment model adopted when they were founded had a higher risk of disbanding or experiencing downgraded performance in the stock market, to the extent that such deviations were seen by stakeholders as a violation of organizational identity.

RESEARCH BRIEF 7.1

Much organizational research is premised on the idea that change is a necessity in fast-paced environments. Change helps organizations discard outdated knowledge and acquire new knowledge. Organizations that are able to change are expected to improve their performance and increase their survival chances. This argument, although plausible on average, overlooks the disruptions caused by change, and the possibility that changing an organization's structure is seen by the constituents as a violation of deep-seated understandings of organizational identity. The study by Hannan et al. (2006) tests the proposition that changes to the structural core features of an organization have destabilizing consequences because they represent a violation of the organization's identity, increasing the chances of organizational dissolution.

Organizations that depend on developing and retaining the intellectual capital of their employees invest heavily in employment relations that institutionalize the flow of knowledge to the point where the organization-specific management of knowledge becomes a central aspect of organizational identity. Drawing on a sample of 154 young technology firms in California's Silicon

Valley, the authors identified four distinct forms of employment relations, reflecting different types of employee attachment to the firm and different recruitment selection criteria: star (professional autonomy and high potential), bureaucracy (formal control and procedures), autocracy (direct surveillance), and commitment (loyalty to the organization and peer control). The founders of these firms were asked to recollect what kind of employment model they had in mind when they established their firm.

The findings of this study show that firms which deviated significantly from the original employment model had a higher probability of failing, and experienced reduced growth in market capitalization, compared to firms that retained their employment model. The reason for this, according to the authors, is that the organizational founders viewed employment relations as a cultural "blueprint" for the organization, determining various structural facets, including the standardization of work practices, the use of formal rules, and the formal specification of managerial roles. Whether employees are managed, say, bureaucratically or professionally plays a key role in the organization's core identity. Identity is a more tacit and elusive property of organizations than, say, a product portfolio or organizational technology. The data in this study indicate that altering identity "blueprints" can have serious destabilizing consequences for the organization, to the extent that changes are seen by the organization's constituents as a violation of basic expectations regarding what the organization should be doing.

Among the limitations of this study is the omission of other effects resulting from the observed changes in employment models. It is possible, for example, that the changes improved the organizations' quality as an employer. Lacking data, it is not known whether disruptions stemming from "identity changes" were offset by improvements in the organizations' fitness in areas other than market capitalization. Also, the study used proxy data for organizational identity and offered no direct information on how the employment models were perceived by employees and external audiences. Some of the firms in the sample may have selected an employment model, for example, to broaden the search for new knowledge, rather than to manage workers' attachment to the firm. It would, therefore, be useful to know how the different employment models were viewed by the employees and external constituents.

Rigid organizational structures provide few incentives for individuals to depart from routines and to explore new knowledge domains (Levinthal and March, 1993). Many people are not inclined to experiment with new ideas, especially under conditions of uncertainty, when they feel ambiguity, stress, and anxiety (Jansen et al., 2006). Instead, they look for solutions that have been applied in the past and they avoid situations where they continuously have to seek new information that is potentially inconsistent with their current understandings (Edmondson, 1999). If such behavior extends to the organizational level, it can lead to path dependency in organizational strategies and structures, with potentially harmful consequences in volatile environments. In times of crisis, organizations often engage in cost cutting and rationalization rather than rewarding experimentation and improvisation (Bozeman and Slusher, 1979). The resulting rigidity in knowledge structures may lead to reduced organizational adaptability and innovation because with less resource slack the organization lacks buffers against downside risk.

The concern for adaptability in knowledge structures raises the question of the location of knowledge in organizations. Those who argue that knowledge resides foremost in the human mind study organizational knowledge by measuring the cognitions and cognitive processes of individuals. For example, they ask survey respondents whether they understand the causal processes in the development of solutions to problems, if the key learning skills are in place, and where performance feedback comes from (McGrath, 2001). When such information is not available from organizational members, researchers may draw on the impressions and understandings of experts outside the organization, such as business journalists and financial analysts (Hayward, 2002). Critics of both approaches argue that studying organizational knowledge through the cognitions of individuals is problematic, given differences and inaccuracies in human perception. Perceptual processes involve cognitive filters that people use to frame information and to create consistency in understanding (Hampton, 1998). In organizations where people use different filters, shared understanding is difficult to obtain and it is difficult to achieve consistency in organizational knowledge. Whether the lack of consistency is harmful to the organization depends on the state of the environment. In stable environments, it pays to increase epistemic efficiency more than in volatile environments. In uncertain environments the search for consistency, by building structures in which everyone reliably produces shareable knowledge, would prematurely truncate the discovery process needed to create a knowledge base with sufficient variation for organizational adaptability (Orton and Weick, 1990).

Given differences in cognitions, it is unlikely that organizational knowledge emerges automatically when individuals work together in the same organizational unit. People may not freely share personal knowledge, even if they work on the same project, have common experiences, or are otherwise similar in outlook and identity. In predicting knowledge sharing, one does not need to go so far as to assume that individuals are always opportunistic, cannot be trusted, and distort the information they make available to others. It is sufficient to assume that they vary in cognitive capacity and bounded rationality. There is always a certain element of randomness in the knowledge that resides at the collective level, even if the collectivity imposes constraints on goal setting, information search, and outcome evaluation. No organization, not even a prison or mental asylum, is structurally so "totalizing" that it leaves no room at all for behavioral deviations from central norms (Goffman, 1961).

There is also an ethical aspect in debates about the "structuring" of knowledge. Organizations that are highly structured (in the sense that there is an elaborate horizontal and vertical division of labor, supported by explicit rules and standard procedures for prioritizing and coordinating work) are often seen negatively as unduly restricting human freedom. Studies indicate that many people do indeed experience rules and hierarchies as "psychic prisons," stifling their creativity (Hirst et al., 2011) or inducing them to seek refuge in self-employment (Bögenhold and Staber, 1991). The negative assessment of structure cuts across organizational levels, since the challenges associated with the structuring of human work are essentially the same in smaller organizational systems as in larger ones. This also includes professional organizations that process complex knowledge and require the commitment of everyone and at all levels where specialized expertise exists (Thomas and Hewitt, 2011), although there are variations in the reliance on hierarchical controls in professional organizations, as in the sample of high-technology firms studied in the research brief above (7.1). Even organizations whose express goal is to practice participatory democracy, such as worker cooperatives or self-help organizations, use hierarchical structures to coordinate the different areas in which members apply their specialized knowledge (Winther and Marens, 1997).

Many studies also offer a positive assessment of the role of hierarchical structures in knowledge creation. While structure constrains action, it also guides action, by creating a sense of meaning and direction, and by providing opportunities for new kinds of behavior. Clear structures are useful not only in routine task settings. Studies have shown that even professional workers, who value personal autonomy, derive benefits from highly structured jobs. First, clearly stated rules and procedures facilitate the work process by enhancing knowledge sharing. Clear authority relations regulate access to the resources that employees need to accomplish their work. In turn, the ability to exchange knowledge with colleagues may increase job satisfaction and improve the interpersonal climate in the organization (Zeitz, 1984). If the existence of formal rules creates problems, it may be due to the manner in which rules are employed. Hierarchy is not a problem *per se*; clear lines of authority are useful as long as superiors remain within their jurisdiction and do not interfere in the day-to-day affairs of knowledgeable employees. Second, working in well-structured jobs reduces role ambiguity. Clearly written and fairly enforced rules provide employees with understandings that increase certainty and reduce anxiety. By institutionalizing personal discretion, formal standards may even have a liberating effect, as in the case of front-line employees in hotels who refer to explicit standards in handling the requests of hotel guests with special needs (Raub, 2008), or in the case of medical doctors working within hospital structures that respect their client orientation and sense of craftsmanship (Stevens et al., 1992). In highly structured settings, employees may perceive more, rather than less, autonomy.

On balance, research suggests that elaborate organizational structures often support rather than hinder knowledge creation and transfer at all levels at which organizations are active, from work groups to inter-organizational systems (Arikan and Schilling, 2011; Bunderson and Boumgarden, 2010). All knowledge is subject to negotiation and revision, and organizational structure provides a context in which revision can take place predictably and reliably. Organizational structure helps reduce uncertainty at the workplace and supports identity building. Highly structured systems are valued especially by people who prefer stability in their organizational engagement over constant change in their knowledge basis. For some people, changes in organizational structure that put more emphasis on individual self-initiative and self-reliance can lead to emotional losses and a sense of insecurity (Sennett, 2006). Other people perceive such changes as creating new opportunities to adapt knowledge to their own needs, thus expanding the realm of choice (Giddens, 1991), as will be discussed in Chapter 8.

5. Theoretical perspectives on organizational knowledge

Organizational economists, institutional theorists, and evolutionary theorists take distinct but, in many ways, complementary approaches to organizational knowledge. Together, they address organizational knowledge as a cross-level phenomenon, ranging from ideas and beliefs as the basic elements of knowledge to the macro-level structures of organizations and inter-organizational systems in which knowledge is situated. Economists explore organizational governance with a view to the efficiency of information processing. Transaction costs are largely knowledge-based, and principal–agent relations are underpinned by knowledge limitations which can make it difficult to enforce contracts. The institutionalist approach to organizations considers shared knowledge an essential ingredient of integration. Because knowledge is a source of power, organizations, in which knowledge does not flow freely can develop into persistent systems of domination, potentially disenfranchising a large part of the membership. Evolutionary theorists view knowledge processes that reproduce domination and control as constraints on variation, limiting the possibility of adaptive change. However, any tendency towards organizational rigidity is checked by the possibility that the individual members of organizations have at least a slightly different set of knowledge. If that knowledge is implicit and not easily articulated, it can be an element of undirected variation, with adaptive potential.

5.1 Organizational economics

Organizational economists argue that knowledge production in the firm is institutionalized in the form of hierarchical governance structures providing the discipline necessary to coordinate the flow of information between specialized units. The economic characterization of hierarchy as a comparatively efficient structuring device for knowledge production, in a context of bounded rationality and environmental uncertainty, draws on Max Weber's (1924/1947) conceptualization of the rational-legal form of authority in organizations. Economists typically follow, albeit often implicitly, Weber's notion of *formal* rationality as a logic based on the use of knowledge to calculate utilities, while recognizing the cognitive limitations regarding the precision of estimates about the future. Standard economic analysis has little to say about *substantive* rationality, downplaying social concerns with difficult-to-calculate utilities, such as ideas about "political correctness" or "preferential treatment" in worker recruitment. When organizational economists address social issues, such as "participatory democracy," they focus typically on the cost effectiveness of different control mechanisms regarding worker ownership – rather than the politics or social legitimacy of control structures (Hansmann, 1990). Value-based substantive rationality in organizational knowledge is a central topic in sociological analyses, exploring issues such as the "deprofessionalization" of work systems in the health care sector (Ritzer and Walczak, 1988) or the institutionalization of therapeutic technologies in rape crisis centers (Zilber, 2002).

The details of economic analyses of organizational knowledge vary from study to study, but they all tend to highlight efficiency considerations in organizational governance. From an economic property rights perspective, those who own organizational assets are seen as having the right to dominate decision-making in organizations. This includes the right to distribute resources such that knowledge can accumulate quickly, while ensuring that it does not leak to outsiders. When there is a possibility of knowledge leakage, firms have an incentive to patent knowledge in order to protect their property rights (Katz and Shapiro, 1987). In cases where specialized knowledge flows between resource interdependent organizations, the possibility of opportunistic behavior on the part of either the knowledge producer (who may withhold critical information) or the knowledge user (who may pass on trade secrets) encourages the more dependent organization to purchase the other organization. Acquisitions are seen as a solution to the transaction cost problem in an exchange relationship characterized by asset specificity.

The principal–agent approach in organizational economics considers the possibility that the principals cannot control the rules of the game the agents are playing between themselves. Each of the agents may respond to different incentives when deciding to share knowledge with others, especially if they have to work with imperfect information or if information is not evenly distributed in the organization (Camerer et al., 1989). Given interdependence between the agents, the optimal decision for one individual depends on the way in which the other individuals make decisions, but this information may not be available, for example because of task uncertainties (Haas, 2010) or physical distance between the actors (Sole and Edmondson, 2002). In non-routine task settings, hierarchical structures may not achieve efficient coordination, if there are no incentives for lower-level workers to transmit their specialized knowledge upwards (Adler, 2001). Organizations may then invest resources to create a shared identity in the workforce that is strong enough to achieve collective discipline without recourse to formal control structures (Ouchi, 1980).

Transaction cost economists focus on the administrative controls afforded by hierarchies, for example in the form of an employment contract in which a worker agrees to offer his or her labor and receives wages in exchange for submitting to a superior officer who has the right to sanction the worker's performance. From a transaction cost perspective, there is no reason to assume perfect goal congruence between the employer and the employee (Ouchi, 1980). All that is required is that the employee endorses the superior's authority and considers the incentive system equitable. Hierarchy does not have to be experienced as an "iron cage." Hierarchical structures can be designed such that people have a sense of community, although this is limited by individual differences regarding commitment, orientation to learning, and so on (Hirst et al., 2011). Individuals who are open to new ideas and are motivated to experiment benefit most from authority structures and formal rules that reduce transaction costs by speeding up communication and decision-making. This is most important for organizations that put a premium on tacit knowledge, when the measurement of individual output is difficult, and there is, therefore, extra pressure on economizing on what people know or claim to know.

Hierarchy and formalization do not necessarily make an organization inflexible. Tacit knowledge hidden in social relations, for instance, can be an important source of change and innovation, encouraging risk-taking and improvisation, and motivating people to search for new knowledge, when required. Formal employment contracts specify obligations, but only imperfectly so. The employment relation represents an *incomplete* form of contracting because it is impossible to stipulate all obligations for every conceivable eventuality. The employee can be induced to accept hierarchical commands only within a "zone of indifference" (Barnard, 1938). The freely formed agreement that the employee will simply "tell and be told" (Williamson, 1985: 221) may leave considerable room for behavioral variations. When situated in an interactionist context in which the individuals believe that reliance on others' knowledge is essential to *collective* epistemic progress, these variations can be an important source of organizational flexibility, inducing employees to realign themselves with others on a case-by-case basis, and thus adding to the organization's knowledge base.

5.2 Organizational institutionalism

Institutional theorists acknowledge the materialistic interests and self-serving motives of individuals in the creation of knowledge, but they also draw attention to the normative framework within which knowledge is situated. Knowledge is not only an instrumental resource; it also has social and symbolic content. For example, when the leaders of organizations experiencing an economic crisis engage external consultants, they do so not necessarily in the hope to discover new solutions but to send a signal to the organization's constituents that "we are doing *something*." Actions like employing consultants or adopting "best-practice" techniques, and rhetorical interventions like championing "progress" or referring to "discoveries" in academic research, can have important symbolic value, with implications for the organization's – and its management's – reputation and legitimacy in the eyes of stakeholders (Kieser, 1997). From the institutional perspective, the search for new knowledge is not a mere technical activity but is driven by social concerns and political interests. Power does not automatically derive from the possession of knowledge; rather, knowledge has to be translated into action if it is to generate power, within structures that may or may not be considered legitimate.

While organizational economics notes the potential efficiency of formal rules, institutional theory highlights the social norms that give stability to rules. Journalism, for example, is a field dominated by rules of investigating and reporting, grounded in norms related to ethics, privacy, duty of honor, and the like. These norms vary widely across some countries and are strongly institutionalized in government regulations and journalism school curricula (Knight and Hawtin, 2010). Because institutions have no determinative character outside the actions that produce them, they are always available for modification in new situations. The transformations in the political economy in post-communist Eastern Europe since the 1990s illustrate the possibility that institutional legacies of the past are not necessarily barriers to change in the future. The social networks, for example, which had regulated the relationship between public ownership and private property in specific sectors of the communist economy, furnished the structure for institutionalizing change in the new market regime (Grabher and Stark, 1997). Similarly, the objective of organizational rules is to organize and preserve knowledge, but this does not mean that they are immune to change or that they cannot be used to initiate change (Feldman, 2000). Changes in rules are often the result of concerted efforts by those who feel disadvantaged by current structures and who use major jolts in the environment as an opportunity to renegotiate their condition. Even when rules are constructed with foresight and with the interests of all organization members in mind, they can have unforeseen consequences in new environments. For example, the formulation of behavioral rules in teams to create a stronger group identity and atmosphere in which the participants freely exchange knowledge may have the opposite effect for minority members who experience the rules as confirmation that they "just don't fit in" (Dipboye and Halverson, 2004). The unintended outcomes of actions taken to create new knowledge structures suggest that knowledge is not "natural" and should not be treated as a phenomenon outside the scope of investigation.

There rarely is a close relationship between intentions and outcomes in the creation of organizational knowledge, not even in tightly structured organizations. Goals are normally not achieved to their full extent; they may even be turned on their head by structures perceived as imposing imperatives. For example, hierarchical structures designed to minimize deviations from organizational goals may eventually lead to their "displacement" in the sense that the means (i.e., hierarchy) to the ends (i.e., goal) become the ends themselves (Merton, 1940). Hierarchical controls that were introduced originally to, say, remove knowledge redundancies may come to be valued over time for their own sake, taking on a life of their own. Once they have become a taken-for-granted feature of the organization, they are no longer recognized as meeting only the original needs and are retained even if environmental circumstances change. Organizational leaders may not even recognize the environmental change because they are narrowly focused on the hierarchical structure rather than the environment or the organization's performance in its environment. In this case, the systemic, *formal* rationality of the organization has swallowed up the *substantive* rationality of decisions at the individual level, with the effect of reducing people's sense of responsibility for the consequences of their actions. Such outcomes transform the organization's knowledge base by drawing attention away from the individual and giving primacy to organizational structure and social context as the source of new value.

5.3 Organizational evolution

Evolutionary theorists view knowledge as a vital resource, embedded in organizational competencies and routines, and developing through the organization's selection and retention processes. Knowledge is also a means to obtain other resources, by providing a cognitive and political basis for decision-making and by building credibility in the eyes of those who control the resources the organization is seeking. While organizational economists emphasize the costs of creating and sharing knowledge, and institutional theorists point to cultural factors as an aid to or an impediment in the flow of knowledge, evolutionary theorists see in knowledge the seeds for improved adaptability in changing environments.

Whether knowledge does in fact improve organizational adaptability is an empirical question in particular instances. Path dependencies in knowledge creation and diffusion may limit opportunities for organizations to act flexibly and innovatively in new environments. Path dependency in knowledge construction means that present knowledge is limited by the knowledge that existed in the past, and that current knowledge shapes the knowledge that can develop in the future. In some cases, social biases (e.g., conformity pressures, traditions) may be so strong that alternative paths are virtually unthinkable (Richerson and Boyd, 2005). Organizations that want to "grow out of" such path dependency require structures that permit the insertion of new actors and new ideas. In other cases, it is mainly cognitive processes that keep learning on a given path and prevent the active consideration of alternative options. Knowledge is normally developed under perceptual constraints (e.g., people's need for consistency) and through filtering mechanisms (e.g., related to sensation and emotion) in the human mind (Thagard, 1996). Rationality is obtained by filtering out ideas, beliefs, and experiences that would otherwise lead to empirical inconsistencies and logical contradictions. When complete consistency cannot be achieved, one often speaks of mysteries or half-truths, but these terms do not necessarily denote irrationality. The idea of mystery is often used as a device to make inconsistent beliefs appear consistent, as when employees rationalize their supervisor's inexplicable behavior by inventing "just-so" stories ("That's just how she is"). Mysteries are an example of responses to exigencies that cannot be checked in fact, so they are interpreted away, thus reinforcing the path along which learning takes place.

On the other hand, knowledge emerging in path-dependent ways should not be taken as "natural." Even the most firmly established evolutionary patterns contain within them fragments of choices ignored, paths not taken, or failed experiments that can be revitalized to support alternative developments. Even in environments that are dominated by a particular organizational form, there is some space for alternative developments. For example, in the northeastern United States during the first half of the twentieth century, different cooperative, not-for-profit forms of production and service provision (e.g., in agriculture, insurance, utilities) could develop alongside the rapid growth of "mainstream" corporate hierarchies in all industries (Schneiberg, 2007). The possibilities for alternative developments may be place-specific, rooted in local institutional and social structures which define the parameters within which innovations can emerge, but they may permit alternative paths to innovation. For example, local institutions may encourage entrepreneurship through spin-offs, outsourcing, labor mobility, or *de novo* organizational foundings (Audia et al., 2006), and each of these mechanisms may have unique consequences for economic and social development. Innovations are often latent in existing structures, especially under conditions of uncertainty when there are risks, but also opportunities.

This raises the question of the role of ideas as constituent elements of knowledge (Camic and Gross, 2004). If evolutionary selection works on ideas, then knowledge is just a temporary bundle of different but related ideas (Weeks and Galunic, 2003). Knowledge then needs to be studied as a composite of ideas bounded by actors, purpose, time, or some other criterion. The more tightly coupled the ideas are in the composite, the more closely tied they are to the fate of the composite. This would imply, for example, that ideas have a specific meaning only in relationship to other ideas. The idea of a handshake has a different meaning depending on whether it is part of the knowledge used in a business negotiation or in a social gathering of friends. Or, a manager may use an ethnic joke successfully in a presentation to colleagues, but the same joke may be harmful in combination with ideas presented in a speech to the members of a charity organization. Similar to genetic fitness, the fitness of an idea is a relative concept: whether an idea survives into the future depends on the adaptive advantage it brings to the organization's knowledge base. The fitness of knowledge is relative to what already exists, and it is not absolute. A manager who believes that women lack leadership skills may apply this belief in any context by denying women promotional opportunities or by ensuring that they are kept out of corporate board rooms (Phillips, 2005). In evolutionary terms, whether this belief survives depends on the environment's receptiveness and on the other beliefs with which it competes for human attention in a particular context.

Knowledge conceived as a population of different but related ideas evolves in the form of changing frequency distributions in the population. For example, in a brainstorming meeting aimed at producing ideas for a client project, new ideas are introduced, while others are dropped, and some of the new ideas are joined with existing ones (Paulus and Yang, 2000). Which ideas in the pool of ideas are selected and retained for further development depends on human cognitive capabilities and on the environment in which people use their capabilities. People may suppress certain ideas, for reasons having to do with self-censorship or risk aversion (Williams, 2002), or they may select certain ideas because they are vulnerable to social pressure (Henrich and Boyd, 2005). This implies that it is not knowledge *per se* that should be studied but rather the properties of ideas, as well as the cognitive orientations of individuals who select and retain the ideas. The ideas that are most likely to survive in the competitive selection process may be those that are novel, outrageous, or catchy, or have some other feature that causes the audience to remember them and pass them on to others. Along these lines, researchers have investigated the diffusion of ideas that are "wrong" or empirically unfounded, such as myths, folktales, and ghost stories (Heath et al., 2001). Some ideas may survive even if they are difficult to implement, for example because they are considered immoral or politically perverse, such as the idea of the "unfettered market" or the "survival of the fittest" in anti-poverty legislation (Somers and Block, 2005). From an evolutionary perspective, knowledge can only develop if there is enough variation and competition in the population of ideas. The academic discourse about business clusters, for instance, has generated a range of ideas concerning flexible specialization, cooperation, collective learning, and so on. These ideas are in a constant struggle for survival; they compete for the attention of scholars, business managers, and government officials, and are passed on in the form of best practice, theoretical understandings, and public policy initiatives (Staber, 2010b).

The evolutionary study of knowledge at the level of ideas reflects a version of human agency that is more socially engaged, with more discretionary, evaluative, and transformative possibilities, than what is offered in many evolutionary accounts at more aggregate levels. The mutation and blending of ideas from different domains, enacted by different actors with different interests, contribute new variation to organizational knowledge. Video games, for example, are produced by organizations in which different actors with specialized competencies (e.g., designers, programmers) combine ideas in an evolutionary process, using inputs from different knowledge domains (e.g., technology, arts, literature) and applying a variety of cultural (e.g., aesthetics, novelty) and economic (e.g., profitability, utility) selection criteria (Tschang and Szczypula, 2006). In a competitive environment of ideas and actors, new variations lead to knowledge boundaries that are constantly changing. Despite people's tendency to compartmentalize, the boundaries of knowledge are rarely clear-cut or fixed. The elements of knowledge "spill over" into one another, creating a reality that is essentially fluid (Zerubavel, 1997: 65–66). Fuzzy knowledge boundaries and boundary crossing are a normal part of organizational life and provide opportunities for innovation, with potential adaptive consequences.

6. Conclusion

Organizations are knowledge-seeking systems. They are not epistemically limited to what people's intuitions tell them. Organizational participants deliberately search for some information and reflect on what they get, while ignoring other data, and effective organizational forms distribute information to those areas where it is needed most. The outcomes of knowledge building can be fragile and highly variable, especially if organizations are designed to encourage people to reflect on structures and practices. Similarly, different theories stress different aspects of knowledge creation; they motivate researchers to look in different places and for different kinds of evidence. For example, to economists, the absence of knowledge or the asymmetric distribution of knowledge is a source of friction, raising transaction costs and leading to instability in economic exchange. The goal of organizing is to find a set of governance structures that minimize these costs. From an institutional perspective, knowledge-based friction is often political, because all knowledge is embedded in social structures where meanings are contested and legitimacy questions are debated. The goal of organizing, from this perspective, is to create structures that regulate the system by providing agreed-upon frameworks for evaluating social and economic action. For evolutionary theorists, knowledge is both a source and outcome of organizational change, mediated by rules, routines, and competencies. The goal of organizing, from an evolutionary perspective, is to create structures that enable the continuous production of new variations, some of which may turn out to have adaptive value in future environments.

An insightful analysis of knowledge in organizations recognizes both the generative and contextual nature of knowledge. There is a large literature highlighting the collectivist nature of organizational knowledge, noting a variety of structural features, as well as the contextual conditions that make structure either limiting or enabling. There is also the recognition of individual-level variations in cognitive capacities and learning behavior, explaining why "the whole is often not simply the sum of its parts." Organizational knowledge is best seen as a phenomenon that exists in the interaction between mental models – that is, the ordering of ideas and concepts in the human mind (Hampton, 1998) – and the way understanding is fueled by external cues – that is, the embeddedness of mental models in the collective mind of organizations (Weick and Roberts, 1993). Knowledge lies at the interface of individual cognition and organizational structure, with implications for employment relations and the social capital of organizations and the larger community in which they exist, as will be discussed in the next chapter.

Recommended further reading

Bourdieu, P. (1993) *The Field of Cultural Production*. New York: Columbia University Press.
Bourdieu argues that knowledge must be deconstructed to reveal how the structures of discourse in the production of culture generate political outcomes.

Greenblatt, S. (2011) *The Swerve: How the Renaissance Began*. New York: W.W. Norton & Company.
This story of the rediscovery during the European "Dark Ages" of ancient Roman scripts demonstrates the influence of political power and social norms on the ideas that people accept as knowledge.

Sperber, D. (1996) *Explaining Culture: A Naturalistic Approach.* Oxford: Blackwell.
An analysis of the cognitive underpinnings of knowledge creation as the foundation of human culture.

Starbuck, W. (2006) *The Production of Knowledge.* Oxford: Oxford University Press.
Starbuck reviews the challenges of new knowledge creation in the social sciences in general, and in organization studies in particular.

 ■ **Practice questions for Anecdote 7.1**

1 In what ways is the routine-oriented behavior of Dr Springfield efficient but not effective?

2 How would you characterize the knowledge processes in the misunderstanding between Dr Springfield and Sally?

3 How would Dr Springfield have to change his approach in his interaction with Sally to learn from her?

8

Conclusion: Private Problems and Public Issues

```
                    ┌──── Learning Objectives ────┐

  This chapter will:

  •  Discuss some of the implications of organizational "flexibilization" for
     employment relations and career building

  •  Discuss the embeddedness of organizations in the social capital of local
     communities

  •  Discuss the emergence of the "unorganized individual" in the "new economy"
```

1. Introduction

This book began with the argument that we live in an "organizational society" in which people's life chances are shaped by their relationships to organizations. Organizations were examined as socio-economic entities that vary along spatial, temporal, structural, and cognitive dimensions, which link them to the surrounding environment. Given the notion of society as a thoroughly organized and differentiated system, it is fitting to conclude the discussion with an examination of some of the social implications of organizational restructuring in the emerging "new economy." As a metaphor, the "new economy" acts as a signal for a particular kind of market economy in which organizational flexibility and individual initiative are considered imperative for success and in which conventional categories (e.g., blue-collar and white-collar) are losing their analytical grip. Efforts at organizational restructuring – popular catchwords include "delayering," "just-in-time production," "lean management," and "downsizing" – over the last few decades have created a situation where the traditional **dual economy** boundaries (e.g., core and periphery sector, primary and secondary labor market) are becoming increasingly blurred.

Following the insights of the "classical" writers in organization studies, such as Marx, Weber, Durkheim, and Tönnies, the problems of organizations can only be understood if the social and economic contexts (e.g., local community, nation-state, international trading blocs) in which they arise are studied dynamically, in their historical transformations. It is through organizations that knowledge is accumulated and diffused, occupational identities are forged, skill requirements are refined, and power differentials are reproduced. In the aggregate, the actions of organizations affect social structures by mobilizing resources, locating production facilities, and shaping income and status opportunities. Through the construction of socially negotiated boundaries between occupations, jobs, technologies, social networks, and so on, organizations contribute dynamically to social inequalities in all spaces in which they are active.

Arguably, there has been more research on the social impact of organizations at the micro-level of individual experiences (e.g., regarding job satisfaction, motivation, and leadership) than at the interface of organization and society. Studies conducted at the micro-level may acknowledge organizations' social embeddedness , but they often hold constant the broader social context in which individual experiences aggregate into larger-scale effects. The objective of this final chapter is to bring this larger context into sharper focus by highlighting some of the key ways in which organizations contribute to what C. Wright Mills (1959: 8–9) described as the "personal troubles of milieu and the public issues of social structure." Organizations are directly implicated in the personal concerns of individuals, such as how to deal with insecurity resulting from irregular employment, and in public matters at the level of society, such as the erosion of community social capital due to organizational restructuring. Consider the issue of employment discrimination. An experienced engineer at the age of 55, who feels she is not being taken seriously in an employment interview because of her advanced age, may interpret this experience as demeaning and a personal failure. But when the large majority of older job applicants are refused a job, in a society that expects people to work until an age well beyond 60, then that is a public issue and a social problem. Organizations play a significant role in the relationship between personal troubles and public issues by creating opportunity structures in which systemic social and economic inequalities can arise.

Organizations are implicated in the production of social inequality in a variety of ways, structurally, spatially, temporally, and cognitively, linking them downwards to individual participants, sideways to competing and cooperating organizations, and upwards to institutional environments. As discussed in previous chapters, the details of these linkages are complex, varying in particular circumstances and necessitating some simplification in the analysis. The discussion below highlights three aspects of these linkages that appear both as "personal troubles" and "public issues": the quality of jobs in organizations that restructure to increase operational flexibility; the role of organizations in the social capital of local communities; and the emergence of the "unorganized individual" in the "new economy." The exact implications of the twin forces of organizational "flexibilization" and social individualization for the social capital of organizations and surrounding communities are not clear, given the available research evidence, but it is worthwhile to contemplate some of the more prominent possibilities.

2. Good jobs and bad jobs

The idea behind the concept of "organizational society" is that organizations are so central to social affairs that, in a sense, they have "absorbed society" (Perrow, 1991). By shaping public opinion, defining uses of technology, determining career opportunities, and so forth they have given relationships in civil society the character of dependent variables. Arguably, organizations have their greatest social impact through the design of jobs and career paths, influencing not only material opportunities for individuals, with implications for career streaming in families and local communities, but also perceptions of insecurity and risk, and thus people's sense of agency.

The large majority of people in the active labor force in the economically most developed societies work for someone else. Although a large proportion of wage-dependent people work in the largest organizations in industry and government, the majority of organizations are small. In the European Union, about 90 percent of firms employ fewer than ten workers, a proportion that is similar in all of the advanced industrial and service societies. Although elaborate job structures and employment systems are typically found only in the largest organizations, small organizations often mimic at least the rudiments of such systems (e.g., formal employment interview, job evaluation, performance assessment), either because they are required to do so through employment legislation or because they see this as a means to enhance their public reputation. Innovations in organizational forms that diffuse easily throughout the economy can, therefore, have a significant impact on employment relations in society at large (Barley and Kunda, 2001).

Until not too long ago, bureaucratic employment structures, enhancing employment stability and rewarding worker loyalty to the organization, were considered the standard in modern corporations. Supported by the growth of mass production and by institutions geared to maximize stability (e.g., labor legislation, import restrictions), bureaucratic forms of employment were the perceived norm, at least in the core sectors of the economy (Piore and Sabel, 1984). In its highly stylized version, the "standard" employment relationship in primary sector organizations (e.g., automobile, oil and mining, banking, government) included career mobility chains, through which employees could pass as they accumulated skills and experience. It also included elaborate training systems and seniority rules, enforced by strong labor unions and professional associations which restricted membership at the point of entry in order to limit competition and increase employment security. The jobs in these arrangements were considered "good" in that they were comparatively well paid, afforded opportunities for career development, and protected against arbitrary discrimination (Kalleberg, 2003). Opportunities were organized in the form of an internal labor market that allocated jobs along stages in career ladders, supported by evaluation systems that rewarded skill development and worker commitment. Because of their greater market power, large employers in the primary sector could generally afford to maintain internal labor markets that gave workers a chance to compete for "good" jobs. They also had little choice but to offer such jobs. Large capital investments, pressures from labor unions, and expectations from the public made it too costly for them not to offer jobs that came with employment security, generous benefit packages, and (re-)training programs. In other words, corporations had a rational interest in creating a well-trained and loyal workforce as a means to maintain their dominant position in product markets.

In recent decades, the growing power of shareholders interested in short-term results, lower-wage foreign competition, and institutional changes in the form of market deregulation, trade liberalization, and privatization of state-owned firms has put enormous pressure on the larger organizations to develop more flexible employment structures. Corporations have sought greater flexibility in a variety of ways (Atkinson, 1987): functionally, by broadening skill requirements and adjusting worker assignments (e.g., multiskilling, project work); numerically, by altering the volume of labor inputs in line with market demand (e.g., labor outsourcing); temporally, by relying more on temporary employment structures (e.g., casual workers); and financially, by moving towards performance-based pay systems (Kalleberg, 2003). Of course, the "standard" employment relationship, as described above, has never been the only or primary form of employment, not even in the core sector of the economy. Opportunities to enter the primary labor force were not equally distributed, and not all jobs in core sector organizations were "good" in the above-described sense. Lower-tier jobs (e.g., secretarial, janitorial, custodial) in these organizations were not too dissimilar from jobs in the peripheral sector of the economy, traded primarily in the secondary labor market and leading to comparatively high employment insecurity. These were also the jobs that large corporations have always tended to outsource in times of economic stress, given the comparatively low transaction costs associated with coordinating routine jobs (Masters and Miles, 2002). Only a small proportion of jobs in core sector organizations could be considered "elite" in the sense of providing opportunities for creativity and exclusivity most cherished by professional workers. Recruitment into such jobs may involve bureaucratic selection procedures, but informal referral systems are used as well, reminiscent more of the affiliative routines of medieval guilds (Kieser, 1989) than the merit-based logic of modern organizations (Baron et al., 2007). Entry into jobs that are difficult to formalize and routinize, because they require intuition, discretion, and judgment, is often circumscribed by incentives for social exclusion, leaving room for arbitrary discrimination. Organizational restructuring to achieve more flexibility creates additional spaces for differential treatment discrimination, with implications for organizational social capital.

2.1 Differential treatment discrimination

According to human capital theory, differences in economic returns reflect different human capital endowments in labor supply (Becker, 1975). The theoretical argument is straightforward: to the extent that worker productivity depends on skills and experience, and to the extent that employers reward productivity, workers with more human capital will receive higher returns on their investment, while organizations can improve their performance by investing in skill-specific training (Ployhart et al., 2011). From this perspective, minorities face restricted access to "good" jobs if they are deficient in the human capital required for such jobs. Plenty of research, however, suggests that the magnitude of income inequalities in industries and occupations exceeds those associated with conventional measures of human capital: years of education and work experience (Tomaskovic-Devey et al., 2005). Despite equal human capital endowments, individuals experience different levels of exposure to labor market risks (e.g., likelihood of unemployment, low pay, hazardous work conditions), with women, the disabled, ethnic minorities, older workers, and other "visible minorities" normally bearing the greatest risks.

One reason for the unequal distribution of labor market risks is that human capital is to a large extent a social product, and not merely the result of an individual investment decision. Employment barriers exist not only at the level of organizations, in decisions related to hiring, appraisal, promotion, and so forth. Barriers are also created at the level of society, where group characteristics like race, age, and sex acquire cultural meaning and become social markers.

Institutional theory points to a number of fields (e.g., schooling, religion) in which social expectations concerning the demographic composition of different jobs are created. These then become the normative source of segregation expectations by employers, who allocate labor supply to activities with different economic and social value. Socialization theory postulates that social conditioning early in people's lives shapes personal identities (Legewie and DiPrete, 2012) and preferences to work in certain kinds of jobs (Hakim, 2000). Socialization effects are considered to be particularly strong in matters related to gender: women are encouraged to take on female-type jobs (e.g., nursing, hairdressing) and jobs that require little training and give them temporal flexibility (e.g., in retailing) so that they can act as family caretakers parallel to wage-employment, while men are encouraged to seek male-type (e.g., firemen, tradesmen) and career-oriented jobs (e.g., pilots) farther away from home. In societies with strong cultural norms rewarding sex-based specialization, one would expect jobs to be segregated, with women seeking employment primarily in organizations offering flexible work hours.

Research finds that socialization does play a significant role in creating segregated employment structures, although the influence of social conditioning norms has been declining, with variations across countries, industries, and occupations. For example, women's participation rates in science-based activities tend to decline as the individuals move from education to employment, but this decline has been much greater in the United States than in Finland (Hanson et al., 1996). Among younger workers in the United States, sex-based differences in job preferences have even increased (Tolbert and Moen, 1998), even in knowledge-intensive professions such as medicine, where job choices are made early in the educational process (Ku, 2011). Numerous studies have shown that in many industries job designers continue to draw heavily on cultural norms when defining task requirements according to who they expect will fill them (Petersen and Saporta, 2004). To the extent that opportunities to develop a satisfactory private solution to inferior employment patterns are not equally distributed in society, labor-market risks become a public structural issue.

Labor market studies show consistently that significant inequalities in employment outcomes (e.g., pay, authority, social status) remain, even after accounting for differences in workers' human capital endowment and the effects of occupational and organizational self-selection (Stainback et al., 2010). Much of this inequality results from discrimination based on employers' arbitrary judgments regarding an applicant's (e.g., for a job, promotion, retraining) personal attributes (e.g., physical appearance, emotional demeanor) or group characteristics (e.g., sex, race, age, immigrant status) (Roscigno et al., 2007). Discriminatory behavior may be subtle and covert, occurring also in organizations that are highly formalized in hiring, training, and performance evaluation, particularly in jobs requiring capabilities that are difficult to measure. Human capital theory is based on the assumption that employers can assess individuals' true economic value. In practice, however, employers often rely on *signals* of ability (Spence, 1974), making selection decisions based on formal educational credentials (e.g., diploma, license) assumed to be "credible," but that may mask structural inequalities in the acquisition of credentials (e.g., through differential access to schooling). In the absence of reliable measures and credentials, employers may use highly visible cues, such as sex and race, to make attributions about applicants' *potential* capabilities. Such practices not only structure the detection and assignment of human capital, and thus constrain its further development in the evolution of a person's career (Rosenbaum, 1990). They also formalize an individual's own personal circumstances, reinforcing past experiences of life and shaping his or her work-based identity (Watson, 2008). In addition to the sub-optimal performance implications for organizations (Backes-Gellner et al., 2011), occupational sex-typing, age-grading, and other forms of differential treatment discrimination in organizational selection and job design can have deep personal as well as public consequences (Weller, 2007).

In cases where legislation is introduced to contain the most extreme manifestations of discrimination, the intervention occurs against the background of firmly institutionalized views on the economic value of employing people from particular categories. Still, legislation intended to equalize employment opportunities may leave considerable room for employers to find an adaptive response that fits their own unique circumstances, thus producing more heterogeneity than would otherwise be expected in strongly institutionalized environments. Under conditions of economic uncertainty, organizations may be particularly likely to resort to sources of familiarity, creating an environment in which clientelism, nepotism, corruption, and other forms of favoritism can flourish. Modern institutions designed to check the most extreme manifestations of patronage include employment legislation to level the playing field on which firms compete for labor, training systems to provide common recruitment standards, and regulations to safeguard skill credentials.

However, institutions may also contribute to the structuring of employment opportunities in ways that are unrelated to actual work performance and, at worst, are discriminatory. For example, institutions may support credentialism as a form of ritual classification, inducing organizations to recruit employees with formal credentials without expending effort in evaluating the economic worth of credentials. Law firms in the United States often recruit associates disproportionately from law schools where most of their existing associates obtained their training. In addition to reducing environmental uncertainty, this practice also facilitates the organizational socialization of new employees in an industry where knowledge sharing is important but difficult to come by

(Tolbert, 1988). From an institutional perspective, recruiting individuals who are similar in outlook to current employees, because they have gone through the same occupational socialization process, facilitates the transmission of organizational culture to new generations of employees. From an economic perspective, such recruitment strategies reduce the transaction costs associated with organizational socialization, while also reducing the agency problem of goal incongruence between employer and employee. Evolutionary theory interprets such strategies with a view to the origins and persistence of variations. Any differences between law schools in belief systems, ideology, and approaches to client relations may be reproduced through the hiring practices of law firms, leading to the institutionalization of employment structures in a given population of organizations and thus turning the private problems of job seekers into a public issue reaching beyond the confines of a particular organization.

In sum, differential treatment discrimination is a widespread phenomenon, even in professional organizations, where one would expect institutional safeguards to be strongest. In the academic profession, for example, studies report many instances of structures and practices in universities that marginalize members of minority groups (Ogbonna and Harris, 2004). In the legal profession, women continue to be underrepresented in the more prestigious and remunerative positions in law firms, even after accounting for differences in educational qualifications, work experience, and personal choices (Hull and Nelson, 2000). In the anecdote below (8.1), Sarah's complaints center on an organizational culture in a law firm in which there is the common belief, institutionalized through the way client projects are allocated, that the ideal lawyer has no responsibilities outside work. She considers founding her own firm to escape from what (she feels) is a discriminatory work environment, and she wonders what kind of social network she could use to help facilitate her plans.

ANECDOTE 8.1

"I've had it," Sarah said to Candace, her long-time friend from their time together as law students. She was furious about having been overlooked in the last promotional round in the law firm in which she had worked since graduating from a reputable law school in the eastern United States. This was now the third year in a row that only men were offered a partnership. As far as she was concerned, this law firm was a "men's club," not a professional organization. In her view, all the men who had been promoted in recent years were no more competent than herself, and some of them had even less work experience than she did.

As far as she was concerned, her superiors had no valid reason for claiming that she was "side-tracked" by familial commitments and, therefore, would not be able to take on big client

(Continued)

projects. Sarah had no plans of becoming a mother or getting married. She had always made that clear to everyone in the firm. If there was anything they could complain about, it was her refusal to do the kinds of activities that many of her male colleagues engaged in to attract clients. This included going to sleazy bars with clients, playing golf with them, going to sports bars, and doing the sorts of things male lawyers often do when they "rub shoulders" with their most valued clients. She hated that kind of "macho culture," she told Candace. "I will never play those games if this is what they mean by job commitment. I love my work, but I don't want it to be the center of my life."

Candace knew what Sarah was talking about. She had similar experiences in her own law firm. Her male colleagues seemed to assume that the ideal lawyer is someone foregoing all external obligations, and that women lawyers were not as committed to their jobs because they had familial obligations. When she challenged her colleagues on this assumption, they would normally blame their clients, saying that clients dictate round-the-clock service and that it was only rational that the law firm would reward lawyers willing to do whatever it takes to meet clients' demands. "We don't have any choice," her male colleagues would say. "Honey, that's just how it is in this business."

To Sarah, these were all bogus arguments. If it was true that the firm offered more interesting work opportunities to its employees who did not have any familial obligations, then why was she not offered more such opportunities, given that she had no family to support? Her performance on her previous client projects was clearly equal to that of her male colleagues, and in some cases it was superior. She felt excluded from the more lucrative projects, for reasons that had nothing to do with her performance but had everything to do with gender-based discrimination.

Sarah felt that she was now very close to starting up her own law firm. Although she was convinced of her capabilities as a lawyer, she knew that it would take several years before her firm would run successfully. Friends had suggested that she could use her former colleagues' social networks to establish a good client base. Under normal circumstances this might be a good idea, she thought, but not in her case. Social networks are great if one wanted to widen one's professional circle, but not all connections are equal. How useful would social ties be if they came from people like her male colleagues?

2.2 Social capital and social network

Social capital is the individual's or organization's capacity to extract value from social networks. Individuals and organizations with more diverse connections to other actors tend to have more expansive repertoires of resources and ideas to work with innovatively. They are better positioned socially, economically, and institutionally, to exploit existing opportunities or explore opportunities in new terrains. Diverse network ties are most critically important in environments with declining resources, where the actors jockey for power or survival. The concept of social capital draws attention to the reach and structural configuration of social networks. When people are embedded in relations rich in social capital, they have occasions for coordinating action, sharing knowledge, developing identity, or building reputation. The social part of social capital highlights the normative and relational aspect of social networks, while the capital part indicates that there is economic value in social relations (Coleman, 1988). If the networked actors are able to coordinate their actions because they are well connected, but are not willing to coordinate, it may be because they see no utility in collaboration, as is often the case in organizations with teams formulated on paper but with no team orientation in practice.

As Sarah in the above anecdote (8.1) suggests, social networks are a critical asset in the organizational formation process, by acting as a channel for identifying business opportunities and procuring the necessary resources. Men and women may compose their social networks differently to achieve the same results, with women often having a higher proportion of kin and females in their networks than men, who draw more on the support from consultants and former work associates (Renzulli et al., 2000). People and organizations rich in social capital have close connections to a variety of others who have access to vital resources and are themselves linked to other resource holders. Social capital is a general resource, useful for a variety of purposes, but there are also risks and liabilities. For example, relations may be so tight that they lead to social closure, preventing innovation and change (Portes and Sensenbrenner, 1993). As such, the consequences of social capital are difficult to predict in the absence of further information about actors, their goals, and the context in which they use social capital. The social gathering shown in Exhibit 8.1 tells the observer nothing about the personal or collective goals these individuals may have in mind. The impression is that of a group of individuals who are oriented to each other, suggesting that they are members of an organization of sorts, but the nature and intensity of social ties is unknown. This group may possess social capital in the sense that existing social relations help the individuals achieve some goal. This goal might be to prepare a strategic plan for a business venture or to organize an illegal betting market at horse racing events. Social capital may be valuable for some people and some purposes (e.g., getting a job, obtaining funding for a new business) but harmful for other people and in other situations (e.g., price-fixing cartels, terrorist networks). One needs to know what the goals of a collectivity are before one can determine what kinds of resources qualify as "capital" and what kinds of relations should be considered "social." While it is *generally* true that people who are well connected improve their chances of obtaining better education, training, and jobs, and well-connected organizations improve their chances of recruiting more valuable employees and building new knowledge, one needs to inquire into the processes by which such outcomes are achieved in specific instances (Lin et al., 2001).

Exhibit 8.1

2.2.1 Inter-organizational network

Employers who are searching for job candidates are limited by the information available to them. They need to collect information about candidates' technical qualifications and attitudinal motivations, and they need to evaluate this information with a view to the likely performance of the person once hired. According to agency theory, any problems of goal incongruence between employers and employees are exacerbated in situations where information is asymmetrically distributed (Eisenhardt, 1989). Job applicants pose a "moral hazard" to employers to the extent that they have an incentive to hide their shortcomings and to overstate their competencies. The likelihood of an applicant creating this risk depends on a variety of factors, including personality, economic need, and the information the person has about the potential employer, all factors which the employer may find difficult to assess. The problem of "adverse selection" for employers arises to the extent that the pool of job applicants contains many individuals who pose a "moral hazard," causing them to offer jobs to applicants who will, on average, not fulfill their promises.

Employers increasingly make use of social media to identify potential job candidates, but this source is subject to noise (e.g., "moral hazard") and may raise ethical and legal problems (e.g., privacy). Employers may find it more effective to draw on their personal connections to sources of information outside the organization, meeting relevant people in social clubs, trade shows, or business associations to collect information about potential job candidates.

Exactly how they use their social ties, and whether they seek information from sources in their own industry or in other industries (Geletkanycz and Hambrick, 1997), depend on the type of job they are seeking to fill, the difficulty of evaluating a candidate's qualifications, and the type of relationship they have with the actors in their network. For example, in cases where the organization needs to maintain a close relationship with another organization, one would expect the external organization to influence the kinds of individuals the organization recruits and the position given to them in the organization's job structure. Law firms, for instance, are more likely to promote women attorneys to partnership positions if the firms' corporate clients have women in visible and important leadership positions and if they are resource dependent on a small number of client firms (Beckman and Phillips, 2005). When strong resource dependence exists, it is important that law firms attend closely to the interests of the client, including the client's views on equity and gender issues in employment. The nature and quality of inter-organizational relations thus influences the employment relations practices in the partner organizations. From the evolutionary perspective, the social networks connecting organizations function as a reproductive mechanism for diffusing models of employment relations throughout a given population of organizations. From the institutional perspective, this diffusion may help to institutionalize a particular model as the "best" one available, even if it is not the most efficient one.

When seeking information through social networks, organizations may either deepen their existing relations or expand their network to include more partners, depending on the type of uncertainty they face (Beckman et al., 2004). Organizations facing *internal* uncertainty, because they have adopted a new technology, are struggling with increased labor turnover, or for some other organizational reason, may form relationships with new network partners out of a desire for risk diversification. When such organizations attempt to recruit new employees with different skills, they may broaden their networks to include partners from domains in which these skills are already in use. New relationships provide them with new information about the type of job applicant they are seeking. Organizations may also experience *environmental* uncertainty, for example because they operate in a tight labor market in their industry or because they face the potential removal of import restrictions for foreign competitors. To cope with this uncertainty, they may strengthen their existing network ties to organizations in their industry, to develop, for example, a joint lobbying strategy (Pfeffer and Salancik, 1978). Strengthening network ties is more important when the source of uncertainty is the supply of non-standard labor skills (e.g., management talent) than the supply of standard labor skills. Management competencies are generally more difficult to evaluate and the search for such competencies often requires tacit knowledge from trustworthy sources.

2.2.2 Interpersonal network

Individuals seeking employment can obtain information about job vacancies and the quality of organizations offering vacancies through formal or informal channels, but both sources have limitations. Information available through formal channels (e.g., organization websites, newspaper advertisements) may be seriously biased by the organization's self-representational tactics, creating a "moral hazard" for the person seeking employment. To compensate for this risk, job seekers may rely more on informal social network ties, such as personal connections to individuals who already work for the organization. However, the usefulness of social ties varies depending on the status, motivation, and resourcefulness of the contact person in the network, as well as the links this person has with others, who may compete for the same job. The social capital that inheres in social networks remains a non-specific resource until it is given concrete value and force through action.

Information about where to find individuals who control access to jobs, or have knowledge of the quality of jobs and employers, is not equally distributed in society. In general, people with more human capital are better informed; they have broader social networks and are more capable of using their social contacts productively. Social class plays an important role as well. People from more privileged social backgrounds tend to have larger and more diverse social networks (Erickson, 1996), and are more likely to use these networks to obtain better jobs (Granovetter, 1995) and self-employment opportunities (Anderson and Miller, 2003). Regarding the use of social networks in wage-employment, one needs to distinguish between their value for obtaining a job and for succeeding on the job. Many members of minority groups have extensive social networks, but they still end up in marginal jobs and in the periphery of the economy. It is not enough to have people in one's social network who are connected to the organization in which one wants to work; one also needs to be able to *mobilize* their active support. Once a contact is made, the job applicant still has to negotiate the conditions of employment. Minorities are at a disadvantage in this for a variety of reasons, including perceived lack of credibility, commitment, and human capital (Seidel et al., 2000). A study of poor blacks in the United States found that for many of those who had job contacts with employed persons, the contact persons were reluctant to recommend them to employers (Smith, 2005). They feared that the person they recommend would perform poorly on the job, and this would reflect badly on themselves. Once recruited, minority members may not derive the same benefits from their social connections as the members of mainstream groups can, or they may experience trade-offs that majority members may not have. For example, having close ties to members of the same ethnic background may provide important social and affective support, but such ties may be viewed negatively by colleagues from different ethnic groups when the ties are used for instrumental purposes, such as seeking promotion to a managerial position (Ibarra, 1995). Social network ties thus do not automatically translate into social capital.

Employers may be interested in attracting workers with rich social capital, particularly those individuals who have close contacts to sources of valuable information outside the organization. One would expect that knowledge-intensive organizations benefit most from members who are well connected to diverse sources of knowledge. Plenty of research suggests that an organization's ability to attract new clients and maintain a positive reputation in society depends not only on its competence to produce high-quality services and low-priced goods but also on the quality and structure of its connections to its external constituents. The study reported in the research brief (8.1) below shows that social capital can be important for the long-term survival chances of firms for which knowledge creation is key (Pennings et al., 1998). The firms in this sample benefited from having individuals in their workforce who maintained strong social ties with potential clients and, in this way, contributed to the organizations' knowledge base. Employees' personal social capital can be a valuable asset for the organization that employs them. From the perspective of the organization, the social ties of employees are evidence of their social credentials and their ability to turn these into economic benefits. From the perspective of the organization's stakeholders, employees' social networks increase the organization's public standing.

RESEARCH BRIEF 8.1

Much research has examined the role of social capital – and of social networks in particular – from the viewpoint of individuals seeking jobs, affective support, or promotional opportunities. Comparatively little research has been conducted on the outcomes for organizations which hire individuals with a view to their personal social capital. The aim of the study by Pennings et al. (1998) was to explore the organizational performance outcomes of recruiting workers with personal networks rich in social capital. The authors reasoned that employees' connectedness with potential clients would help attract clients for the organization, and that this would have consequences for the organization's long-term survival chances. They argued that a workforce rich in social capital is beneficial for the organization, especially in those cases where clients lack information about service quality. In the absence of reliable information, clients face higher transaction costs, so they place extra value on interacting with those firms that employ people already known to them from previous relations in other contexts.

The authors tested arguments about the relative importance of firm-specific and industry-specific social capital for organizational performance, using data on the complete population of Dutch accounting firms for the period from 1880 to 1990. One of the main findings was that the social

(Continued)

(Continued)

capital accumulated by partners in the firms reduced the likelihood of organizational failure, whereas the social capital of lower-ranked associates was inconsequential. Also, it was partners' firm-specific experience that reduced failure rates, rather than the industry experience they had accumulated from working in a range of different organizations. The explanation given was that when employees leave a firm and find employment in the client's environment, they have strong incentives to take advantage of the social capital they had built up in the previous firm. They will, therefore, prefer to continue business relationships with clients known to them from their previous employment.

This study offers insights into the structure of social capital at the aggregate level of organizations. However, given available data, it cannot say anything about the workings of social capital at the micro-level of actual behavior. For example, the study included no measures of information exchange or influence attempts in employee–client exchanges. Nor were there any measures to assess the strength or types of relationships between employees and clients. Also, the researchers used the firm's age as a proxy for knowledge accumulation, but they could not measure knowledge building through employees' social networks directly. A direction for future research is to develop and test hypotheses about the mechanisms by which social networks yield knowledge benefits to the organization, and the mechanisms by which these knowledge outcomes translate into improved organizational survival chances.

In summary, conventional wisdom tells us that whom you know is often as important as what you know, but in order to understand why it matters whom you know, one needs to appreciate the many different ways in which social networks of various types and structures confer different kinds of advantages. Building social capital at the aggregate level involves variable processes at the individual level of cognition and action, related to interpretation, competence, and motivation. Individual actions may or may not translate into collective social capital, with benefits for knowledge sharing, innovation, and the like. How individuals build social capital for their own purposes may be their private problem, without necessarily becoming a public issue at the organizational level. To understand how individual social capital translates into organizational social capital, one needs to know how attitudinal orientations and behavioral routines in a given network arise and become socially shared among the actors, to the point where social relations produce new options and opportunities both for the individuals and the collectivity in which they are engaged. Informal social gatherings, such as those shown in Exhibit 8.1, may very well be a mechanism by which collective goals are developed and enforced, but the processes involved may differ widely across individuals and situational contexts. Factors at the individual level, such as cognitive ability, perceptions of self-efficacy, and approaches to risk all play a role in the construction of organizational social capital, as do the structural attributes of organizations, such as the configuration of positional authority and the distribution of units with specialized responsibility. Likewise, to understand the evolution of social capital at the level of organizational populations, one needs to know the structure and quality of social relations between individuals who link the organizations in their role as boundary spanners. These linkages play a key role in the flow of resources between organizations, with implications for the social capital of local social communities as the environment in which organizations are most directly embedded. The contribution of organizations to local social capital can be a critical public issue.

3. Community social capital

Much writing about "knowledge societies" highlights the role of organizational and institutional infrastructures in relationally bounded agglomerations, because knowledge creation often requires close interpersonal and inter-organizational interaction between actors with different competencies. Various assets have to come together in local space to form a rich resource environment in which the exploration of new knowledge can flourish (Gertler and Wolfe, 2004). These assets include the specialized knowledge of individuals and organizations, the capabilities of collective-service institutions like funding arrangements (e.g., venture capital) and educational programs (e.g., retraining), and the shared mindset of actors embedded in social networks. The experience of many regions around the world suggests that it is possible for local communities to enhance their social and economic development by nurturing an organizational system that includes the above assets (Asheim et al., 2006), although the specific combination of these assets can vary greatly across industrial and cultural contexts (Staber, 2007). Evolutionary variety in competencies, technologies, and organizational governance forms provides fertile ground for innovations, as long as the selected innovation does not foreclose alternative paths of development with potentially greater adaptive value in a new environment.

In the ideal-typical conception of community social capital, shared norms, values, and understandings facilitate cooperation among individuals and organizations to their mutual advantage. Civic-mindedness in the form of solidarity, trust, and tolerance of alternative visions and perspectives, as well as a civic culture built on collective action in the form of voluntary citizenship engagements and overlapping interest associations, are the key ingredients of local social capital (Putnam, 2000). The actors are linked in multiple ways, such as overlapping memberships in organizations, with some of these organizations acting as bridges between competency areas (Burt, 2005). Community social capital contributes to an innovative milieu within which organizations can experiment (Fromhold-Eisebith, 2004), while organizations contribute to local social capital through resource exchanges with local suppliers and institutions. Dysfunctional organizational behaviors (e.g., favoritism, arbitrary discrimination) can arise when organizations are not effectively embedded in the social community, especially in areas where direct customer contact is critical, as in education or health care. For example, the ethnic diversity of hospital staff can improve the quality of service delivery, if such diversity is representative of the ethnic demography of the local community (King et al., 2011). Dysfunctional behaviors are more likely to occur in organizations that view themselves as entities operating autonomously and without regard to local concerns.

Scholars working from different theoretical perspectives highlight different aspects of local social capital, such as the efficiency of different forms of governance or the construction of a shared identity, but they tend to agree on the central insight that the knowledge embedded in social capital is a tradable asset whose utility depends on how individuals and organizations are connected (Uzzi, 1996). What kinds of network structures – how densely the actors are connected, the presence of strategic leaders, the global reach of relations, and so on – connecting individuals, organizations, and institutions, are most conducive to entrepreneurship, business innovation, and community economic development depends on the particular historical, political, technological, and cultural context in which the networks exist. In some regions, it may be the constellation of political and religious interests which govern development. In other regions, it may be the linkages between local producers and international firms which determine local investment behavior. Research suggests that there is no single developmental path of local communities to which social capital contributes (Staber, 2007).

Local social capital plays a key role in community studies informed by arguments from organizational economics, institutionalism, and evolutionary theory. Economists often refer to the "alignment hypothesis" from transaction cost theory when proposing that firms match modes of collective governance to the features of individual transactions. Whether firms and support institutions use more informal governance forms, relying on interpersonal trust, social norms, and implicit understandings, or whether they use more hierarchical forms, relying on explicit contracts or the authoritative intervention of a "principal" acting as a broker (e.g., government-appointed third-party arbitrator), depends on the constellation of transaction attributes, such as the tacitness of the knowledge that is exchanged or the specificity of the firms' investments in the exchange (Bell et al., 2009). Because tacit knowledge creates strong demands on the interpretation of information, one would expect organizations with structures supporting trust-based informal relations between boundary spanners to be at an advantage (Asheim et al., 2007). By contrast, when organizations make specialized investments in a relationship that is dedicated to particular uses, it is costly to switch partners. In this case, organizations have a stronger incentive to safeguard their investments through hierarchical control mechanisms (Geyskens et al., 2006).

Transaction cost economists often turn to institutional theory to explain the influence of a larger culture on exchange relations between economic actors. If the actors are embedded in an institutional environment providing a milieu for informal communication, transactions are easier to monitor and enforce if they occur through trust-based social mechanisms. Hierarchical governance may be efficient for routine and standard tasks, but it encounters difficulties if there is demand for new knowledge. The high-tech industrial complex in Silicon Valley is an example of a local organizational field of highly specialized firms and institutional support organizations that can flexibly adjust their transactions because they operate within a macro-culture rich in social capital. The social capital in Silicon Valley is grounded in shared norms regarding the value of competitiveness and innovation based on the actors' calculative performance-oriented trust and confidence in the reliability of exchange partners (Cohen and Fields, 1999). By contrast, the social capital in industrial districts in northern Italy is based more on kinship ties between business owners and on worker communities held together by local cultural traditions and political and religious ideologies, although there has been growing pressure recently towards a more market-driven approach to collaboration (Rinaldi, 2005). Thus, while social capital is important to innovation and local economic development in general, its meaning and its structural and temporal features can vary significantly across regions. Such differences make it difficult to transplant the experiences of one region to other regions, without developing new forms of governance.

Institutional theorists explore differences in collective governance with a view to the identity orientations of organizations in local communities. In economically successful communities, so the argument goes, the most prominent institutional forces tend to revolve around a collective identity, which the organizations reproduce in their everyday interactions. Without such interaction, there is a risk that the common identity disintegrates into nothing more than a nominal label. If, however, it is actively mobilized and experienced as a central ingredient of social capital, it can be a powerful tool for collective governance. A strong community identity is often demonstrated to the outside world in the form of a collective image with reputational effects (Staber and Sautter, 2011), used by firms as a mechanism for recruiting labor, and by local governments for marketing purposes and for attracting new investments (Romanelli and Khessina, 2005). Many studies have documented the advantages of a distinct local identity as a source of regional competitive advantage, especially for industries and regions subject to strong globalization pressures (Gertler and Wolfe, 2004). Sustainable advantage requires that the identity is a unique and difficult-to-imitate aspect of local social capital, which takes time to develop. A distinct identity, giving rise to robust images, such as Bangkok as the "City of Angels," Hollywood as "Tinsel Town", or Rome as the "Eternal City," cannot be purchased; it evolves from the bottom up and over the long term, and is, therefore, difficult to copy.

Identification with other actors in the same community can be a powerful cognitive mechanism for coordination, providing a cognitive link between organization and community. In the face of ambiguity, organizations often take their cues from what other organizations are doing, and they pay particular attention to those organizations that are similar to themselves and are located in close vicinity. For example, firms often adopt particular employment relations approaches (e.g., "bureaucratic" versus "professional") or management compensation models (e.g., "golden parachutes") to the extent that other firms in the same community do so (Davis et al., 2003; Hannan et al., 2006). Adopting similar models signals legitimacy in the eyes of constituencies located in geographic proximity. A study of the largest US industrial corporations found that firms were more likely to share governing board members with firms located in the same city if the city had a greater number of upper-class social clubs (Kono et al., 1998). Research in other countries has revealed similar patterns. In the Netherlands, for example, executives tend to forge social relations locally, using informal gatherings in places like dinner clubs and stadium skyboxes to build close intercorporate ties (Heemskerk, 2007). In a New Zealand boat-building district, knowledge sharing among the firms takes place in local sailing clubs and sports clubs (Chetty and Agndal, 2008). Such studies show that a common identity does not merely exist; it is constructed through the everyday interactions of individuals, involving trust and trust-building, but also power and political struggle. In some cases, identification with the local environment is strong enough to maintain social relations even with direct competitors. In the ship-building cluster in the Scottish Clyde River region, for example, kinship relations between the owners of companies have been the main mechanism by which a strong local identity and social cohesiveness in the business community were reproduced over the last three centuries (Ingram and Lifschitz, 2006).

Evolutionary theory sees in such historical legacies the potential for structural inertia in the development of local economies. Business cultures, labor relations systems, and collective governance systems cannot be created overnight, and they cannot be changed every time there is an environmental shock. Difficulties of adaptation can sometimes be traced to a region's longstanding dependence on a single industry and to historically sedimented social structures. Tight social structures can lead to a certain degree of "trained incapacity" to read new signals in a changed environment. In some regional clusters it is strong family connections between companies that inhibit change, as in some Italian industrial districts where extended family networks, which had once stimulated the growth of the industry, have became a source of inertia when market conditions changed (Rinaldi, 2005). In other clusters it is the progressive standardization of technology that makes transformations difficult, as in the Swiss watchmaking cluster in the 1980s (Kebir and Crevoisier, 2008). Tradition can have powerful effects, keeping organizations from strategic change, as in some German textile clusters, where some firms take elaborate measures to reproduce a local business culture based on interpersonal rivalry and mistrust, rather than switching to more cooperative actions to ward off common threats to their local industry (Staber, 2009).

In some cases, the community conditions at the time an organization is founded have a strong imprinting effect on organizational forms, explaining why the original forms persist over extended periods of time even if environments change dramatically. For example, the way organizational founders deal with environmental demands (e.g., imitating particular organizations, following some institutional rules but not others) during the founding process defines the basic framework for organizational design and labor relations (Hannan et al., 2006). A study of the geography of corporate governance forms in the United States found that business clusters created before the advent of air travel maintained more densely connected corporate networks and interlocking directorates into the twenty-first century than younger communities of comparable size (Marquis, 2003). The network imprinting effect, in this case, reflected the impact of local norms regarding business conduct, which the leading local companies passed on to firms that newly entered the community. A company joining an established business community was more likely to appoint directors to its board from the cluster of local companies than was a comparable new company in a younger business community. This practice had the effect of creating a particular pattern of inter-organizational relations that was reproduced over time, independent of changes in the environment.

Stability in local business cultures and institutional structures is part of the explanation why organizational communities often find it difficult to switch to a different path of development, as illustrated by the cluster of vertically integrated high-tech firms near Boston after World War II (Saxenian, 1994). Thus, if one wants to understand the construction and maintenance of local social capital, one needs to study how the actors relate to local institutions to achieve their particular objectives. Whether they operate on the basis of norms that enforce trust-based mutualism and cooperation, or distrust-based individualism and competitive rivalry, is a question requiring attention to the institutions through which the actors' orientations are reproduced. It makes a difference if government regulations, financing arrangements, public media engagements, and so on reward, say, cooperative or competitive labor relations in organizations. In the former case, one would expect more labor–management cooperation and a stronger worker welfare orientation, with a greater emphasis on helping workers advance their career and supporting their identification with the organization as a source of self-identity. In the latter case, one would expect more antagonistic labor relations and a stronger "do-it-yourself" attitude to career building, encouraging workers to construct their own environment for self-identity. If one views organizations as networks of differentiated positions as the context in which individuals create an identity, it becomes clear that fundamental structural changes in these networks can affect the maintenance of personal identities. Organizational restructuring intended to increase the level of functional, numerical, temporal, and financial flexibility in the employment of labor can have far-reaching implications for workers' sense of security and well-being, to the point where some people may feel "disembedded" from organizations, depending on whether weakened attachments are seen as voluntary or involuntary. Clearly, the labor force includes people who actively seek opportunities for contingent work because they value independence. Bernhard, in Anecdote 4.1, is among those people who use whatever positional power they have in the organization to defend a distinct personal identity. He acts to create distance between himself and his former colleagues, erecting categories and sharpening boundaries to defend his autonomy, but he is not "unorganized." He feels a strong connection to the organization that employs him. Sam in Anecdote 2.1, by contrast, seeks new opportunities to connect to a range of different individuals and organizations in order to build a dynamic identity.

4. The "unorganized individual"

The relationship between social capital and employment structures at the level of organizations and organizational communities raises questions about the nature of workers' embeddedness in the life of organizations and the implications for personal identity building. The basic nexus between the members of an economic enterprise and the organization itself is, for most people, the fact of employment. Whatever else workers may be doing in the organization that employs them (e.g., getting entertainment, seeking comradeship, finding a mate), they are essentially there to earn a living and to derive a sense of self- and well-being from the fact of employment. In this view, the "organized individual" is a person who derives meaning from organizational attachment as an *employed* person. Work in the employing organization is central to the individual's condition of life: it carries moral prestige, reflects the person's long-term strategic thinking, and builds character. The "*un*organized individual," by contrast, is not a person who is disoriented or chaotic, but an individual who actively and reflexively creates meaning out of his or her *disconnection* from the organization. This individual may have an irregular status in the labor market and may be employed on an ephemerally contingent basis, but does not depend on organizations for building a strong sense of self.

With respect to the meaning of employment for the "organized individual," one may distinguish between two perspectives: the organization seen as a central source of identity for individual members, and the organization seen as a means of material sustenance. Regarding the former view, organizations provide a classification system for individuals to build self-identity by differentiating positions horizontally and vertically, and by endowing positions with different resources and authority. Recruitment, socialization, evaluation, and task assignment are some of the ways in which members come to occupy organizational identity spaces which may or may not be consistent with their personal identity (Watson, 2008). The individual's self-conception may, for example, collide with the organization's identity, as when practicing Catholics find it difficult to work in an organization that expects its employees to work on Sundays because it wants to project the image of a customer-friendly organization. Alternatively, individual and organizational identities may be related consistently, as in the case of a sports club offering opportunities for employees to act out their competitive personality. People may join specific organizations to maintain a self-conception closely tied to the kind of work they are doing and the kind of people they interact with while on the job. They may see their membership in the organization as a means to consolidate their personal identity or to give it more visibility. Working for a social movement organization like Greenpeace or Amnesty International may carry more authenticity for some people than being merely a fee-paying member. Research shows that an employee's identification with the organization can significantly reduce the agency costs associated with ensuring that employee actions do not harm the organization (Boivie et al., 2011). For this reason, organizations may seek mechanisms that encourage sustained member identification. Some organizations engage in heavy-handed rituals to dramatize their exclusivity and to reaffirm and celebrate – both for newcomers and existing members – the value of "being one of us," such as military organizations "hazing" new recruits (Pershing, 2006) or hospitals "overworking" newly hired nurses (Evans et al., 2010). The view of organizational employment constituting a powerful source of self-identity is thus to argue that the private issue of identity-building is inextricably tied to the public problem of regulating the collective outcomes of identity-building. To ward off public intervention, organizations will want to avoid the impression that the individual or organizational identity maintenance efforts are inconsistent with the "public interest."

The alternative perspective on the meaning of employment for the "organized individual" emphasizes employment as a means of material sustenance. In this view, the main purpose that keeps the person tied to the organization is the prospect of obtaining money and other material rewards, to ensure a sense of ontological security, and to prevent feelings of anxiety. Whether employees like their job, appreciate their colleagues, or worry about the organization's mission is largely irrelevant. In the extreme case, employees care about the organization only to the extent that it survives long enough to provide them with material support, which is more specific and divisible than intangible rewards (e.g., sociability, having fun). They feel bound to the organization only if the financial bribes are large enough to extract their commitment, which will vanish as soon as they perceive that there is no external confirmation of their contributions ("No one appreciates me around here"). If they remain with the organization, they will then either seek a larger or a different set of bribes (e.g., favoritism in promotion, assignment to a more interesting task) or will engage in sabotage or more subtle forms of "voice" (e.g., working-to-rule, backstabbing colleagues).

Both of these perspectives on the meaning of organizational employment reflect on the "organized individual's" sense of attachment to an organization, but they provide only a partial picture. Although employment is one of the most important classificatory principles in society, with deep implications for people's life chances and the way they deal with private problems, the employment-centered image of the "organized individual" – regardless of whether it is seen from a social identity or an economic-calculative perspective – is unrealistic if it is based on a binary distinction between employed and unemployed and ignores what people actually do *within* these categories. Employment and unemployment are socially constructed categories, similar to other social categories (e.g., occupations, job titles) that are ranked, reproduced, imposed, defended, and resisted, and are given meaning through action. Individuals may or may not have particular feelings about their employment status, but this status is only made *socially* real by virtue of their being a member of this category, even if they are not aware of their membership. Employment categories, such as skilled/unskilled, mental/manual, or blue-collar/white-collar, may be distant from the people to whom they refer. It would be fairly uncommon, for example, for managers to spend much time wondering whether they are members of the "managerial class," "power elite," or some other social stratum, although many of them probably behave *as if* they belonged to a distinct category of people, as Bernhard does in Anecdote 4.1. While "management" denotes an individual identity, it is also a *social* category, referring to a class of people who "belong" together even if they don't know of each other and don't interact as members of this category. As a social category, "management" becomes a public issue regarding social concerns such as domination or responsibility.

The notion of category is complicated by the fact that there is a distinction between the general definition of the category and its culturally specific construction in a particular instance. Employment categories have general value (e.g., for research, public policy, official statistics), but it is not clear what the implications are for actual behavior. There are many different ways in which people identify with and behave with reference to social categories. One is not born into an employment category in the same way that one is born into a family or a residential neighborhood. A manager, for example, is *made* into the person that he or she is, socially through everyday social encounters (e.g., meetings with consultants, presentations to clients) and institutionally through rituals (e.g., press conferences) and political relationships (e.g., lobbying). Social construction of employment categories means that the individual's identity is spatially situated in terms of relations *vis-à-vis* others, and these relations may vary across organizational sites. Organizational participants create their identity through social encounters both on the organization's public frontstage and private backstage (Goffman, 1959: 106–140). Identity work may involve formal actions and routines (e.g., chairing taskforce meetings, e-mails to colleagues), but much behavior is also habitual or improvised, rather than calculated and rule-governed (Berger and Luckmann, 1966). Some of the actions taking place frontstage – where one would normally expect people to follow formal rules – may be improvised to cope with unforeseen events, but improvisation may be seen as legitimate only if it remains within the framework of existing formal routines. Some of the behavior backstage – where one would normally expect people to behave more informally – may be strategically calculated to safeguard one's identity or to promote one's self-image, but calculative behavior may turn into a habit. Restaurant waiters may retreat to the backstage of a kitchen to let off steam about a "terrible customer," managers may have a "private talk" with an employee to restore authority, and school principals may criticize a teacher publicly in front of parents to demonstrate change management. Identity work may involve different kinds of behaviors in different sites, which make sense to the individual, but in the eyes of audiences, the individual's actions may not add up to consistency across situations. The image of the "organized person" has long been that of a person who has an unambiguous and stable identity based on his or her orientation to rules, standards, and routines, and reinforced by consistent behavior, both in public and private spaces, but there are many contexts and situations where the actual evidence contradicts this image.

An example of the "organized individual" is the "*Organization Man*" (Whyte, 1956), a person who is so utterly committed to the job and loyal to the organization that he (*sic!*) is not looking for choices and is unaware of whatever options there may be in even the most "totalizing" organization to pursue an identity of his own. The "organization man" has long been the image of the "perfect bureaucrat," a mostly dull, apathetic, and compliant individual who works in an equally one-dimensional organization, as depicted in writings about organizations during the mid-1900s, in which authors categorized male employees as "white collar men" (Mills, 1951) or "men in gray flannel suits" (Wilson, 1955), and distinguished between women employed as "tokens" and non-employed women as "office wives" (Kanter, 1977). This image has gradually been replaced by another image of the individual worker as a "free agent." In this alternative image, a person's commitment to the organization is driven by the search for opportunities to practice individual initiative, decision-making autonomy, and self-responsibility. This is the image of individuals who thrive on independence, are creative when given the chance to develop new ideas, cherish mobility of any kind, and take risks whenever the opportunity arises to improve their lot. Many of these people are self-employed (e.g., artists, financial advisors, copyeditors), while others are wage-employed in organizations which are increasingly under pressure to adopt more entrepreneurial and flexible structures, variously referred to as "network organizations," "boundaryless organizations," or "learning organizations" (Barley and Kunda, 2001; Smith, 1997). In an environment that rewards innovativeness and adaptability, the ideal-typical "postmodern" organization, according to this view, is one that supports individuals to pursue their independence, by providing structures offering such incentives as empowerment, participative management, quality circles, job enrichment, and 360-degree feedback.

In some cases this transformation towards organizational flexibility has indeed taken place, as evidenced by the increased use of team work, cross-functional project work, and flat hierarchies (Thompson and Warhurst, 1998). In many other cases, however, the assumed liberation from the bureaucratic regime of mass production and strict hierarchy has not materialized (Vallas, 1999). In many businesses (e.g., eateries, bakeries, call centers), there has been a resurgence of the old principles of scientific management and bureaucratic control systems, coupled with low wages and limited-duration work engagements (Kalleberg, 2009). The most visible developments in the macro-economy point to fundamental structural changes in the labor market of many of the advanced "postindustrial" countries, in which "neo-liberal" public policies have gone hand in hand with the image of the creative-innovative and self-reliant individual as the role model for market-conforming self-realization. Looking at the work histories of people, one observes that an increasing proportion of people in the younger cohorts are no longer playing out their careers from beginning to end in a single organization. People are moving between organizations at unprecedented rates, and in many industries this movement is more often horizontal or downwards than upwards. Episodes of employment are becoming shorter, as firms attempt to cut costs by relying more on contingent labor, employing people on short-term contracts, as needed. On the whole, the employment relationship has become more temporary, precarious, and individualized (Cappelli, 2008; Kalleberg, 2009; Sennett, 2006), with implications for personal autonomy and self-identity (Sennett, 1998).

4.1 Personal autonomy and self-control

The question that follows from the long-term trend towards "flexible specialization" in production (Storper and Christopherson, 1987) and precarious employment structures in organizations and industries (Kalleberg, 2003) is what happens to people who become disconnected from organizations and are forced into irregular patterns of economic activity at the periphery of an economy (Kalleberg, 2009), or are pushed into precarious self-employment as an alternative to unemployment (Bögenhold and Staber, 1991)? What are the meanings that people attach to a volatile career pattern characterized by extreme uncertainty and insecurity, and how do they build identities under such conditions (Webb, 2004)?

One argument is that irregular career patterns provide new opportunities for people with a calculative orientation to life (Giddens, 1991). For these people, market-oriented work relations are occasions to practice personally meaningful autonomy and self-control. Rather than eroding one's sense of self-worth, the socio-economic changes that accompany organizational restructuring create new opportunities for people to shape their own identity in ways that link variable experiences at work with those in other social domains. New technologies in communication and information processing (e.g., social media, mobile telephony, blogging software) provide new possibilities for moving in and out of contingent spaces (e.g., occupation, social clique, entertainment, training), while picking up elements of identity along the way. This is in line with the argument that social networks are not static structures for encounters of a specific kind, but are tools for building new options in continually evolving environments (White, 1992). "Persons themselves are not simply stationary nodes in a network, but are flexible constellations of identities-on-the-move" (Sheller, 2004: 49).

From this perspective, opportunities to develop latent talents, learn new skills, and explore challenges in new territories are seen as basically positive: humanizing, liberating, and empowering. Working in new environments and in diverse groups of people and social networks allows people to adapt their knowledge to their own purposes and capabilities, and creates occasions for learning how to deal with uncertainty and risk and how to improve their control over the terms of social relations. This may also expand people's general public realm and enhance the quality of their embeddedness in the social structures of local communities. The result is a self-identity that is reflexively and actively achieved rather than imposed or ascribed from the outside. The alternative would be, from this stylized model, a society in which people and organizations continue to work – bee-like in goal-directness and industriousness – on the construction of their bureaucratic prisons, in the end exhausted and no longer able to regenerate out of their own cultural reserves.

Some studies have explored these arguments with empirical data. They find that for many people, organizational restructuring towards greater flexibility has been accompanied by an increase in skills or the diversification of skills. Studies of subcontractors in technical professions (e.g., engineers, medical specialists, computer consultants) indicate extensive horizontal mobility for this group of workers who use informal social networks and temporary employ-ment agencies to locate new opportunities for improving their professional expertise and reputation (Kunda et al., 2002). Many of these workers view their career as a sequence of projects, and they use organizations mostly as a context for practicing their skills and developing further social contacts. Studies of self-employed workers find that many of them use the challenges of surviving in the "new economy" as an opportunity to carve out new spaces in which they flourish socially, intellectually, and emotionally (Fenwick, 2002). The more successful self-employed people are flexibly embedded in local social capital, benefiting from social support systems and institutions that pro-vide an environment in which creativity can flourish. Self-employed artists, for example, tend to cluster near a variety of organizations like galleries, work-shops, arts schools, and arts fairs to seek new social and professional contacts (Bain, 2005), as described in Anecdote 2.1. Freelancers sometimes share "co-working spaces" to access different knowledge sources and to facilitate social integration in fast-paced environments, while also minimizing transaction costs in production (Shirky, 2009). And an increasing number of academic teachers move worldwide between universities, and from contract to contract, to build a career (Dobbie and Robinson, 2008). Reliable data are not available to determine the proportion of people who perceive this new environment as emancipating, as opposed to those who consider it mere drudgery or a loss of cherished security.

4.2 Erosion of social bonds

An opposing view on the "liberating" identity implications of "flexible speciali-zation" in the "new economy" draws attention to the corrosive effects for social bonds (Sennett, 1998). Representatives of this view see in labor-market fragmentation and organizational flexibilization an intensification of tenden-cies that novelists during the 1800s described as "increasing uncertainty in an increasingly unknowable world." The consequences of being forced on to irregular career trajectories are considered corrosive in the sense that inter-rupted work biographies limit people's ability to plan for the future and to create sustainable social relations. In the stylized version of the old "standard" employment and career systems, people could develop a sense of attachment to others and were given enough time to develop the competencies required in a particular domain of knowledge. By investing in labor training for the long-term and by rewarding seniority, organizations could nurture loyalty in the workforce and build "competitive advantage through people" (Pfeffer, 1994).

The "sense of belonging" and mutual dependence, so the argument goes, is declining in an economy driven by short-term market orientations and resource requirements that make it difficult to build the social capital necessary for sustainable innovations. Developing social capital takes time and patience, but organizations that pursue a strategy of flexibility don't have time. Employees are expected to constantly update their skills to be able to accomplish many different things on short notice, in line with shifting tasks and projects, while those who commit to craftsmanship – characterized by depth, authenticity, and self-criticism – tend to be devalued, and may even be regarded with suspicion (Sennett, 2006). To the extent that people value stability and security, the foundation for their creativity is weakening when they feel no longer strongly embedded in organizations rich in social capital. The risk then is that they experience irregular employment episodes and career interruptions as personal failure and a threat to their sense of self-worth, with paralyzing consequences for society and economy. In so far as organizations are structured such that employment is short term, precarious, and constantly shifting, the problem of insecurity becomes incapable of a purely private solution, at least for those people who have difficulty dealing with uncertainty. To that extent, the private problem of insecurity becomes a public issue for government intervention.

Research has explored these issues at various levels. At the cognitive level, some studies have noted an increase in the number of people who say they "drift in isolation" (Sennett, 2006: 27) and feel less valued and more disposable. When such people have to create their own biography, they experience anxiety, if not existential dilemmas. At the level of organizations, studies indicate that some people react to flexibilization and individualization by becoming either cynical or by artificially over-stating their commitment to the organization's instrumental economic goals (Padavic, 2005). At the industry level, some studies note an increase in labor segmentation along gender and ethnic lines, as well as the closing down, rather than opening up, of "old boy networks." In the multimedia sector, for example, an environment normally associated with openness to innovation and tolerance for ambiguity, career survival depends heavily on "whom you know" (Christopherson, 2008). And at the local community level, some commentators note that the "new economy" leads many people to reduce their social engagement, evidenced in declining membership in voluntary associations and community organizations (Putnam, 2000). The erosion of local social capital can have broad-sweeping social and economic implications, related, for example, to the ability of local governments to attract new industries and to create jobs for the poor, and the ability of institutions to socially integrate immigrant populations (Kalleberg, 2009). For the members of some ethnic groups, the social capital they derive from their social networks may be the only source of economic opportunities, but to the extent that these networks are disconnected from the mainstream economy, they are merely taking the place of the old exclusionary organizational structures (Reingold, 1999). If the "new economy" is such that more responsibility is placed on the individual to create his or her own work biography, then the members of minority groups at the periphery of the economy are even more disadvantaged in the distribution of opportunities.

Debates about what kind of individual emerges in an "organizational society" that offers fewer opportunities for stable life-long employment careers in one or a few organizations can be situated within the context of discussions about some of the catchwords constituting the current *Zeitgeist* in politics, arts, literature, and so on. After some period of silence, which began at about the time when the communist regimes in Eastern Europe collapsed, scholars in various social theory camps have now resurrected old questions about the governance of a society that may have seen its best days already. These are questions about post-democracy, such as what room is left for truly democratic decision-making in a regime of financial imperatives and global competition in which organizational restructuring undermines individuals' capacity to form sound political judgments (Crouch, 2004). There are also questions about postmodernism (Bauman, 2002), such as whether the "anything goes" mentality of the "new" independent individual is a sign of emancipated creativity or of market-driven helplessness. Related to this are questions about the post-social individual (Knorr Cetina, 2001), a person who is no longer embedded in society through face-to-face relations "on the ground", but is someone who asks himself, "How do I adapt to an external world over which I have no influence?" The post-social individual finds security less in human bonds than in relations with non-human objects, such as computer screens and iPhones, and in technical-social media, such as internet platforms and chat rooms in virtual space. If this individual has a negative relationship to the organization that employs him or her, it is less informed by the type of dread and joylessness that is popularly associated with large-scale bureaucracy than by the ontological anxiety that is induced by organizational flexibilization and fragmentation (Sennett, 2006). The postsocial individual may survive through participation in social networks, but these networks are not necessarily of the type that creates robust social capital, providing collective strength and security. The image is that of people constantly "on the move," in search of events, happenings, and experiences, constantly reconstructing network connections that, because they are thin and ephemeral, mirror the volatile "organizational society" that gives rise to them in the first place.

5. Conclusion

Studies which focus on the cognitive or micro-interactional aspects of organizational phenomena often ignore macro-level factors, and vice versa. This makes it difficult to derive generalizations from evidence collected in the specific contexts of organizations, industries, and communities. Isolated studies of phenomena in specific situations have little potential for yielding generalizable principles. Instead, the goal should be theorizing in the "middle range" (Merton, 1967), to generate hypotheses that can be tested through comparative investigation. When examined in relation to specific social, economic, and technological contexts, it is clear that the relationship between organizations and individuals is multifaceted, dynamic, and largely indeterminate. For many people there are choices, but these are more or less constrained by the environment in which they carve out a livelihood for themselves. Whether these choices are "character building" or "character corroding" is difficult to say without knowing the particular context in which they emerge. For organizational analysis this means that investigators should use contextualization to avoid falling into the trap of testing hypotheses to "prove" that some theories are correct and some theories are wrong. The goal should be to discover the pattern of contexts in which the limiting assumptions of each theory become apparent, thus reaching a more sophisticated understanding of the multiple factors and mechanisms that operate across a spectrum of situations (McGuire, 1999: 407).

Since the beginnings of organization studies as a distinct academic discipline some fifty years ago, researchers have devoted their energies to exploring how much in the organizational world is driven by regularities and how much is driven by idiosyncratic conditions. What we can say in general is that whatever social regularities exist, they are not the result of deterministic laws of behavior but are the aggregate consequences of the purposive actions of individuals, interacting in environments that pose constraints as well as opportunities. A given organizational form can be realized in different ways, but there are certain principles (e.g., division of labor, decision heuristics) that can be identified in most situations. Similarly, if we want to discover the patterns in individuals' responses to organizational restructuring, we should not merely study the particular realizations of individual actions but rather the features that these actions share.

Much research on organizations has focused on individual behavior subject to structural constraints. Organizational structures impact on individuals in many different ways: they channel information for individual decision-making, create rules for task coordination, and create routines for individuals to pursue their goals. However, structures are lifeless until they are interpreted and acted upon by individuals with specific interests and capabilities. Structures are instantiated by individuals who perceive and give meaning to them, typically in interaction with other individuals operating under the same constraints. Some actions strengthen existing structures, as studied by institutional theorists who focus on the persistence of social order. Other actions transform structures to create something new, as noted by evolutionary theorists who regard variation as the raw material for change. And for organizational econo-mists a key issue concerns the cognitive limitations in individual action, leading to transaction costs and agency problems. For theorists working in all three camps, the understanding of individual behavior in organizations requires knowledge of how individuals turn sheer behavior into *meaningful* action, in spaces that must be filled through interpretations and practices.

Turning to the organizational level of analysis, it is clear that organizations will continue to be center stage in modern or postmodern society, even if developments in markets and institutions are such that more responsibility is placed on individuals. Scholars working on issues at the organizational level have investigated the manifold ways in which organizations create knowledge, mobilize resources, and legitimate their actions. Institutional theorists have examined how organizational forms become a taken-for-granted feature of the social landscape; evolutionary theorists have studied how organizational struc-tures co-evolve with the forces and organizations in their relevant environ-ments; and organizational economists have examined the conditions under which different forms of governance minimize agency problems and econo-mize on transaction costs. If one were to study organizations only in terms of individual action, one would miss the context in which action acquires mean-ing. The social structure of organizations imposes constraints on the shape of social relations. Understanding the mechanisms that create and reproduce these constraints is central to understanding a wide range of organizational phenomena, from the workings of an organization's internal labor market to the creation of social capital.

At the population level, the performance of organizations is influenced by the kind of linkages they maintain to institutions. Background institutions, such as industrial relations systems and labor legislation, affect organizational performance by defining incentive structures for labor training, shaping the parameters for labor–management cooperation, and so forth. Such institu-tions are broad enough to influence the innovative capacity of entire industries and regional economies, but the interventions of key people and organiza-tions in aggregating and reconciling the diverse interests "on the ground" matter as well. Institutional theory highlights the shared norms and values that facilitate coordination among the actors, while evolutionary theory draws attention to the possibility that too much institutional homogeneity can reduce adaptability by stifling the search for new solutions. For organi-zational economists, diversity is a source of friction between principals and their agents, and between specialized organizations in decentralized produc-tion systems. The advantage of a production system rich in social capital is that it makes the most of diversity, while keeping transaction costs to a minimum. Evolutionary theorists suggest that social capital is an asset only if it reproduces enough ambiguity and variability to prevent organizations from getting locked on to a developmental path that is too costly – economically or socially – to leave.

The risk of evolutionary dead-ends exists also at the level of society at large, if pressures towards stability are so strong that they hinder the reproduction of diversity. The intermediation by organizations in all institutionally relevant domains is a precondition for the governance of society. Societies with well-functioning democratic institutions have organizations that contribute to the innovative capacity of civil society, not by following a singular political or pure market logic, but by responding to a variety of interests and by permitting a variety of interpretations of the same activity. Differentiation plays a key role in the discovery process taking place in all subdomains of society. Organizations are central to horizontal differentiation in society, by sorting activities in industries, occupations, and jobs, and they contribute to vertical differentiation, by distributing decision-making rights in the form of hierarchies of authority and responsibility. The continued production of organizational diversity, in populations with sufficient competition to allow organizations to fail, is critical for the adaptability of society, because a system with more organizational diversity has a higher probability of having in hand some form that helps cope with conditions in changing environments (Hannan and Freeman, 1989: 8). At the level of theoretical understanding as well, organizational diversity in evolving environments creates plenty of opportunities for an insightful, multi-perspectival approach to the study of organizations, driving productive theorizing in new directions.

Recommended further reading

Amin, A. and Roberts, J. (eds) (2008) *Community, Economic Creativity, and Organization.* Oxford: Oxford University Press.
The contributions in this volume use the concept of "communities of practice" to explore the dynamic relationship between organizational innovation, economic creativity, and local economic development.

Krause, E. (1996) *Death of the Guilds: Professions, States, and the Advance of Capitalism, 1930 to the Present.* New Haven, CT: Yale University Press.
Using the case of medicine, law, engineering, and the professoriate in Britain, France, Germany, Italy, and the United States, the author suggests that the organized power of professions has been declining with the growth of capitalism and the state.

Marschall, D. (2012) *The Company We Keep: Occupational Community in the High-tech Network Society.* Philadelphia, PA: Temple University Press.

This study of the experiences of workers in a fast-changing high-tech company examines the reproduction of a distinct occupational culture in a volatile labor market.

Urry, J. (2008) *Mobilities*. Malden, MA and Cambridge: Polity Press.
A discussion of how the physical, virtual, and imaginative movement of people, ideas, objects, and information produces a densely networked social life.

 ■ **Practice questions for Anecdote 8.1** ▬▬▬▬▬▬

1 How would you characterize the social capital of the law firm in which Sarah works?

2 What could Sarah do to draw personal benefits from participating in this law firm's social network?

3 If this law firm were more bureaucratic in its employment relations, there would be less gender-based discrimination. Do you agree?

Glossary

Actors are discrete entities capable of practice, such as individuals, groups, and organizations. In network analysis, actors also include non-human entities, such as events or ideas.

Administrative school is a subfield of "classical management" approaches, summarizing a small number of administrative principles of governing an organization, such as division of labor and unity of command.

Agency refers to the ability to make a difference in a social situation and to affect the circumstances in which one finds oneself.

Authority is the legitimate right to exercise control over others. The effective exercise of authority requires the endorsement of those who are subject to it.

Boundary spanner is a person connecting the organization or organizational unit with individuals in other units or in the organization's environment. Boundary spanners may specialize in such roles as liaison positions, investor relations, public relations, or supplier relations.

Bureaucracy is a specific form of organization characterized by a strict division of labor, a focus on formal rules and discipline, and an orientation to rationality based on a clear relationship between means and ends.

Causal agent is a basic unit of action that makes things happen. The properties of the agent bring about outcomes.

Competitive advantage is conferred by structures and practices that make an organization more successful than rival organizations. Organizational forms that are distinct, valuable, and difficult to imitate can be a source of competitive advantage.

Concept is an abstract mental construct that represents some aspect of the world in a simplified, general form.

Constructivism is an epistemological approach based on the premise that social actors are capable of reflection, creating their own biographies.

Contingency analysis specifies the conditions under which something happens. In organization studies, the contingency approach suggests that there is no one best way to organize a system. The "best" organizational form depends on the situation in which the system exists.

Core competency is the set of skills that are regarded as central to an organization and in which the organization has a relative advantage in performing them.

Determinism is an approach that emphasizes constraints on choices and argues that the future of an entity, like an organization, is preordained to unfold in fixed ways.

Dual economy refers to the distinction between a core sector of the economy, dominated by large corporations with significant political and market power, and a periphery sector, populated by small businesses facing intense competition.

Ecology refers to the distribution of resources in a system and the terms on which they are available to the members of the system.

Emergence refers to a process by which some collective phenomenon is created through the actions of an entity at a lower level, but the outcome is not reducible to only these actions. A property of a collectivity (e.g., group sociability) is emergent if its existence depends on an entity at a lower level (e.g., individual disposition) without being fully predictable from the properties of this lower-level entity.

Empiricist researchers use formal modeling and statistical procedures of data interpretation. They apply such procedures to organizational phenomena that are immediately observable and measurable.

Environment is what exists outside the boundaries of an organization. This includes resources exchanged in product markets, financial markets, and labor markets. It also includes the demands and expectations that external actors like governments and social movement organizations have of organizations.

Epistemology addresses questions about the nature of knowledge and how to obtain knowledge, such as the question of generalizability of findings from samples and cases.

Focal organization   is the organization seen from the perspective of those who study it, work in it, invest in it, or relate to it in some other meaningful way.

Functionalism   is an approach based on the premise that phenomena exist to fulfill some function. Consensus on functional goals is often presumed to be the natural state of affairs.

Heuristic   refers to an experience-based technique of problem solving. In organizations, heuristic devices are often used in decision-making situations where an exhaustive search for optimal solutions is impractical or too time-consuming.

Human capital   refers to attributes with economic value for individuals, such as education and work experience.

Human Relations   is a school of thought based on the premise that people have social needs. A key argument is that organizational structures, which are oriented to workers' social concerns, have motivating effects.

Inducements–contributions   refer to the relationship between what organizational members receive in return for their investments in the organization.

Institution   refers to established rules and patterns of activity, fulfilling functions considered indispensable. Institutions persist over the long term, shaping what people do and how they interpret what they do.

Instrumental rationality   refers to the deliberate calculation of the means available to achieve a given goal. In an organizational setting. It usually refers to calculated activities related to task accomplishment.

Intended rationality   includes limitations in the human capacity to collect and process information. Humans intend to be rational in their decision-making but are constrained by the availability of information and the inability to process all information correctly.

Interest   refers to an individual's wish to improve his or her well-being. Interest is socially constructed, based on the individual's interpretation of his or her social, political, and economic situation.

Interlocking directorate   is a form of inter-organizational coordination in which organizations share one or more external representatives on their governing board.

Internal labor market   denotes an exchange system in organizations for allocating individuals to jobs, using incentives in the form of wages, training opportunities, and career routes as mechanisms to match individuals and jobs.

Inter-organizational network   refers to the set of ties connecting a group of organizations. Network ties may be in the form of exchange relations based on personal friendship, information, or contractual authority.

Labor process   refers to the complex of relations between labor and management regarding the design, control, and monitoring of tasks, and the opportunities available for workers to resist or evade managerial controls.

Logic   is a set of principles or mutually enhancing rules used in discourse and decision-making. One may distinguish, for example, between a market logic based on economic criteria and a cultural logic based on ethical criteria.

Matrix design   is an organizational structure that arranges work simultaneously by different criteria, such as functional (e.g., marketing, research, finance) and product criteria. (e.g., fiction and non-fiction books, commercial and military aircraft)

Mechanism   refers to a causal force that regularly brings about certain outcomes. Mechanisms are the driving forces connecting initial conditions to outcomes.

Mechanistic structure   emphasizes stability and control. Mechanistically structured organizations have a highly specialized division of labor within which each individual performs a precisely defined task, and they employ formal rules for enforcing expected behaviors.

Metaphor   is a term used to describe an unfamiliar entity in terms of a familiar entity. For example, characterizing an organization as a brain allows one to see the organization *as if* it were a brain, suggesting features normally associated with a brain, such as complexity, flexibility, and adaptability.

Moral hazard   exists in social situations, such as an employment relationship, if there is a risk that individuals will not put forth the agreed-upon effort or will not comply with the terms of a contract.

Narratives   are story-like accounts of experiences in the form of texts and conversations. They are an integral part of meaning construction.

Normative   is what is commonly accepted as normal or appropriate in a given situation. Social norms denote the regular expectations that people hold in society.

Ontology refers to claims about the existence of some entity. The question is: What is there to know?

Organic solidarity is a concept Emile Durkheim used to describe the interdependence between actors with different but complementary interests or competencies. In a dynamic organization, organic solidarity is often seen as a source of integration.

Organic structure emphasizes adaptability rather than adaptation, and emergence rather than imposition. In organic structures, rules, processes, and relationships evolve in line with the changing contexts in which they exist.

Organization describes an evolving activity system, oriented towards collective goals and struggling to maintain a more or less distinct identity in an uncertain resource environment.

Organization science is the study of organizations based on the systematic observation of organizational actions and of human behavior in organizations.

Organizational culture refers to the shared values, beliefs, and expectations of the members of an organization.

Organizational field refers to populations of resource interdependent and functionally related organizations in a specific domain. The organizations are bound together by an orientation to shared norms and rules.

Organizational form refers to the complex of structural characteristics and practices of organizations in a given context.

Organizational inertia is a condition, rooted in structures and practices, reflecting the inability of an organization to adjust rapidly to new conditions in the environment.

Organizing is an ongoing process of adapting the organization to changing circumstances. It involves activities related to planning, coordinating, and evaluating, and so on.

Paradigm refers to a distinct way of studying a given subject matter, based on a coherent set of assumptions about the nature of the subject and the methods for studying them. Paradigmatic consensus exists when researchers agree on the central questions, concepts, and methodological approaches.

Paradox   is a situation or condition that implies contradiction. Things are paradoxical if they contain elements that cannot both be true, such as the argument that creativity is both spontaneous and regulated.

Path dependence   refers to a developmental feature in organizations, industries, technologies, and social relations, suggesting that choices made in the past constrain possibilities for the future.

Practice   refers to the actions that people engage in to accomplish things, without necessarily following deliberate plans and strategies. Practice involves agentic creativity and is bound by structural constraints.

Property right   is a judicial and sociological concept denoting the right to ownership of tangible and intangible things, and the right to deal on the basis of ownership.

Rational   and rationality refer to the logic adopted by individuals who act to maximize their personal interests, whatever these may be. Economic versions of rationality refer to the calculus of costs and benefits, while sociological versions of rationality include substantive values.

Rational choice theory   is based on the premise that people are essentially self-interested and goal-oriented individuals. They choose between alternative options based on the information available to them and the incentives provided in the setting in which they exist.

Rationalization   refers to the application of principles to a particular situation, for example to explain or justify behavior in that situation.

Reciprocity   refers to a sense of obligation in a situation where two individuals return a favor. When reciprocity expectations are strong, they can govern mutual behavior even without the intervention of a third party.

Relation   is the connection between elements of a system. From a relational perspective, an organization is a web of relations between different units, rather than a set of attributes. Actors derive social meaning from their position with respect to one another, and not from their intrinsic characteristics.

Routine   is behavior that is learned, repetitious, and highly patterned. Organizational routines are evident in standards, rules, procedures, programs, habits, and conventions.

Rule   is a device denoting possibilities for interpretation and action. Behavioral rules ("You must always be on time") link individual action to expectations in a given context. Cognitive rules ("Pay most attention to what you heard last") provide frames for action by filtering external cues.

Scientific management   is a school of thought that emphasizes the systematic selection and training of workers, based on the premise that people are rational and respond to monetary incentives.

Social capital   is the value a person, group, or organization derives from the close contacts and understandings of mutually oriented actors. Social communities rich in social capital are often referred to as clans, clubs, or cliques.

Social construction   describes the process by which people actively and creatively shape their own reality, in interaction with salient others. To the extent that each participant in this process has somewhat different ideas about what reality should be, social construction involves contestation and negotiation.

Social fact   is a term used for patterns and occurrences that have an objective reality beyond the interpretations of individuals. People experience social facts as conditions shaping their lives and decisions.

Social legitimacy   is the generalized perception that the actions of an entity, such as a person, group, or organization, meet social definitions of desirability and acceptability.

Social network   is a set of regular connections or contacts between individuals through which resources are exchanged.

Sociality   refers to mutual awareness in a group of individuals, potentially leading to solidarity and joint action.

Socialization   is the process by which individuals develop an understanding of social expectations in the social unit of which they are members. Organizational socialization is the process by which members take on the beliefs and values of the organization through such mechanisms as instruction, evaluation, and promotion.

Stakeholder   is an individual or group of individuals with a strong interest in the performance of an entity, such as an organization or a project.

Structuralist   theorists argue that the opportunity constraints in a system, such as an organization, industry, social class, or kinship network, are grounded in the structure of relationships and may be so strong that they leave no meaningful room for individual variation.

Structure refers to the patterned arrangement of things, reflected, for example, in chains of events or in regularities in behavior.

Symbol is an item used to stand for or represent another item. Texts, signs, actions, names, and so on can all have symbolic meanings.

Task technology refers both to the knowledge that is embedded in a task and to the techniques by which the performance requirements of a task are executed.

Theoretical pluralism refers to sets of theories that retain their distinctiveness, yet all contribute to debates and discussions about issues and phenomena.

Theory is a coherent system of statements about how, why, and under what conditions the entities under investigation are related.

Typology refers to a form of classification that involves grouping entities according to mutually exclusive themes or dimensions.

Variable refers to a characteristic of an entity that varies in the degree to which it is present. Variables that change in response to an independent variable are called dependent variables.

References

Abbott, A. (1995) Sequence analysis: New methods for old ideas, *Annual Review of Sociology*, 21: 93–113.

Adler, P. (2001) Market, hierarchy, and trust: The knowledge economy and the future of capitalism, *Organization Science*, 12: 215–234.

Adler, P. and Borys, B. (1996) Two types of bureaucracy: Enabling and coercive, *Administrative Science Quarterly*, 41: 61–89.

Agarwal, R., Sarkar, M., and Echambadi, R. (2002) The conditioning effect of time on firm survival: An industry life cycle approach, *Academy of Management Journal*, 45: 971–994.

Aharonson, B., Baum, J., and Feldman, M. (2007) Desperately seeking spillovers? Increasing returns, industrial organization and the location of new entrants in geographic and technological space, *Industrial and Corporate Change*, 16: 89–130.

Ahmadjian, C. and Robbins, G. (2005) A clash of capitalisms: Foreign shareholders and corporate restructuring in 1990s Japan, *American Sociological Review*, 70: 451–471.

Akerlof, G. and Kranton, R. (2005) Identity and the economics of organizations, *Journal of Economic Perspectives*, 19: 9–32.

Alchian, A. and Demsetz, H. (1972) Production, information costs, and economic organization, *American Economic Review*, 62: 777–795.

Aldrich, H. (1971) Organizational boundaries and inter-organizational conflict, *Human Relations*, 24: 279–293.

Aldrich, H. (1979) *Organizations and Environments*. Englewood Cliffs, NJ: Prentice-Hall.

Aldrich, H. and Fiol, C.M. (1994) Fools rush in? The institutional context of industry creation, *Academy of Management Review*, 19: 645–670.

Aldrich, H. and Herker, D. (1977) Boundary spanning roles and organization structure, *Academy of Management Review*, 2: 217–230.

Aldrich, H. and Martinez, M. (2001) Many are called but few are chosen: An evolutionary perspective for the study of entrepreneurship, *Entrepreneurship Theory and Practice*, 25: 41–56.

Aldrich, H. and McKelvey, B. (1983) Populations, natural selection, and applied organizational science, *Administrative Science Quarterly*, 28: 101–128.

Aldrich, H. and Ruef, M. (2006) *Organizations Evolving*. London: Sage.

Aldrich, H., Zimmer, C., Staber, U., and Beggs, J. (1994) Minimalism, mutualism, and maturity: The evolution of the American trade association population in the 20th century, in J. Baum and J. Singh (eds), *Evolutionary Dynamics of Organizations*. New York: Oxford University Press, pp. 223–239.

Alvesson, M. (2003) Beyond neopositivists, romantics, and localists: A reflexive approach to interviews in organizational research, *Academy of Management Review*, 28: 13–33.

Alvesson, M. and Robertson, M. (2006) The best and the brightest: The construction, significance and effects of elite identities in consulting firms, *Organization*, 13: 195–224.

Ambrosini, V. and Bowman, C. (2009) What are dynamic capabilities and are they a useful construct in strategic management? *International Journal of Management Reviews*, 11: 29–49.

Amin, A. and Cohendet, P. (2004) *Architectures of Knowledge: Firms, Capabilities, and Communities*. Oxford: Oxford University Press.

Amin, A. and Thrift, N. (2007) Cultural-economy and cities, *Progress in Human Geography*, 31: 143–161.

Ancona, D., Okhuysen, G., and Perlow, L. (2001) Taking time to integrate temporal research, *Academy of Management Review*, 26: 512–529.

Anderson, A. and Miller, C. (2003) Class matters: Human and social capital in the entrepreneurial process, *Journal of Socio-Economics*, 32: 17–36.

Annesi, J. (1999) Effects of minimal group promotion on cohesion and exercise adherence, *Small Group Research*, 30: 542–557.

Aoki, M., Gustafsson, B., and Williamson, O. (eds) (1990) *The Firm as a Nexus of Treaties*. London: Sage.

Argote, L. and Miron-Spektor, E. (2011) Organizational learning: From experience to knowledge, *Organization Science*, 22: 1123–1137.

Arikan, A. and Schilling, M. (2011) Structure and governance in industrial districts: Implications for competitive advantage, *Journal of Management Studies*, 48: 772–803.

Arzaghi, M. and Henderson, J. (2008) Networking off Madison Avenue, *Review of Economic Studies*, 75: 1011–1038.

Asheim, B. and Coenen, L. (2005) Knowledge bases and regional innovation systems: Comparing Nordic clusters, *Research Policy*, 34: 1173–1190.

Asheim, B., Cooke, P., and Martin, R. (eds) (2006) *Clusters and Regional Development: Critical Reflections and Explorations*. London: Routledge.

Asheim, B., Coenen, L., and Vang, J. (2007) Face-to-face, buzz and knowledge bases: Socio-spatial implications for learning, innovation, and innovation policy, *Environment and Planning C: Government and Policy*, 25: 655–670.

Atkinson, J. (1987) Flexibility or fragmentation? The United Kingdom labour market in the eighties, *Labour and Society*, 12: 87–105.

Audia, P., Freeman, J., and Reynolds, P. (2006) Organizational foundings in community context: Instruments manufacturers and their interrelationship with other organizations, *Administrative Science Quarterly*, 51: 381–419.

Audretsch, D. and Feldman, M. (1996) R&D spillovers and the geography of innovation and production, *American Economic Review*, 86: 630–640.

Bacharach, S. (1989) Organizational theories: Some criteria for evaluation, *Academy of Management Review*, 14: 496–515.

Backes-Gellner, U., Schneider, M., and Veen, S. (2011) Effect of workforce age on quantitative and qualitative organizational performance: Conceptual framework and case study evidence, *Organization Studies*, 32: 1103–1121.

Bahr, D. and Rosenfeld-Johnson, S. (2010) Treatment of children with speech oral placement disorders (OPDs): A paradigm emerges, *Communication Disorders Quarterly*, 31: 131–138.

Bain, A. (2005) Constructing an artistic identity, *Work, Employment and Society*, 19: 25–46.

Barley, S. and Kunda, G. (2001) Bringing work back in, *Organization Science*, 12: 76–95.

Barnard, C. (1938) *The Functions of the Executive*. Cambridge, MA: Harvard University Press.

Barnes, J. (1984) Cognitive biases and their impact on strategic planning, *Strategic Management Journal*, 5: 129–137.

Barney, J. and Hesterly, W. (1996) Organizational economics: Understanding the relationship between organizations and economic analysis, in S. Clegg, C. Hardy, and W. Nord (eds), *Handbook of Organization Studies*. London: Sage, pp. 115–147.

Barney, J. and Ouchi, W. (eds) (1986) *Organizational Economics*. San Francisco: Jossey-Bass.

Baron, J., Jennings, P., and Dobbin, F. (1988) Mission control? The development of personnel systems in U.S. industry, *American Sociological Review*, 53: 497–514.

Baron, J., Hannan, M., Hsu, G., and Koçak, Ö. (2007) In the company of women: Gender inequality and the logic of bureaucracy In start-up firms, *Work and Occupations*, 34: 35–66.

Bathelt, H. and Glückler, J. (2003) Toward a relational economic geography, *Journal of Economic Geography*, 3: 117–144.

Baum, J. (1996) Organizational ecology, in S. Clegg, C. Hardy, and W. Nord (eds), *Handbook of Organization Studies*. London: Sage, pp. 77–114.

Baum, J. (ed.) (2002) *The Blackwell Companion to Organizations*. Malden, MA: Blackwell Publishers.

Baum, J. and Mezias, S. (1992) Localized competition and organizational failure in the Manhattan hotel industry, 1898–1990, *Administrative Science Quarterly*, 37: 580–604.

Baum, J. and Oliver, C. (1991) Institutional linkages and organizational mortality, *Administrative Science Quarterly*, 36: 187–218.

Bauman, Z. (2002) The 20th century: The end or a beginning? *Thesis Eleven*, 70: 15–25.

Beck, N. and Walgenbach, P. (2005) Technical efficiency or adaptation to institutionalized expectations? The adoption of ISO 9000 standards in the German mechanical engineering industry, *Organization Studies*, 26: 841–866.

Becker, G. (1975) *Human Capital: A Theoretical and Empirical Analysis*. New York: National Bureau of Economic Research.

Beckman, C. and Phillips, D. (2005) Interorganizational determinants of promotion: Client leadership and the attainment of women attorneys, *American Sociological Review*, 70: 678–701.

Beckman, C., Haunschild, P., and Phillips, D. (2004) Friends or strangers? Firm-specific uncertainty, market uncertainty, and network partner selection, *Organization Science*, 15: 259–275.

Bell, S., Tracey, P., and Heide, J. (2009) The organization of regional clusters, *Academy of Management Review*, 34: 623–642.

Benjamin, W. (1973) The work of art in an age of mechanical reproduction, in W. Benjamin, *Illuminations*. London: Fontana, pp. 219–254.

Benner, C. (2003) Learning communities in a learning region: The soft infrastructure of cross-firm learning networks in Silicon Valley, *Environment and Planning A*, 35: 1809–1830.

Bennett, A. (2006) Reincarnation, sect unity, and identity among the Druze, *Ethnology*, 45: 87–104.

Benneworth, P. and Henry, N. (2004) Where is the value added in the cluster approach? Hermeneutic theorising, economic geography and clusters as a multiperspectival approach, *Urban Studies*, 41: 1011–1023.

Benson, R. and Saguy, A. (2005) Constructing social problems in an age of globalization: A French–American comparison, *American Sociological Review*, 70: 233–259.

Berger, P. and Luckmann, T. (1966) *The Social Construction of Reality*. Garden City, NY: Doubleday.

Bielby, W. and Bielby, D. (1994) "All hits are flukes": Institutionalized decision making and the rhetoric of network prime-time program development, *American Journal of Sociology*, 99: 1287–1313.

Birnholtz, J., Cohen, M., and Hoch, S. (2007) Organizational character: On the regeneration of camp poplar grove, *Organization Science*, 18: 315–332.

Bishop, M. and Thompson, D. (1992) Privatisation in the UK: Internal organization and productive efficiency, *Annals of Public and Cooperative Economics*, 63: 171–188.

Blackler, F. (1995) Knowledge, knowledge work and organizations: An overview and interpretation, *Organization Studies*, 16: 1021–1046.

Blair, H. (2003) Winning and losing in flexible labour markets: The formation and operation of networks of interdependence in the UK film industry, *Sociology*, 37: 677–694.

Blau, P. and Schoenherr, R. (1971) *The Structure of Organizations*. New York: Basic Books.

Blitz, D. (1992) *Emergent Evolution: Qualitative Novelty and the Levels of Reality*. Dordrecht: Kluwer.

Bögenhold, D. and Staber, U. (1991) The decline and rise of self-employment, *Work, Employment and Society*, 5: 223–239.

Boivie, S., Lange, D., McDonald, M., and Westphal, J. (2011) Me or we: The effects of CEO organizational identification on agency costs, *Academy of Management Journal*, 54: 551–576.

Borgatti, S. and Cross, R. (2003) A relational view of information seeking and learning in social networks, *Management Science*, 49: 432–445.

Boswell, W., Zimmerman, R., and Swider, B. (2012) Employee job search: Toward an understanding of search context and search objectives, *Journal of Management*, 38: 129–163.

Bozeman, B. (2010) Hard lessons from hard times: Reconsidering and reorienting the "managing decline" literature, *Public Administration Review*, 70: 557–563.

Bozeman, B. and Slusher, E. (1979) Scarcity and environmental stress in public organizations: A conjectural essay, *Administration and Society*, 2: 335–355.

Brickson, S. (2005) Organizational identity orientation: Forging a link between organizational identity and organizations' relations with stakeholders, *Administrative Science Quarterly*, 50: 576–609.

Brown, A., Kornberger, M., Clegg, S., and Carter, C. (2010) "Invisible walls" and "silent hierarchies": A case study of power relations in an architecture firm, *Human Relations*, 63: 525–549.

Brown, G., Lawrence, T., and Robinson, S. (2005) Territoriality in organizations, *Academy of Management Review*, 30: 577–594.

Brown, S. and Eisenhardt, K. (1997) The art of continuous change: Linking complexity theory and time-paced evolution in relentlessly shifting organizations, *Administrative Science Quarterly*, 42: 1–34.

Bunderson, J. and Boumgarden, P. (2010) Structure and learning in self-managed teams: Why "bureaucratic" teams can be better learners, *Organization Science*, 21: 609–624.

Burke, P. and Franzoi, S. (1988) Studying situations and identities using experiential sampling methodology, *American Sociological Review*, 53: 559–568.

Burns, L. and Wholey, D. (1993) Adoption and abandonment of matrix management programs: Effects of organizational characteristics and interorganizational networks, *Academy of Management Journal*, 36: 106–138.

Burroni, L. and Trigilia, C. (2001) Italy: Economic development through local economies, in C. Crouch, P. Le Galès, C. Trigilia, and H. Voelzkow (eds), *Local Production Systems in Europe: Rise or Demise?* Oxford: Oxford University Press, pp. 46–78.

Burt, R. (2005) *Brokerage and Closure*. New York: Oxford University Press.

Camerer, C., Loewenstein, G., and Weber, M. (1989) The curse of knowledge in economic settings: An experimental analysis, *Journal of Political Economy*, 97: 1232–1254.

Camic, C. and Gross, N. (2004) The new sociology of ideas, in J. Blau (ed.), *The Blackwell Companion to Sociology*. Malden, MA–Oxford: Blackwell, pp. 236–249.

Campbell, D. (1969) Variation and selective retention in socio-cultural evolution, *General Systems*, 14: 69–85.

Campbell, J. (1998) Institutional analysis and the role of ideas in political economy, *Theory and Society*, 27: 377–409.

Cappelli, P. (2008) *Talent on Demand: Managing Talent in an Age of Uncertainty.* Boston, MA: Harvard Business School Press.

Cappelli, P. and Sherer, P. (1991) The missing role of context in OB: The need for a meso-level approach, *Research in Organizational Behavior*, 13: 55–110.

Carpenter, R. (2003) Women and children first: Gender, norms, and humanitarian evacuation in the Balkans 1991–95, *International Organization*, 57: 661–694.

Carroll, G. and Hannan, M. (1989) Density dependence in the evolution of populations of newspaper organizations, *American Sociological Review*, 54: 524–541.

Carroll, G. and Harrison, J. (1991) Keeping the faith: A model of cultural transmission in formal organizations, *Administrative Science Quarterly*, 36: 552–582.

Carroll, G. and Harrison, J. (1994) On the historical efficiency of competition between organizational populations, *American Journal of Sociology*, 100: 720–749.

Carroll, G. and Mosakowski, E. (1987) The career dynamics of self-employment, *Administrative Science Quarterly*, 32: 570–589.

Carroll, G. and Swaminathan, A. (2000) Why the microbrewery movement? Organizational dynamics of resource partitioning in the U.S. brewing industry, *American Journal of Sociology*, 106: 715–762.

Carroll, G., Preisendoerfer, P., Swaminathan, A., and Wiedenmayer, G. (1993) Brewery and brauerei: The organizational ecology of brewing, *Organization Studies*, 14: 155–188.

Carsten, M., Bradley, M., West, J., Patera, J., and McGregor, R. (2010) Exploring social constructions of followership: A qualitative study, *The Leadership Quarterly*, 21: 543–562.

Cattani, G., Ferriani, S., Negro, G., and Perretti, F. (2008) The structure of consensus: Network ties, legitimation, and exit rates of U.S. feature film producer organizations, *Administrative Science Quarterly*, 53: 145–182.

Chai, S. and Rhee, M. (2010) Confucian capitalism and the paradox of closure and structural holes in East Asian firms, *Management and Organization Review*, 6: 5–29.

Chen, H. and Naquin, S. (2006) An integrative model of competency development, training design, assessment center, and multi-rater assessment, *Advances in Developing Human Resources*, 8: 265–282.

Chetty, S. and Agndal, H. (2008) Role of inter-organizational networks and interpersonal networks in an industrial district, *Regional Studies*, 42: 175–187.

Child, J. and McGrath, R. (2001) Organizations unfettered: Organizational form in an information-intensive economy, *Academy of Management Journal*, 44: 1135–1148.

Christopherson, S. (2008) Beyond the self-expressive creative worker: An industry perspective on entertainment media, *Theory, Culture and Society*, 25: 73–95.

Chugh, S. and Hancock, P. (2009) Networks of aestheticization: The architecture, artefacts and embodiment of hairdressing salons, *Work, Employment and Society*, 23: 460–476.

Clegg, S., Hardy, C., and Nord, W. (eds) (1996) *Handbook of Organization Studies*. London: Sage.

Coase, R. (1937) The nature of the firm, *Economica*, 4: 386–405.

Cohen, S. and Fields, G. (1999) Social capital and capital gains in Silicon Valley, *California Management Review*, 41: 108–130.

Cohen, W. and Levinthal, D. (1990) Absorptive capacity: A new perspective on learning and innovation, *Administrative Science Quarterly*, 35: 128–153.

Coleman, J. (1988) Social capital in the creation of human capital, *American Journal of Sociology*, 94: S95–S120.

Collinson, D. and Collinson, M. (1997) "Delayering managers": Time-space surveillance and its gendered effects, *Organization*, 4: 375–407.

Collinson, J. (2006) Just "non-academics"? Research administrators and contested occupational identity, *Work Employment and Society*, 20: 267–288.

Crossan, M., Cunha, M., Vera, D., and Cunha, J. (2005) Time and organizational improvisation, *Academy of Management Review*, 30: 129–145.

Crouch, C. (2004) *Post-Democracy*. Cambridge: Polity Press.

Czarniawska, B. (2004) On time, space, and action nets, *Organization*, 11: 773–791.

Dacin, M., Munir, K., and Tracey, P. (2010) Formal dining at Cambridge colleges: Linking ritual performance and institutional maintenance, *Academy of Management Journal*, 53: 1393–1418.

Daft, R. and Lengel, R. (1986) Organizational information requirement, media richness and structural design, *Management Science*, 32: 554–571.

Dahrendorf, R. (1959) *Class and Class Conflict in Industrial Society*. London: Routledge and Kegan Paul.

Davis, G., Yoo, M., and Baker, W. (2003) The small world of the American corporate elite, 1982–2001, *Strategic Organization*, 1: 301–326.

Dean, A. and Kretschmer, M. (2007) Can ideas be capital? Factors of production in the postindustrial economy: A review and critique, *Academy of Management Review*, 32: 573–594.

Dearborn, D. and Simon, H. (1958) Selective perception: A note on the departmental identification of executives, *Sociometry*, 21: 140–144.

Dennett, D. (1995) *Darwin's Dangerous Idea*. New York: Simon & Schuster.

Dent, M. (2003) *Remodelling Hospitals and Health Professions in Europe: Medicine, Nursing and the State*. Basingstoke: Palgrave Macmillan.

DeRue, D. and Ashford, S. (2010) Who will lead and who will follow? A social process of leadership identity construction in organizations, *Academy of Management Review*, 35: 627–647.

De Vany, A. and Walls, W. (1999) Uncertainty in the movie business: Does star power reduce the terror of the box office? *Journal of Cultural Economics*, 23: 285–318.

Dewey, J. (1910) *How We Think*. Lexington, MA: D.C. Heath.

Dieleman, M. and Boddewyn, J. (2012) Using organization structure to buffer political ties in emerging markets: A case study, *Organization Studies*, 33: 71–95.

DiMaggio, P. and Powell, W. (1983) The iron cage revisited: Institutional isomorphism and collective rationality in organizational fields, *American Sociological Review*, 48: 147–160.

DiMaggio, P. and Powell, W. (1991) Introduction, in W. Powell and P. DiMaggio (eds), *The New Institutionalism in Organizational Analysis*. Chicago, IL: University of Chicago Press, pp. 1–38.

Dipboye, R. and Halverson, S. (2004) Subtle (and not so subtle) discrimination in organizations, in R. Griffin and A. O'Leary-Kelly (eds), *The Dark Side of Organizational Behavior*. San Francisco: Jossey-Bass, pp. 131–158.

Djelic, M. and Ainamo, A. (1999) The coevolution of new organizational forms in the fashion industry: A historical and comparative study of France, Italy, and the United States, *Organization Science*, 10: 622–637.

Djelic, M. and Quack, S. (2003) *Globalization and Institutions: Redefining the Rules of the Economic Game*. Cheltenham: Edward Elgar.

Dobbie, D. and Robinson, I. (2008) Reorganizing higher education in the United States and Canada: The erosion of tenure and the unionization of contingent faculty, *Labor Studies Journal*, 33: 117–140.

Dobrev, S., Kim, T., and Hannan, M. (2001) Dynamics of niche width and resource partitioning, *American Journal of Sociology*, 106: 1299–1337.

Docco, G., Wilk, S., and Rothbard, N. (2009) Unpacking prior experience: How career history affects job performance, *Organization Science*, 20: 51–68.

Donaldson, L. (1996) The normal science of structural contingency theory, in S. Clegg, C. Hardy, and W. Nord (eds), *Handbook of Organization Studies*. London: Sage, pp. 57–76.

Doolin, B. (2002) Enterprise discourse, professional identity and the organizational control of hospital clinicians, *Organization Studies*, 23: 369–390.

Dougherty, D. (1992) Interpretive barriers to successful product innovation in large firms, *Organization Science*, 3: 179–202.

Duncan, R. (1972) Characteristics of organizational environments and perceived environmental uncertainty, *Administrative Science Quarterly*, 17: 313–327.

Durkheim, E. (1893/1949) *Division of Labor in Society*. Glencoe, IL: Free Press.

Durkheim, E. (1982) *The Rules of Sociological Method*. London: Macmillan.

Dyck, B. and Wiebe, E. (2012) Salvation, theology and organizational practices across the centuries, *Organization*, 19: 299–324.

Edmondson, A. (1999) Psychological safety and learning behavior in work teams, *Administrative Science Quarterly*, 44: 350–383.

Eisenhardt, K. (1989) Agency theory: An assessment and review, *Academy of Management Review*, 14: 57–74.

Eliasoph, N. and Lichterman, P. (2003) Culture in interaction, *American Journal of Sociology*, 108: 735–794.

Elsbach, K. and Kramer, R. (1996) Members' responses to organizational identity threats: Encountering and countering the *Business Week* rankings, *Administrative Science Quarterly*, 41: 442–476.

Elsbach, K., Barr, P., and Hargadon, A. (2005) Identifying situated cognition in organizations, *Organization Science*, 16: 422–433.

Elster, J. (2007) *Explaining Social Behavior*. New York: Cambridge University Press.

Emirbayer, M. (1997) Manifesto for a relational sociology, *American Journal of Sociology*, 103: 281–317.

Emirbayer, M. and Mische, A. (1998) What is agency? *American Journal of Sociology*, 103: 962–1023.

Erickson, B. (1996) Class, culture, and connections, *American Journal of Sociology*, 102: 217–251.

Evans, G. (2009) Creative cities, creative spaces and urban policy, *Urban Studies*, 46: 1003–1040.

Evans, J., Bell, J., Sweeney, A., Morgan, J., and Kelly, H. (2010) Confidence in critical care nursing, *Nursing Science Quarterly*, 23: 334–340.

Faulconbridge, J. (2006) Stretching tacit knowledge beyond a local fix? Global spaces of learning in advertising professional service firms, *Journal of Economic Geography*, 6: 517–540.

Feldman, M. (2000) Organizational routines as a source of continuous change, *Organization Science*, 11: 611–629.

Felin, T. and Hesterly, W. (2007) The knowledge-based view, nested heterogeneity, and new value creation: Philosophical considerations on the locus of knowledge, *Academy of Management Review*, 32: 195–218.

Fenwick, T. (2002) Transgressive desires: New enterprising selves in the new capitalism, *Work, Employment and Society*, 16: 703–723.

Fine, G. (2009) *Kitchens: The Culture of Restaurant Work*. Berkeley, CA: University of California Press.

Fineman, S. (2011) *Organizing Age*. Oxford: Oxford University Press.

Flaherty, M. and Seipp-Williams, L. (2005) Sociotemporal rhythms in e-mail: A case study, *Time and Society*, 14: 39–49.

Folgerø, I. and Fjeldstad, I. (1995) On duty–off guard: Cultural norms and sexual harassment in service organizations, *Organization Studies*, 16: 299–313.

Franzosi, R. (1998) Narrative analysis – or why (and how) sociologists should be interested in narrative, *Annual Review of Sociology*, 24: 517–554.

Freeman, J. (1973) Environment technology, and administrative intensity of manufacturing organizations, *American Sociological Review*, 38: 750–763.

Freeman, J. and Hannan, M. (1983) Niche width and the dynamics of organizational populations, *American Journal of Sociology*, 88: 1116–1145.

Frew, M. and McGillivray, D. (2005) Health and fitness clubs and body politics: Aesthetics and the promotion of physical capital, *Leisure Studies*, 24: 161–175.

Fromhold-Eisebith, M. (2004) Innovative milieu and social capital: Complementary or redundant concepts of collaboration-based regional development? *European Planning Studies*, 12: 747–765.

Galunic, C. and Rodan, S. (1998) Resource recombinations in the firm: Knowledge structures and the potential for Schumpeterian innovation, *Strategic Management Journal*, 19: 1193–1201.

Galunic, C. and Weeks, J. (2002) Intraorganizational ecology, in J. Baum (ed.), *The Blackwell Companion to Organizations*. Malden, MA: Blackwell, pp. 75–97.

Gavetti, G. (2005) Cognition and hierarchy: Rethinking the microfoundations of capabilities' development, *Organization Science*, 16: 599–617.

Gaziano, E. (1996) Ecological metaphors as scientific boundary work: Innovation and authority in interwar sociology and biology, *American Journal of Sociology*, 101: 874–907.

Geletkanycz, M. and Hambrick, D. (1997) The external ties of top executives: Implications for strategic choice and performance, *Administrative Science Quarterly*, 42: 654–681.

George, A. and McKeown, T. (1985) Case studies and theories of organizational decision-making, *Advances in Information Processing in Organizations*, 2: 21–58.

Geppert, M. and Matten, D. (2006) Institutional influences on manufacturing organization in multinational corporations: The "cherrypicking" approach, *Organization Studies*, 27: 491–515.

Gertler, M. (1995) "Being there": Proximity, organization and culture in the development and adoption of advanced manufacturing technologies, *Economic Geography*, 71: 1–26.

Gertler, M. and Wolfe, D. (2004) Local social knowledge management: Community actors, institutions and multilevel governance in regional foresight exercises, *Futures*, 36: 45–65.

Geyskens, I., Steenkamp, J., and Kumar, N. (2006) Make, buy, or ally: A transaction cost theory meta-analysis, *Academy of Management Journal*, 49: 519–543.

Gibson, D. (2005) Taking turns and talking ties: Network structure and conversational sequences, *American Journal of Sociology*, 110: 1561–1597.

Giddens, A. (1971) *Capitalism and Modern Social Theory: An Analysis of the Writings of Marx, Durkheim and Max Weber*. Cambridge: Cambridge University Press.

Giddens, A. (1984) *The Constitution of Society: Outline of the Theory of Structuration*. Cambridge: Polity Press.

Giddens, A. (1991) *Modernity and Self-Identity: Self and Society in the Late Modern Age*. Stanford, CA: Stanford University Press.

Gieryn, T. (2000) A space for place in sociology, *Annual Review of Sociology*, 26: 463–496.

Gill, M., Hearnshaw, S., and Turbin, V. (1998) Violence in schools: Quantifying and responding to the problem, *Educational Management Administration and Leadership*, 26: 429–442.

Gioia, D. and Corley, K. (2002) Being good versus looking good: Business school rankings and the Circean transformation from substance to image, *Academy of Management Learning and Education*, 1: 107–120.

Girard, M. and Stark, D. (2003) Heterarchies of value in Manhattan-based new media firms, *Theory, Culture and Society*, 20: 77–105.

Giuliani, E. and Bell, M. (2005) The micro-determinants of meso-level learning and innovation: Evidence from a Chilean wine cluster, *Research Policy*, 34: 47–68.

Glaeser, A. (2000) *Divided in Unity: Identity, Germany, and the Berlin Police*. Chicago, IL: University of Chicago Press.

Glynn, M. (2008) Configuring the field of play: How hosting the Olympic Games impacts civic community, *Journal of Management Studies*, 45: 1118–1146.

Godart, F. and White, H. (2010) Switchings under uncertainty: The coming and becoming of meanings, *Poetics*, 38: 567–586.

Goffman, E. (1959) *The Presentation of Self in Everyday Life*. New York: Anchor Books.

Goffman, E. (1961) *Encounters: Two Studies in the Sociology of Interaction*. Indianapolis, IN. Bobbs-Merrill.

Gospodini, A. (2009) Post-industrial trajectories of Mediterranean European cities: The case of post-Olympics Athens, *Urban Studies*, 46: 1157–1186.

Gouldner, A. (1954) *Patterns of Industrial Bureaucracy*. New York: Free Press.

Grabher, G. (2004) Temporary architectures of learning: Knowledge governance in project ecologies, *Organization Studies*, 25: 1491–1514.

Grabher, G. and Stark, D. (1997) Organizing diversity: Evolutionary theory, network analysis, and Post-socialism, *Regional Studies*, 31: 533–544.

Granovetter, M. (1985) Economic action and social structure: The problem of embeddedness, *American Journal of Sociology*, 91: 481–510.

Granovetter, M. (1995) *Getting a Job: A Study of Contracts and Careers* (2nd edn). Chicago: University of Chicago Press.

Grant, R. (1996) Toward a knowledge-based theory of the firm, *Strategic Management Journal*, 17: 109–122.

Greiner, L. (1998) Evolution and revolution as organizations grow, *Harvard Business Review*, 76: 55–68.

Griffin, R. and O'Leary-Kelly, A. (eds) (2004) *The Dark Side of Organizational Behavior*. San Francisco: Jossey-Bass.

Gulati, R. (1995) Does familiarity breed trust? The implications of repeated ties for contractual choice in alliances, *Academy of Management Journal*, 38: 85–112.

Guthrie, D. and Roth, L. (1999) The state, courts, and maternity policies in U.S. organizations: Specifying institutional mechanisms, *American Sociological Review*, 64: 41–63.

Haas, M. (2010) The double-edged swords of autonomy and external knowledge: Analyzing team effectiveness in a multinational organization, *Academy of Management Journal*, 53: 989–1008.

Hacker, J. (1998) The historical logic of national health insurance: Structure and sequence in the development of British, Canadian, and U.S. medical policy, *Studies in American Political Development*, 12: 57–130.

Hakim, C. (2000) *Work-Lifestyle Choices in the 21st Century: Preference Theory*. New York: Oxford University Press.

Hall, E. (1959) *The Silent Language*. Garden City, NY: Doubleday.

Hambrick, D., Cho, T., and Chen, M. (1996) The influence of top management team heterogeneity on firms' competitive moves, *Administrative Science Quarterly*, 41: 659–684.

Hampton, J. (1998) Similarity-based categorization and fuzziness of natural categories, *Cognition*, 65: 137–165.

Hannan, M. (1997) Inertia, density and the structure of organizational populations: Entries in European automobile industries, 1886–1981, *Organization Studies*, 18: 193–228.

Hannan, M. and Freeman, J. (1984) Structural inertia and organizational change, *American Sociological Review*, 49: 149–164.

Hannan, M. and Freeman, J. (1989) *Organizational Ecology*. Cambridge, MA: Harvard University Press.

Hannan, M., Baron, J., Hsu, G., and Koçak, Ö. (2006) Organizational identities and the hazard of change, *Industrial and Corporate Change*, 15: 755–784.

Hansmann, H. (1990) The viability of worker ownership: An economic perspective on the political structure of the firm, in M. Aoki, B. Gustafsson, and O. Williamson (eds), *The Firm as a Nexus of Treaties*. London: Sage, pp. 162–184.

Hanson, S., Schaub, M., and Baker, D. (1996) Gender stratification in the science pipeline: A comparative analysis of seven countries, *Gender and Society*, 10: 271–290.

Harzing, A. and Sorge, A. (2003) The relative impact of country of origin and universal contingencies on internationalization strategies and corporate control in multinational enterprises: Worldwide and European perspectives, *Organization Studies*, 24: 187–214.

Haveman, H. (1992) Between a rock and a hard place: Organizational change and performance under conditions of fundamental environmental transformation, *Administrative Science Quarterly*, 37: 48–75.

Hawley, A. (1986) *Human Ecology*. Chicago, IL: University of Chicago Press.

Hayward, M. (2002) When do firms learn from their acquisition experience? Evidence from 1990–1995, *Strategic Management Journal*, 23: 21–39.

Heath, C. and Staudenmayer, N. (2000) Coordination neglect: How lay theories of organizing complicate coordination in organizations, *Research in Organizational Behavior*, 22: 155–193.

Heath, C., Larrick, R., and Klayman, J. (1998) Cognitive repairs: How organizational practices can compensate for individual shortcomings, *Research in Organizational Behavior*, 20: 1–37.

Heath, C., Hindmarsh, J., and Luff, P. (1999) Interaction in isolation: The dislocated world of the London Underground train driver, *Sociology*, 33: 555–575.

Heath, C., Bell, C., and Sternberg, E. (2001) Emotional selection in memes: The case of urban legends, *Journal of Personality and Social Psychology*, 81: 1028–1041.

Heemskerk, E. (2007) *Decline of the Corporate Community: Network Dynamics of the Dutch Business Elite*. Amsterdam: Amsterdam University Press.

Henrich, J. and Boyd, R. (2005) *Not by Genes Alone: How Culture Transformed Human Evolution*. Chicago, IL: Chicago University Press.

Hertle, H. (1996) *Chronik des Mauerfalls: Die dramatischen Ereignisse um den 9. November 1989*. Berlin: Ch. Links Verlag.

Hill, V. and Carley, K. (1999) An approach to identifying consensus in a subfield: The case of organizational culture, *Poetics*, 27: 1–30.

Hirsch, P. and Lounsbury, M. (1997) Ending the family quarrel: Toward a reconciliation of "old" and "new" institutionalisms, *American Behavioral Scientist*, 40: 406–418.

Hirst, G., van Knippenberg, D., Chen, C., and Sacramento, C. (2011) How does bureaucracy impact individual creativity? A cross-level investigation of team contextual influences on goal orientation-creativity relationships, *Academy of Management Journal*, 54: 624–641.

Hodgson, G. (2004) *The Evolution of Institutional Economics: Agency, Structure and Darwinism in American Institutionalism*. London: Routledge.

Hodgson, G. and Knudsen, T. (2006) Why we need a generalized Darwinism, and why a generalized Darwinism is not enough, *Journal of Economic Behavior and Organization*, 61: 1–19.

Hofstede, G. (1980) *Culture's Consequences: International Differences in Work-Related Values*. Newbury Park, CA: Sage.

Hogg, M. and Terry, D. (2000) Social identity and self-categorization processes in organizational contexts, *Academy of Management Review*, 25: 121–141.

Hollingsworth, J. (1997) Continuities and changes in systems of production: The cases of Japan, Germany, and the United States, in J. Hollingsworth and R. Boyer (eds), *Contemporary Capitalism: The Embeddedness of Institutions*. Cambridge: Cambridge University Press, pp. 265–310.

Holmstrom, B. (1982) Moral hazard in teams, *Bell Journal of Economics*, 13: 324–340.

Hopkins, J. (1994) Orchestrating an indoor city: Ambient noise inside a mega-mall, *Environment and Behavior*, 26: 785–812.

Hsu, G. (2006) Jacks of all trades and masters of none: Audiences' reactions to spanning genres in feature film production, *Administrative Science Quarterly*, 51: 420–450.

Hsu, G. and Hannan, M. (2005) Identities, genres, and organizational forms, *Organization Science*, 16: 474–490.

Hsu, G., Hannan, M., and Koçak, Ö. (2009) Multiple category memberships in markets: An integrative theory and two empirical tests, *American Sociological Review*, 74: 150–169.

Hull, K. and Nelson, R. (2000) Assimilation, choice, or constraint? Testing theories of gender differences in the careers of lawyers, *Social Forces*, 79: 229–264.

Huygens, M., Baden-Fuller, C., van den Bosch, F., and Volberda, H. (2002) Co-evolution of firm capabilities and industrial competition: Investigating the music industry, 1877–1997, *Organization Studies*, 22: 971–1012.

Hwang, H. and Suarez, D. (2005) Lost and found in the translation of strategic plans and websites, in B. Czarniawska and G. Sevón (eds), *Global Ideas: How Ideas, Objects and Practices Travel in the Global Economy*. Copenhagen: Copenhagen Business School Press, pp. 71–93.

Ibarra, H. (1995) Race, opportunity, and diversity of social circles in managerial networks, *Academy of Management Journal*, 38: 673–703.

Ibarra, H. (1999) Provisional selves: Experimenting with image and identity in professional adaptation, *Administrative Science Quarterly*, 44: 764–791.

Ingram, P. (1996) Organizational form as a solution to the problem of credible commitment: The evolution of naming strategies among U.S. hotel chains, 1896–1980, *Strategic Management Journal*, 17: 85–98.

Ingram, P. and Clay, K. (2000) The choice-within-constraints new institutionalism and implications for sociology, *Annual Review of Sociology*, 26: 525–546.

Ingram, P. and Lifschitz, A. (2006) Kinship in the shadow of the corporation: The inter-builder network in Clyde River shipbuilding, 1711–1990, *American Sociological Review*, 71: 334–352.

Ingram, P. and Roberts, P. (2000) Friendships among competitors in the Sydney hotel industry, *American Journal of Sociology*, 106: 387–423.

Jablonka, E. and Lamb, M. (2005) *Evolution in Four Dimensions: Genetic, Epigenetic, Behavioral, and Symbolic Variation in the History of Life*. Cambridge, MA: MIT Press.

Janicik, G. and Larrick, R. (2005) Social network schemas and the learning of incomplete networks, *Journal of Personality and Social Psychology*, 88: 348–364.

Jansen, J., van den Bosch, F., and Volberda, H. (2006) Exploratory innovation, exploitative innovation, and performance: Effects of organizational antecedents and environmental moderators, *Management Science*, 52: 1661–1674.

Jenkins, R. (2004) *Social Identity* (2nd edn). London: Routledge.

Jensen, M. and Meckling, W. (1976) Theory of the firm: Managerial behavior, agency costs, and ownership structure, *Journal of Financial Economics*, 3: 305–360.

Jepperson, R. (1991) Institutions, institutional effects, and institutionalism, in W. Powell and P. DiMaggio (eds), *The New Institutionalism in Organizational Analysis*. Chicago, IL: University of Chicago Press, pp. 143–163.

Johns, G. (2006) The essential impact of context on organizational behavior, *Academy of Management Review*, 31: 386–408.

Johnson, B., Lorenz, E., and Lundvall, B.-Å. (2002) Why all this fuss about codified and tacit knowledge? *Industrial and Corporate Change*, 11: 245–262.

Johnson, V. (2007) What is organizational imprinting? Cultural entrepreneurship in the founding of the Paris Opera, *American Journal of Sociology*, 113: 97–127.

Jones, A. (2008) Beyond embeddedness: Economic practices and the invisible dimensions of transnational business activity, *Progress in Human Geography*, 32: 71–88.

Kahneman, D. (2011) *Thinking, Fast and Slow*. London: Penguin Books.

Kalleberg, A. (2003) Flexible firms and labor market segmentation: Effects of workplace restructuring on jobs and workers, *Work and Occupations*, 30: 154–175.

Kalleberg, A. (2009) Precarious work, insecure workers: Employment relations in transition, *American Sociological Review*, 74: 1–22.

Kanter, R. (1977) *Men and Women of the Corporation*. New York: Basic Books.

Katz, D. and Kahn, R. (1966) *The Social Psychology of Organizations*. New York: Wiley.

Katz, J. and Gartner, W. (1988) Properties of emerging organizations, *Academy of Management Review*, 13: 429–441.

Katz, M. and Shapiro, C. (1987) R&D rivalry with licensing or imitation, *American Economic Review*, 77: 402–421.

Kaufman, J. (2002) The political economy of interdenominational competition in late nineteenth-century American cities, *Journal of Urban History*, 28: 445–465.

Kebir, L. and Crevoisier, O. (2008) Cultural resources and regional development: The case of the cultural legacy of watchmaking, *European Planning Studies*, 16: 1189–1205.

Kerr, C. (2001) *The Uses of the University* (5th edn). Cambridge, MA: Harvard University Press.

Kieser, A. (1989) Organizational, institutional, and societal evolution: Medieval craft guilds and the genesis of formal organizations, *Administrative Science Quarterly*, 34: 540–564.

Kieser, A. (1997) Rhetoric and myth in management fashion, *Organization*, 4: 49–74.

Kijkuit, B. and van den Ende, J. (2010) With a little help from our colleagues: A longitudinal study of social networks for innovation, *Organization Studies*, 31: 451–479.

Kilduff, M., Angelmar, R., and Mehra, A. (2000) Top management-team diversity and firm performance: Examining the role of cognitions, *Organization Science*, 11: 21–34.

Kilduff, M., Elfenbein, H., and Staw, B. (2010) The psychology of rivalry: A relationally dependent analysis of competition, *Academy of Management Journal*, 53: 943–969.

King, E., Dawson, J., West, M., Gilrane, V., Peddie, C., and Bastin, L. (2011) Why organizational and community diversity matter: Representativeness and the emergence of incivility and organizational performance, *Academy of Management*, 54: 1103–1118.

Klaas, B., Gainey, T., McClendon, J., and Yang, H. (2005) Professional employer organizations and their impact on client satisfaction with human resource outcomes: A field study of human resource outsourcing in small and medium enterprises, *Journal of Management*, 31: 234–254.

Klein Woolthuis, R., Hillebrand, B., and Nooteboom, B. (2005) Trust, contract and relationship development, *Organization Studies*, 26: 813–840.

Knight, M. and Hawtin, C. (2010) The new global j-school: Issues arising from the internationalization and monetization of journalism education, *Journalism and Mass Communication Educator*, 65: 250–264.

Knoke, D. (1990a) *Organizing for Collective Action: The Political Economies of Associations*. Hawthorne, NY: Aldine de Gruyter.

Knoke, D. (1990b) *Political Networks: The Structural Perspective*. Cambridge: Cambridge University Press.

Knorr Cetina, K. (2001) Postsocial relations: Theorizing sociality in a postsocial environment, in G. Ritzer and B. Smart (eds), *Handbook of Social Theory*. London: Sage, pp. 520–537.

Koçak, Ö. and Carroll, G. (2008) Growing church organizations in diverse U.S. communities, 1890–1926, *American Journal of Sociology*, 113: 1272–1315.

Kogut, B. and Zander, U. (1996) What firms do? Coordination, identity, and learning, *Organization Science*, 7: 502–518.

Kolb, D. (2008) Exploring the metaphor of connectivity: Attributes, dimensions and duality, *Organization Studies*, 29: 127–144.

Kono, C., Palmer, D., Friedland, R., and Zafonte, M. (1998) Lost in space: The geography of corporate interlocking directorates, *American Journal of Sociology*, 103: 863–911.

Kraatz, M. (1998) Learning by association? Interorganizational networks and adaptation to environmental change, *Academy of Management Journal*, 41: 621–643.

Ku, M. (2011) When does gender matter? Gender differences in specialty choice among physicians, *Work and Occupations*, 38: 221–262.

Kunda, G., Barley, S., and Evans, J. (2002) Why do contractors contract? The experience of highly skilled technical professionals in a contingent labor market, *Industrial and Labor Relations Review*, 55: 234–261.

Laestadius, S. (1998) Technology level, knowledge formation and industrial competence in paper manufacturing, in G. Eliasson et al. (eds), *Microfoundations of Economic Growth*. Ann Arbor, MI: University of Michigan Press, pp. 212–226.

Langlois, R. and Robertson, P. (1989) Explaining vertical integration: Lessons from the American automobile industry, *Journal of Economic History*, 49: 361–375.

Lawrence, P. and Edwards, V. (2000) *Management in Western Europe*. Basingstoke: Macmillan.

Lawrence, P. and Lorsch, J. (1967) *Organization and Environment: Managing Differentiation and Integration*. Boston, MA: Graduate School of Business Administration, Harvard University.

Lazerson, M. (1995) A new phoenix? Modern putting-out in the Modena knitwear industry, *Administrative Science Quarterly*, 40: 34–59.

Lazzeretti, L. (2004) *Art Cities, Cultural Districts and Museums*. Florence: Firenze University Press.

Legewie, J. and DiPrete, T. (2012) School context and the gender gap in educational achievement, *American Sociological Review*, 77: 463–485.

Lemley, M. (2003) Place and cyberspace, *California Law Review*, 91: 521–542.

Levesque, L., Wilson, J., and Wholey, D. (2001) Cognitive divergence and shared mental models in software development project teams, *Journal of Organizational Behavior*, 22: 135–144.

Levine, R. (1997) *A Geography of Time*. New York: Basic Books.

Levinthal, D. and March, J. (1993) The myopia of learning, *Strategic Management Journal*, 14: 95–112.

Lewin, K. (1951) *Field Theory in Social Science*. New York: Harper.

Liden, R., Martin, C., and Parsons, C. (1993) Interviewer and applicant behaviors in employment interviews, *Academy of Management Journal*, 36: 372–366.

Lienhardt, G. (1954) Modes of thought, in E. Evans-Pritchard (ed.), *The Institutions of Primitive Society*. Oxford: Basil Blackwell, pp. 95–107.

Lin, N., Cook, K., and Burt, R. (eds) (2001) *Social Capital: Theory and Research*. New Brunswick, NJ: Aldine Transactions.

Lockwood, D. (1964) Social integration and system integration, in G. Zollschan and W. Hirsch (eds), *Explorations in Social Change*. London: Routledge & Kegan Paul, pp. 244–257.

Lorenzi, P., Sims, H., and Slocum, J. (1981) Perceived environmental uncertainty: An individual or environmental attribute? *Journal of Management*, 7: 27–41.

Lundvall, B.-Å. (1998) Why study national systems and national styles of innovations? *Technology Analysis and Strategic Management*, 10: 407–421.

Lundvall, B.-Å. and Johnson, B. (1994) The learning economy, *Journal of Industry Studies*, 1: 23–42.

Maclean, M., Harvey, C., and Chia, R. (2010) Dominant corporate agents and the power elite in France and Britain, *Organization Studies*, 31: 327–348.

Malmberg, A. and Maskell, P. (2006) Localized learning revisited, *Growth and Change*, 37: 1–18.

March, J. and Simon, H. (1958) *Organizations*. New York: Wiley.

Marquis, C. (2003) The pressure of the past: Network imprinting in intercorporate communities, *Administrative Science Quarterly*, 48: 655–689.

Martine, J. and Jones, G. (2000) The role of time in theory and theory building, *Journal of Management*, 26: 657–684.

Marx, K. (1867/1954) *Capital*. Trans. Moscow: Foreign Languages Publishing House.

Masters, J. and Miles, G. (2002) Predicting the use of external labor arrangements: A test of the transaction costs perspective, *Academy of Management Journal*, 45: 431–442.

Mayr, E. (2001) *What Evolution Is*. New York: Basic Books.

McGrath, R. (2001) Exploratory learning, innovative capacity, and managerial oversight, *Academy of Management Journal*, 44: 118–131.

McGregor, D. (1960) *The Human Side of Enterprise*. New York: McGraw-Hill.

McGuire, W. (1999) *Constructing Social Psychology*. New York: Cambridge University Press.

McPherson, M. (2004) A Blau space primer: Prolegomenon to an ecology of affiliation, *Industrial and Corporate Change*, 13: 263–280.

Merton, R. (1940) Bureaucratic structure and personality, *Social Forces*, 18: 560–568.

Merton, R. (1967) *On Theoretical Sociology: Five Essays, Old and New*. New York: Free Press.

Meyer, J. (1994) Institutional and organizational rationalization in the mental health system, in W.R. Scott and J. Meyer (eds), *Institutional Environments and Organizations*. Thousand Oaks, CA: Sage, pp. 215–227.

Meyer, J. and Jepperson, R. (2000) The "actors" of modern society: The cultural construction of social agency, *Sociological Theory*, 18: 100–120.

Meyer, J. and Rowan, B. (1977) Institutionalized organizations: Formal structure as myth and ceremony, *American Journal of Sociology*, 83: 340–363.

Meyer, J. and Scott, W.R. (eds) (1983) *Organizational Environments: Ritual and Rationality*. Beverly Hills, CA: Sage.

Meyer, J., Boli, J., and Thomas, G. (1994a) Ontology and rationalization in the Western cultural account, in W.R. Scott and J. Meyer (eds), *Institutional Environments and Organizations*. Thousand Oaks, CA: Sage, pp. 9–27.

Meyer, J., Scott, W.R., and Strang, D. (1994b) Centralization, fragmentation, and school district complexity, in W.R. Scott and J. Meyer (eds), *Institutional Environments and Organizations*. Thousand Oaks, CA: Sage, pp. 160–178.

Meyer, M. and Zucker, L. (1989) *Permanently Failing Organizations*. Newbury Park, CA: Sage.

Miles, R. and Snow, C. (1978) *Organizational Strategy, Structure, and Process*. New York: McGraw-Hill.

Miller, D. and Shamsie, J. (1996) The resource-based view of the firm in two environments: The Hollywood film studios from 1936 to 1965, *Academy of Management Journal*, 39: 519–543.

Milliken, F. (1987) Three types of perceived uncertainty about the environment: State, effect, and response uncertainty, *Academy of Management Review*, 12: 133–143.

Mills, C.W. (1951) *White Collar: The American Middle Classes*. New York: Oxford University Press.

Mills, C.W. (1959) *The Sociological Imagination*. Oxford: Oxford University Press.

Milton, L. and Westphal, J. (2005) Identity confirmation networks and cooperation in work groups, *Academy of Management Journal*, 48: 191–212.

Miner, A. (1990) Structural evolution through idiosyncratic jobs: The potential for unplanned learning, *Organization Science*, 1: 195–210.

Miner, A. and Mezias, S. (1996) Ugly duckling no more: Pasts and futures of organizational learning research, *Organization Science*, 7: 88–99.

Mische, A. and Pattison, P. (2000) Composing a civic arena: Publics, projects, and social settings, *Poetics*, 27: 163–194.

Mohr, J. (1998) Measuring meaning structures, *Annual Review of Sociology*, 24: 345–370.

Mohr, J. (2012) Implicit terrains: Meaning, measurement, and spatial metaphors in organizational theory, Unpublished paper, Department of Sociology, University of California, Santa Barbara.

Mohr, J. and Duquenne, V. (1997) The duality of culture and practice: Poverty relief in New York City, 1888–1917, *Theory and Society*, 26: 305–356.

Mommaas, H. (2004) Cultural clusters and the post-industrial city: Towards the remapping of urban cultural policy, *Urban Studies*, 41: 507–532.

Montgomery, K. and Oliver, A. (2007) A fresh look at how professions take shape: Dual-directed networking activities and social boundaries, *Organization Studies*, 28: 661–687.

Moodysson, J., Coenen, L., and Asheim, B. (2008) Explaining spatial patterns of innovation: Analytical and synthetic modes of knowledge creation in the Medicon Valley life-science cluster, *Environment and Planning A*, 40: 1040–1056.

Morgan, G. and Quack, S. (2005) Institutional legacies and firm dynamics: The growth and internationalization of British and German law firms, *Organization Studies*, 26: 1765–1785.

Murmann, J. (2003) *Knowledge and Competitive Advantage: The Coevolution of Firms, Technology and National Institutions*. Cambridge: Cambridge University Press.

Mutch, A., Delbridge, R., and Ventresca, M. (2006) Situating organizational action: The relational sociology of organizations, *Organization*, 13: 607–625.

Naurin, D. and Lindahl, R. (2010) Out in the cold? Flexible integration and the political status of Euro opt-outs, *European Union Politics*, 11: 485–509.

Nelson, R. (2006) Evolutionary social science and universal Darwinism, *Journal of Evolutionary Economics*, 16: 491–510.

Nelson, R. and Winter, S. (1982) *An Evolutionary Theory of Economic Change*. Cambridge, MA: Harvard University Press.

Nicholson, N. (2010) The design of work: An evolutionary perspective, *Journal of Organizational Behavior*, 31: 422–431.

Nijsmans, M. (1991) Professional culture and organizational morality: An ethnographic account of a therapeutic organization, *British Journal of Sociology*, 42: 1–19.

Nilsson, K. (1996) Practice, myths and theories for change: The reconstruction of an East German organization, *Organization Studies*, 17: 291–309.

North, D. (2005) *Understanding the Process of Economic Change*. Princeton, NJ: Princeton University Press.

Norton, R. (1992) Agglomeration and competitiveness: From Marshall to Chinitz, *Urban Studies*, 29: 155–170.

Ogbonna, E. and Harris, L. (2004) Work intensification and emotional labour among UK university lecturers: An exploratory study, *Organization Studies*, 25: 1185–1203.

Oishi, S., Diener, E., Scollon, C., and Biswas-Diener, R. (2004) Cross-situational consistency of affective experiences across cultures, *Journal of Personality and Social Psychology*, 86: 460–472.

Orton, J. and Weick, K. (1990) Loosely coupled systems: A reconceptualization, *Academy of Management Review*, 15: 203–223.

Oswick, C., Keenoy, T., and Grant, D. (2002) Metaphor and analogical reasoning in organization theory: Beyond orthodoxy, *Academy of Management Review*, 27: 294–303.

Ouchi, W. (1980) Markets, bureaucracies, and clans, *Administrative Science Quarterly*, 25: 129–141.

Pachucki, M. and Breiger, R. (2010) Cultural holes: Beyond relationality in social networks and culture, *Annual Review of Sociology*, 36: 205–224.

Padavic, I. (2005) Laboring under uncertainty: Identity renegotiation among contingent workers, *Symbolic Interaction*, 28: 111–134.

Pascale, R. (1984) Perspectives on strategy: The real story behind Honda's success, *California Management Review*, 26: 47–72.

Paulus, P. and Yang, H. (2000) Idea generation in groups: A basis for creativity in organizations, *Organizational Behavior and Human Decision Processes*, 82: 76–87.

Pennings, J. and Wezel, F. (2010) Faraway, yet so close: Organizations in demographic flux, *Organization Science*, 21: 451–468.

Pennings, J., Lee, K., and van Witteloostuijn, A. (1998) Human capital, social capital, and firm dissolution, *Academy of Management Journal*, 41: 425–440.

Pentland, B. and Feldman, M. (2007) Narrative networks: Patterns of technology and organization, *Organization Science*, 18: 781–795.

Perl, P. and Olson, D. (2000) Religious market share and intensity of church involvement in five denominations, *Journal for the Scientific Study of Religion*, 39: 12–31.

Perretti, F. and Negro, G. (2007) Mixing genres and matching people: A study in innovation and team composition in Hollywood, *Journal of Organizational Behavior*, 28: 563–586.

Perrow, C. (1967) A framework for the comparative analysis of organizations, *American Sociological Review*, 32: 194–208.

Perrow, C. (1986) *Complex Organizations: A Critical Essay* (3rd edn). New York: Random House.

Perrow, C. (1991) A society of organizations, *Theory and Society*, 20: 725–762.

Perry, N. (1998) Indecent exposures: Theorizing whistleblowing, *Organization Studies*, 19: 235–257.

Pershing, J. (2006) Men and women's experiences with hazing in a male-dominated elite military institution, *Men and Masculinities*, 8: 470–492.

Petersen, T. and Saporta, I. (2004) The opportunity structure for discrimination, *American Journal of Sociology*, 109: 852–901.

Peterson, R. and Kern, R. (1996) Changing highbrow taste: From snob to omnivore, *American Sociological Review*, 61: 900–907.

Pfeffer, J. (1994) *Competitive Advantage through People*. Boston, MA: Harvard Business School Press.

Pfeffer, J. and Salancik, G. (1978) *The External Control of Organizations*. New York: Harper & Row.

Phillips, D. (2005) Organizational genealogies and the persistence of gender inequality: The case of Silicon Valley law firms, *Administrative Science Quarterly*, 50: 440–472.

Pierson, P. (2004) *Politics in Time: History, Institutions and Social Analysis*. Princeton, NJ: Princeton University Press.

Piore, M. and Sabel, C. (1984) *The Second Industrial Divide*. New York: Basic Books.

Ployhart, R., van Iddekinge, C., and Mackenzie, W. (2011) Acquiring and developing human capital in service contexts: The interconnectedness of human capital resources, *Academy of Management Journal*, 54: 353–368.

Polanyi, M. (1966) *The Tacit Dimension*. New York: Doubleday.

Popper, K. (1959) *The Logic of Scientific Discovery*. New York: Harper & Row.

Porter, M. (2000) Location, competition, and economic development: Local clusters in a global economy, *Economic Development Quarterly*, 14: 15–34.

Portes, A. and Sensenbrenner, J. (1993) Embeddedness and immigration: Notes on the determinants of social action, *American Journal of Sociology*, 98: 1320–1350.

Powell, W. and Colyvas, J. (2008) Microfoundations of institutional theory, in R. Greenwood, C. Oliver, R. Suddaby, and K. Sahlin-Andersson (eds), *Handbook of Organizational Institutionalism*. London: Sage, pp. 276–298.

Powell, W. and Snellman, K. (2004) The knowledge economy, *Annual Review of Sociology*, 30: 199–220.

Powell, W., Koput, K., and Smith-Doerr, L. (1996) Inter-organizational collaboration and the locus of innovation: Networks of learning in biotechnology, *Administrative Science Quarterly*, 41: 116–145.

Pratt, A. (2002) Hot jobs in cool places: The material cultures of new media product spaces: The case of South of the Market, San Francisco, *Information, Communication and Society*, 5: 27–50.

Pratt, M. and Foreman, P. (2000) Classifying managerial responses to multiple organizational identities, *Academy of Management Review*, 25: 18–42.

Putnam, R. (2000) *Bowling Alone: The Collapse and Revival of American Community.* New York: Simon & Schuster.

Raab, J. and Milward, H. (2003) Dark networks as problems, *Journal of Public Administration Research and Theory*, 13: 413–439.

Rafaeli, A., Dutton, J., Harquail, C., and Mackie-Lewis, S. (1997) Navigating by attire: The use of dress by female administrative employees, *Academy of Management Journal*, 40: 9–45.

Rao, H., Monin, P., and Durand, R. (2005) Border crossing: Bricolage and the erosion of categorical boundaries in French gastronomy, *American Sociological Review*, 70: 968–991.

Raub, S. (2008) Does bureaucracy kill individual initiative? The impact of structure on organizational citizenship behavior in the hospitality industry, *International Journal of Hospitality Management*, 27: 179–186.

Reay, T. and Hinings, C. (2009) Managing the rivalry of competing institutional logics, *Organization Studies*, 30: 629–652.

Reingold, D. (1999) Social networks and the employment problems of the urban poor, *Urban Studies*, 36: 1907–1932.

Renzulli, L., Aldrich, H., and Moody, J. (2000) Family matters: Gender, networks, and entrepreneurial outcomes, *Social Forces*, 79: 523–546.

Rerup, C. and Feldman, M. (2011) Routines as a source of change in organizational schemata: The role of trial-and-error learning, *Academy of Management Journal*, 54: 577–610.

Reskin, B. (2003) Including mechanisms in our models of ascriptive inequality: 2002 presidential address, *American Sociological Review*, 68: 1–21.

Richerson, P. and Boyd, R. (2005) *Not by Genes Alone.* Chicago, IL: University of Chicago Press.

Rinaldi, A. (2005) The Emilian model revisited: Twenty years after, *Business History*, 47: 244–266.

Ritzer, G. and Walczak, D. (1988) Rationalization and the deprofessionalization of physicians, *Social Forces*, 67: 1–22.

Romanelli, E. and Khessina, O. (2005) Regional industrial identity: Cluster configurations and economic development, *Organization Science*, 16: 344–358.

Ron, N., Lipshitz, R., and Popper, M. (2006) How organizations learn: Post-flight reviews in an F-16 fighter squadron, *Organization Studies*, 27: 1069–1089.

Roscigno, V., Garcia, L., and Bobbitt-Zeher, D. (2007) Social closure and processes of race/sex employment discrimination, *The ANNALS of the American Academy of Political and Social Science*, 609: 16–48.

Rosenbach, W. and Gregory, R. (1982) Job attitudes of commercial and U.S. Air Force pilots, *Armed Forces and Society*, 8: 615–628.

Rosenbaum, J. (1990) Structural models of organizational careers: A critical review and new directions, in R. Breiger (ed.), *Social Mobility and Social Structure*. Cambridge: Cambridge University Press, pp. 272–307.

Rosenkopf, L. and Almeida, P. (2003) Overcoming local search through alliances and mobility, *Management Science*, 49: 751–766.

Ross, J. and Staw, B. (1993) Organizational escalation and exit: Lessons from the Shorehand nuclear power plant, *Academy of Management Journal*, 36: 701–732.

Roth, P. (1986) *The Counterlife.* New York: Farrar, Straus and Giroux.

Rowley, T. (1997) Moving beyond dyadic ties: A network theory of stakeholder influences, *Academy of Management Review*, 22: 887–910.

Ruef, M. and Patterson, K. (2009) Credit and classification: The impact of industry boundaries in nineteenth century America, *Administrative Science Quarterly*, 54: 486–520.

Runciman, W. (2009) *The Theory of Cultural and Social Selection*. Cambridge: Cambridge University Press.

Rynes, S., Brown, K., and Colbert, A. (2002) Seven common misconceptions about human resource practices: Research findings versus practitioner beliefs, *Academy of Management Executive*, 16: 92–102.

Sanchez, R., Bauer, T., and Paronto, M. (2006) Peer-mentoring freshmen: Implications for satisfaction, commitment, and retention to graduation, *Academy of Management Learning and Education*, 5: 25–37.

Sauder, M. and Espeland, W. (2009) The discipline of rankings: Tight coupling and organizational change, *American Sociological Review*, 74: 63–82.

Sawyer, R. (2001) Emergence in sociology: Contemporary philosophy of mind and some implications for sociological theory, *American Journal of Sociology*, 107: 551–585.

Saxenian, A. (1994) *Regional Advantage: Culture and Competition in Silicon Valley and Route 128*. Cambridge, MA: Harvard University Press.

Saxenian, A. and Quan, Y. (2002) *Local and Global Networks of Immigrant Professionals in Silicon Valley*. San Francisco: Public Policy Institute of California.

Scheid, T. and Greenley, J. (1997) Evaluations of organizational effectiveness in mental health programs, *Journal of Health and Social Behavior*, 38: 403–426.

Schneiberg, M. (2007) What's on the path? Path dependence, organizational diversity and the problem of institutional change in the US economy, 1900–1950, *Socio-Economic Review*, 5: 47–80.

Schulz, M. (1998) Limits to bureaucratic growth: The density dependence of organizational rule births, *Administrative Science Quarterly*, 43: 845–876.

Schulz, S. (2008) Our lady hates viscose: The role of the customer image in high street fashion production, *Cultural Sociology*, 2: 385–405.

Schweingruber, D. and Berns, N. (2005) Shaping the selves of young salespeople through emotion management, *Journal of Contemporary Ethnography*, 34: 679–706.

Scott, A. (2000) *The Cultural Economy of Cities*. London: Sage.

Scott, A. and Pope, N. (2007) Hollywood, Vancouver, and the world: Employment relocation and the emergence of satellite production centers in the motion-picture industry, *Environment and Planning A*, 39: 1364–1381.

Scott, W.R. (1987) The adolescence of institutional theory, *Administrative Science Quarterly*, 32: 493–511.

Scott, W.R. (2004) Reflections on a half-century of organizational sociology, *Annual Review of Sociology*, 30: 1–21.

Scott, W.R. (2008) *Institutions and Organizations*. Los Angeles: Sage.

Searle, J. (1976) A classification of illocutionary acts, *Language in Society*, 5: 1–23.

Sedita, S. (2008) Interpersonal and inter-organizational networks in the performing arts: The case of project based organizations in the live music industry, *Industry and Innovation*, 15: 493–511.

Seidel, M., Polzer, J., and Stewart, K. (2000) Friends in high places: The effects of social networks on discrimination in salary negotiations, *Administrative Science Quarterly*, 45: 1–24.

Sennett, R. (1998) *The Corrosion of Character: The Personal Consequences of Work in the New Capitalism*. New York: W.W. Norton.

Sennett, R. (2006) *The Culture of the New Capitalism*. New Haven, CT: Yale University Press.

Sennett, R. (2008) *The Craftsman*. New Haven, CT: Yale University Press.

Shaw, J., Duffy, M., Johnson, J., and Lockhart, D. (2005) Turnover, social capital losses, and performance, *Academy of Management Journal*, 48: 594–606.

Sheller, M. (2004) Mobile publics: Beyond the network perspective, *Environment and Planning D*, 22: 39–52.

Shirky, C. (2009) *Here Comes Everybody: The Power of Organizing without Organizations*. London: Penguin Books.

Shorter, E. (1997) *A History of Psychiatry*. New York: John Wiley & Sons.

Shorter, E. (2009) *Before Prozac: The Troubled History of Mood Disorders in Psychiatry*. Oxford: Oxford University Press.

Simmel, G. (1908/1922/1955) *Conflict and the Web of Group-Affiliations*. Glencoe, IL: Free Press.

Simmie, J. (2002) Knowledge spillovers and reasons for the concentration of innovative SMEs, *Urban Studies*, 39: 885–902.

Singh, H. and Harianto, F. (1989) Management-board relationships, takeover risk, and the adoption of golden parachutes, *Academy of Management Journal*, 32: 7–24.

Slaughter, J. and Zickar, M. (2006) A new look at the role of insiders in the newcomer socialization process, *Group and Organization Management*, 31: 264–290.

Smith, E. (2011) Identities as lenses: How organizational identity affects audiences' evaluation of organizational performance, *Administrative Science Quarterly*, 56: 61–94.

Smith, S. (2005) "Don't put my name on it": Social capital activation and job finding assistance among the black urban poor, *American Journal of Sociology*, 111: 1–57.

Smith, V. (1997) New forms of work organization, *Annual Review of Sociology*, 23: 315–339.

Sole, D. and Edmondson, A. (2002) Situated knowledge and learning in dispersed teams, *British Journal of Management*, 13: S17–S34.

Somers, M. and Block, F. (2005) From poverty to perversity: Ideas, markets, and institutions over 200 years of welfare debate, *American Sociological Review*, 70: 260–287.

Soofi, E., Nystrom, P., and Yasai-Ardekani, M. (2009) Executives' perceived environmental uncertainty shortly after 9/11, *Computational Statistics and Data Analysis*, 53: 3502–3515.

Sorensen, J. (2004) Recruitment-based competition between industries: A community ecology, *Industrial and Corporate Change*, 13: 149–170.

Sorenson, O. and Audia, P. (2000) The social structure of entrepreneurial activity: Geographic concentration of footwear production in the United States, 1940–1989, *American Journal of Sociology*, 106: 424–462.

Sosteric, M. (1996) Subjectivity and the labour process: A case study in the restaurant industry, *Work, Employment and Society*, 10: 297–318.

Spanou, C. (2008) State reform in Greece: Responding to old and new challenges, *International Journal of Public Sector Management*, 21: 150–173.

Spence, M. (1974) *Market Signaling: Information Transfer in Hiring and Related Processes*. Cambridge, MA: Harvard University Press.

Spender, J.-C. (1998) Pluralist epistemology and the knowledge-based theory of the firm, *Organization*, 5: 233–256.

Staber, U. (1992) Organizational interdependence and organizational mortality in the cooperative sector: A community ecology perspective, *Human Relations*, 45: 1191–1212.

Staber, U. (2001) Spatial proximity and firm survival in a declining industrial district: The case of knitwear firms in Baden-Württemberg, *Regional Studies*, 35: 329–341.

Staber, U. (2007) Contextualizing research on social capital in regional clusters, *International Journal of Urban and Regional Research*, 31: 505–521.

Staber, U. (2009) Collective learning in clusters: Mechanisms and biases, *Entrepreneurship and Regional Development*, 21: 553–573.

Staber, U. (2010a) Imitation without interaction: How firms identify with clusters, *Organization Studies*, 31: 153–174.

Staber, U. (2010b) A social-evolutionary perspective on regional clusters, in R. Boschma and R. Martin (eds), *The Handbook of Evolutionary Economic Geography*. Cheltenham: Edward Elgar, pp. 221–238.

Staber, U. (2012) The ecological foundations of creativity, in F. Belussi and U. Staber (eds), *Managing Networks of Creativity*. New York: Routledge, pp. 30–45.

Staber, U. and Sautter, B. (2011) Who are we, and do we need to change? Cluster identity and life cycle, *Regional Studies*, 45: 1349–1361.

Staber, U. and Sydow, J. (2002) Organizational adaptive capacity: A structuration perspective, *Journal of Management Inquiry*, 11: 408–424.

Stainback, K., Tomaskovic-Devey, D., and Skaggs, S. (2010) Organizational approaches to inequality: Inertia, relative power, and environments, *Annual Review of Sociology*, 36: 225–247.

Starbuck, W. (1992) Learning by knowledge-intensive firms, *Journal of Management Studies*, 29: 713–740.

Starbuck, W. and Mezias, J. (1996) Opening Pandora's box: Studying the accuracy of managers' perceptions, *Journal of Organizational Behavior*, 17: 99–117.

Staw, B. and Epstein, L. (2000) What bandwagons bring: Effects of popular management techniques on corporate performance, reputation, and CEO pay, *Administrative Science Quarterly*, 45: 523–556.

Stevens, F., Diederiks, J., and Philipsen, H. (1992) Physician satisfaction, professional characteristics and behavior formalization in hospitals, *Social Science and Medicine*, 35: 295–303.

Stigler, G. (1951) The division of labor is limited by the extent of the market, *Journal of Political Economy*, 59: 185–193.

Stinchcombe, A. (1997) On the virtues of the old institutionalism, *Annual Review of Sociology*, 23: 1–18.

Storper, M. and Christopherson, S. (1987) Flexible specialization and regional industrial agglomerations: The case of the U.S. motion picture industry, *Annals of the Association of American Geographers*, 77: 104–117.

Storper, M. and Venables, A. (2004) Buzz: Face-to-face contact and the urban economy, *Journal of Economic Geography*, 4: 351–370.

Stuart, T., Hoang, H., and Hybels, R. (1999) Interorganizational endorsements and the performance of entrepreneurial ventures, *Administrative Science Quarterly*, 44: 315–349.

Sullivan-Taylor, B. and Wilson, D. (2009) Managing the threat of terrorism in British travel and leisure organizations, *Organization Studies*, 30: 251–276.

Swidler, A. and Arditi, J. (1994) The new sociology of knowledge, *Annual Review of Sociology*, 20: 305–329.

Sydow, J. and Staber, U. (2002) The institutional embeddedness of project networks: The case of content production in German television, *Regional Studies*, 36: 215–227.

Sydow, J., Schreyögg, G., and Koch, J. (2009) Organizational path dependence: Opening the black box, *Academy of Management Review*, 34: 689–789.

Sydow, J., Windeler, A., Wirth, C., and Staber, U. (2010) Foreign market entry as network entry: A relational-structuration perspective on internationalization in television content production, *Scandinavian Journal of Management*, 26: 13–24.

Szulanski, G. (1996) Exploring internal stickiness: Impediments to the best practice within the firm, *Strategic Management Journal*, 17: 27–43.

Taylor, F. (1911) *The Principles of Scientific Management*. New York: Harper.

Taylor, P. (1999) Places, spaces and Macy's: Place–space tensions in the political geography of modernities, *Progress in Human Geography*, 23: 7–26.

Thagard, P. (1996) *Mind: Introduction to Cognitive Science*. Cambridge, MA: MIT Press.

Thiétart, R. and Forgues, B. (1997) Action, structure and chaos, *Organization Studies*, 18: 119–143.

Thomas, P. and Hewitt, J. (2011) Managerial organization and professional autonomy: A discourse-based conceptualization, *Organization Studies*, 32: 1373–1393.

Thompson, P. and Warhurst, C. (1998) *Workplaces of the Future*. Basingstoke: Macmillan.

Tilly, C. (2006) *Why? What Happens When People Give Reasons … and Why?* Princeton, NJ: Princeton University Press.

Tilly, C. (2008) *Explaining Social Processes*. Boulder, CO: Paradigm Publishers.

Tolbert, P. (1988) Institutional sources of organizational culture in major law firms, in L. Zucker (ed.), *Institutional Patterns and Organizations: Culture and Environment*. Cambridge, MA: Ballinger, pp. 101–113.

Tolbert, P. and Moen, P. (1998) Men's and women's definitions of "good" jobs: Similarities and differences by age and across time, *Work and Occupations*, 25: 168–194.

Tolbert, P. and Zucker, L. (1996) The institutionalization of institutional theory, in S. Clegg, C. Hardy, and W. Nord (eds), *Handbook of Organization Studies*. London: Sage, pp. 175–190.

Tomaskovic-Devey, D., Thomas, M., and Johnson, K. (2005) Race and the accumulation of human capital across the career: A theoretical model and fixed-effects application, *American Journal of Sociology*, 111: 58–89.

Torres, D. (1988) Professionalism, variation, and organizational survival, *American Sociological Review*, 53: 380–394.

Town, R., Wholey, D., Feldman, R., and Burns, L. (2007) Revisiting the relationship between managed care and hospital consolidation, *Health Services Research*, 42: 219–238.

Traganou, J. (2010) National narratives in the opening and closing ceremonies of the Athens 2004 Olympic Games, *Journal of Sport and Social Issues*, 34: 236–251.

Tsang, E. and Yip, P. (2009) Competition, agglomeration, and performance of Beijing hotels, *Service Industries Journal*, 29: 155–171.

Tschang, F. and Szczypula, J. (2006) Idea creation, constructivism and evolution as key characteristics in the videogame artefact design process, *European Management Journal*, 24: 270–287.

Tsoukas, H. and Knudsen, C. (eds) (2003) *The Oxford Handbook of Organization Theory: Meta-Theoretical Perspectives*. Oxford: Oxford University Press.

Tsoukas, H. and Mylonopoulos, N. (eds) (2003) *Organizations as Knowledge Systems: Knowledge, Learning and Dynamic Capabilities*. New York and Basingstoke: Palgrave Macmillan.

Tuan, Y. (1977) *Space and Place*. London: Arnold.

Tuma, N., Hannan, M., and Groeneveld, L. (1979) Dynamic analysis of event histories, *American Journal of Sociology*, 84: 820–854.

Tyler, M. and Abbott, P. (1998) Chocs away: Weight watching in the contemporary airline industry, *Sociology*, 32: 433–450.

Tylor, E. (1871) *Primitive Culture*. New York: J.P. Putnam's Sons.

Uzzi, B. (1996) The sources and consequences of embeddedness for the economic performance of organizations: The network effect, *American Sociological Review*, 61: 674–698.

Vallas, S. (1999) Rethinking Post-Fordism: The meaning of workplace flexibility, *Sociological Theory*, 17: 68–101.

Warren, R. (1967) The interorganizational field as a focus for investigation, *Administrative Science Quarterly*, 12: 396–419.

Watson, T. (2008) Managing identity: Identity work, personal predicaments and structural circumstances, *Organization*, 15: 121–143.

Webb, J. (2004) Organizations, self-identities and the new economy, *Sociology*, 38: 719–738.

Weber, K. (2005) A toolkit for analyzing corporate cultural toolkits, *Poetics*, 33: 227–252.

Weber, K., Heinze, K., and deSoucey, M. (2008) Forage for thought: Mobilizing codes in the movement for grass-fed meat and dairy products, *Administrative Science Quarterly*, 53: 529–567.

Weber, M. (1904/1958) *The Protestant Ethic and the Spirit of Capitalism*. Trans. T. Parsons. New York: Scribner's.

Weber, M. (1924/1947) *The Theory of Social and Economic Organization*. Trans. and edited A. Henderson and T. Parsons. New York: Free Press.

Weber, M. (1949) *The Methodology of the Social Sciences*. Trans. and edited E. Shils and H. Finch. Glencoe, IL: Free Press.

Webster, J. and Starbuck, W. (1988) Theory building in industrial and organizational psychology, in C. Cooper and I. Robertson (eds), *International Review of Industrial and Organizational Psychology*. London: John Wiley, pp. 93–138.

Weeks, J. and Galunic, C. (2003) A theory of the cultural evolution of the firm: The intra-organizational ecology of memes, *Organization Studies*, 24: 1309–1352.

Weick, K. (1969) *The Social Psychology of Organizing*. Reading, MA: Addison-Wesley.

Weick, K. (1993) The collapse of sensemaking in organizations: The Mann Gulch disaster, *Administrative Science Quarterly*, 38: 628–652.

Weick, K. (2001) *Making Sense of the Organization*. Malden, MA: Blackwell.

Weick, K. and Roberts, K. (1993) Collective minds in organizations: Heedful interrelating on flight decks, *Administrative Science Quarterly*, 38: 357–381.

Weick, K., Sutcliffe, K., and Obstfeld, D. (2005) Organizing and the process of sensemaking, *Organization Science*, 16: 409–421.

Weller, S. (2007) Discrimination, labour markets and the labour market prospects of older workers: What can a legal case teach us? *Work, Employment and Society*, 21: 417–437.

Whetten, D., Felin, T., and King, B. (2009) The practice of theory borrowing in organizational studies: Current issues and future directions, *Journal of Management*, 35: 537–563.

White, H. (1992) *Identity and Control: A Structural Theory of Social Action*. Princeton, NJ: Princeton University Press.

Whittington, K., Owen-Smith, J., and Powell, W. (2009) Networks, propinquity, and innovation in knowledge-intensive industries, *Administrative Science Quarterly*, 54: 90–122.

Wholey, D. and Brittain, J. (1989) Characterizing environmental variation, *Academy of Management Journal*, 32: 867–882.

Whyte, W. (1956) *The Organization Man*. New York: Simon & Schuster.

Wilkinson, B. (1996) Culture, institutions and business in East Asia, *Organization Studies*, 17: 421–447.

Williams, S. (2002) Self-esteem and the self-censorship of creative ideas, *Personnel Review*, 31: 495–503.

Williamson, O. (1985) *The Economic Institutions of Capitalism*. New York: Free Press.

Williamson, O. (1994) Transaction cost economics and organization theory, in N. Smelser and R. Swedberg (eds), *The Handbook of Economic Sociology*. Princeton, NJ: Princeton University Press, pp. 77–107.

Wilson, S. (1955) *The Man in the Gray Flannel Suit*. Cambridge, MA: Da Capo Press.

Wilson, T. and Brekke, N. (1994) Mental contamination and mental correction, *Psychological Bulletin*, 116: 117–142.

Wilson, T. and Hodges, S. (1992) Attitudes as temporary constructions, in L. Martin and A. Tesser (eds), *The Construction of Social Judgments*. Hillsdale, NJ: Lawrence Erlbaum Associates, pp. 37–65.

Winter, S. and Szulanski, G. (2001) Replication as strategy, *Organization Science*, 12: 730–743.

Winther, G. and Marens, R. (1997) Participatory democracy may go a long way: Comparative growth performance of employee ownership firms in New York and Washington States, *Economic and Industrial Democracy*, 18: 393–422.

Witman, Y., Smid, G., Meurs, P., and Willems, D. (2010) Doctor in the lead: Balancing between two worlds, *Organization*, 18: 477–495.

Yang, H., Phelps, C., and Steensma, H. (2010) Learning from what others have learned from you: The effects of knowledge spillovers on originating firms, *Academy of Management Journal*, 53: 371–389.

Yu, J., Engleman, R., and Van de Ven, A. (2005) The integration journey: An attention-based view of the merger and acquisition integration process, *Organization Studies*, 26: 1501–1528.

Zaheer, S., Albert, S., and Zaheer, A. (1999) Time scales and organizational theory, *Academy of Management Review*, 24: 725–741.

Zaidman, N., Goldstein-Gidoni, O., and Nehemya, I. (2009) From temples to organizations: The introduction and packaging of spirituality, *Organization*, 16: 597–621.

Zajac, E. (1988) Interlocking directorates as an interorganizational strategy: A test of critical assumptions, *Academy of Management Journal*, 31: 428–438.

Zajac, E. and Bazerman, M. (1991) Blind spots in industry and competitor analysis: Implications of interfirm (mis)perceptions for strategic decisions, *Academy of Management Review*, 16: 37–56.

Zajac, E. and Westphal, J. (1996) Who shall succeed? How CEO/board preferences and power affect the choice of new CEOs, *Academy of Management Journal*, 39: 64–90.

Zald, M. and Lounsbury, M. (2010) The Wizards of Oz: Towards an institutional approach to elites, expertise and command posts, *Organization Studies*, 31: 963–996.

Zeitz, G. (1984) Bureaucratic role characteristics and member affective response in organizations, *The Sociological Quarterly*, 25: 301–318.

Zerubavel, E. (1976) Timetables and scheduling: On the social organization of time, *Sociological Inquiry*, 46: 87–94.

Zerubavel, E. (1997) *Social Mindscapes: An Invitation to Cognitive Sociology*. Cambridge, MA: Harvard University Press.

Zhou, X. (1993) The dynamics of organizational rules, *American Journal of Sociology*, 98: 1134–1166.

Zilber, T. (2002) Institutionalization as an interplay between actions, meanings, and actors: The case of a rape crisis center in Israel, *Academy of Management Journal*, 45: 234–254.

Zucker, L. (1977) The role of institutionalization in cultural persistence, *American Sociological Review*, 42: 726–743.

Zucker, L. (1987) Institutional theories of organization, *Annual Review of Sociology*, 13: 443–464.

Zucker, L. (1989) Combining institutional theory and population ecology: No legitimacy, no history, *American Sociological Review*, 54: 542–545.

Zuckerman, E. and Kim, T. (2003) The critical trade-off: Identity assignment and box-office success in the feature film industry, *Industrial and Corporate Change*, 12: 27–67.

Zuckerman, E., Kim, T., Ukanwa, K., and von Rittmann, J. (2003) Robust identities or nonentities? Typecasting in the feature-film labor market, *American Journal of Sociology*, 108: 1018–1074.

Index

knowledge
    accuracy vs. generality, 175
    codification, 127, 153, 176–178, 181–185
    explicit vs. tacit, 176–182, 192, 216
knowledge base, 109–110, 188, 192, 194,
    196, 213
    analytical, symbolic, synthetic knowledge,
      182–185
knowledge-intensive organization,
    112, 174–176
knowledge spillover, 98, 185, 197

labor market, 35, 68, 69, 94, 97, 123, 163, 204,
    205, 211, 220, 224, 226
    internal and external labor market,
      4, 203, 230
    primary and secondary labor market,
      201, 203
labor process, 79
law firms, 16, 71, 105, 112, 137, 149,
    206–208, 211
life-cycle, 128–129
location, 7, 8, 91, 93, 97–99, 106, 108, 112,
    113, 120, 123, 129, 173, 184, 188
logic, 3, 39, 43, 71, 74, 78, 104, 105, 107, 111,
    137, 147, 157, 167, 185, 191, 204, 231

management, 16, 20, 34–35, 43, 62, 86, 87,
    91, 92, 94, 102, 118, 156, 161, 166, 193,
    211, 222
market, 2, 4, 19–20, 23–24, 33–38, 49, 58,
    64, 70, 74–75, 100–102, 124–125, 134,
    145–148
matrix design, 120, 133
meaning, 2, 3, 6, 9, 14, 20, 25, 27, 38–40, 48,
    55–59, 79, 91– 94, 99, 104–113, 121–133,
    136, 138–140, 149, 160, 163, 165, 173,
    176, 180, 184, 196, 198, 204, 217,
    220–222, 225, 230
mechanism,13, 18, 64, 141, 229
    causal, 16, 32, 54, 62, 78, 107, 140, 185
mechanistic structure, 13, 14, 168
mental health, 40, 103, 104, 183
metaphor, 3, 13–15
minorities, 168, 194, 204, 207, 212, 228
monochronism vs. polychronism, 131–132
moral hazard, 34, 210, 212
multi-media, 42, 70, 96, 100, 175, 227
museums, 68–69, 81, 112, 147, 175, 180
myth, 40–41, 180, 196

narrative, 9, 133
neo-classical economic theory, 19, 33
network
    inter-organizational, 70, 98–99, 108, 210–211
    social, 4, 31, 71, 76–77, 92, 105, 185, 193,
      207–210, 213–215, 225–228

network *cont.*
    niche, 94, 99–103, 107, 110
    fundamental vs. realized, 100–101
    overlap, 103, 112
    partitioning, 100–101, 125
    width, 100, 125, 175
normative, 4, 21, 42, 82, 121, 193, 205, 209

Olympic Games, 78–79, 130, 180
ontology, 30, 141
opportunism, 35–37, 50, 52, 58, 73, 80, 85, 87,
    134–135, 149, 152, 166, 188, 191
organic solidarity, 145
organic structure, 14, 54, 168
organization, defined, 3
organization science, 32
organizational culture, 51, 53, 111, 118, 207
organizational design, 2, 3, 14, 26, 31, 36, 47,
    55, 81, 87, 94, 120, 138, 149, 152, 159,
    169–170, 192, 194, 197, 219
organizational economics, 19–20, 33–38
organizational failure, 50, 69, 83, 87, 135, 140,
    186, 214
organizational field, 94–95, 105, 111, 137, 217
    defined, 104
    structuration, 105–106
organizational form, 10–12, 20–22, 37, 40,
    43, 48–49, 53, 59, 63, 67, 77, 88, 101,
    104–106, 112, 118, 134–140, 168, 195,
    202, 219, 229, 230
organizational founding, 64, 69, 83, 120, 122,
    135, 195, 207, 219
organizational inertia, 51, 186, 218
outsourcing, 67, 74–75, 86, 97, 166, 195, 204

paradigm, 16, 180
paradox, 3, 81, 136, 157
path dependence, 126–128, 141, 187, 194–195
perception, 3, 9, 15, 25, 31, 52, 85–87,
    102, 135, 151, 163, 172–173, 182, 188,
    202, 214
performance, organizational, 4, 23–24, 54, 64,
    67, 69, 76, 80–81, 86, 99, 129, 135, 158,
    186, 194
    measurement, 19, 20, 35, 40, 43, 102,
      136, 162
politics, organizational, 15, 21, 38, 43–44, 50,
    51, 70, 72, 74, 78–79, 81, 94, 112, 120,
    156, 173, 191, 193, 198, 218, 223, 231
population
    boundary, 102
    organizational, 12, 40, 48–50, 71, 73, 100,
      107, 138–139, 158, 207, 211
position, 2, 8, 55, 67, 69, 72, 92, 108, 144,
    155–158, 183, 207, 211, 215, 220–221
post-communism, 193, 228
postmodern organization, 5, 224